LOUISIANA

OFF THE BEATEN PATH®

OFF THE BEATEN PATH® SERIES

ELEVENTH EDITION

LOUISIANA

OFF THE BEATEN PATH®

DISCOVER YOUR FUN

JACKIE SHECKLER FINCH

Globe
Pequot
Guilford, Connecticut

All the information in this guidebook is subject to change. We recommend that you call ahead to obtain current information before traveling.

Globe Pequot

An imprint of The Rowman & Littlefield Publishing Group, Inc.
4501 Forbes Blvd., Ste. 200
Lanham, MD 20706
www.rowman.com

Distributed by NATIONAL BOOK NETWORK

Copyright © 2015 The Rowman & Littlefield Publishing Group, Inc.
This Globe Pequot edition 2020
Maps by Equator Graphics

British Library Cataloguing in Publication Information available

Library of Congress Cataloging-in-Publication Data available

ISBN 978-1-4930-4267-8 (paperback)
ISBN 978-1-4930-4268-5 (e-book)

∞™ The paper used in this publication meets the minimum requirements of American National Standard for Information Sciences—Permanence of Paper for Printed Library Materials, ANSI/NISO Z39.48-1992

Contents

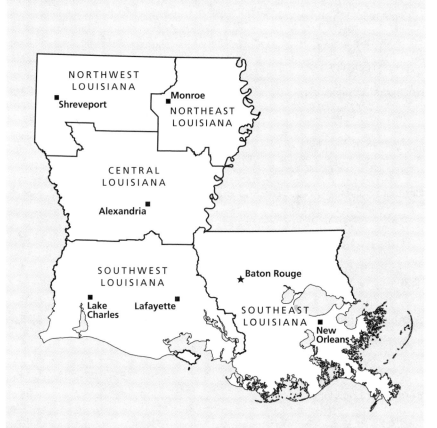

Acknowledgments

As I crisscrossed Louisiana while researching this book, many people helped me discover the beautiful treasures this state offers. Thanks to the wonderful tourism folks of Louisiana for answering my endless questions–Celine Alis, Ben Berthelot, Stacy Brown, Lauren Frye, Shelley Johnson, Donna O'Daniels, Will Precht, Carrie Stansbury, and Kelly Parks Strenge.

My appreciation to the Louisiana residents and business owners who took the time to share what makes Louisiana special.

Gratitude to Sarah Parke, Emily Chiarelli, and the friendly and professional staff at Globe Pequot Press for inviting me to take this joy-filled trip through Louisiana. It has been a delight and a pure pleasure.

My gratitude to my family for their encouragement: Kelly Rose; Sean and Emma Rose; Stefanie, Will, Trey, and Arianna Scott; and Logan and Grayson Peters. A special remembrance to my husband, Bill Finch, whose spirit goes with me every step of the way through life's amazing journey.

—Jackie Sheckler Finch

About the Author

An award-winning journalist and photographer, Jackie Sheckler Finch has covered a wide array of topics—from birth to death, with all the joy and sorrow in between. She has written for numerous publications and has been the author of more than a dozen books. She has been named the Mark Twain Travel Writer of the Year by the Midwest Travel Journalists Association a record five times, in 1998, 2001, 2003, 2007, and 2011. She also belongs to the Society of American Travel Writers. She shares her home with resident guard and entertainer, a rescued pooch named Pepper. One of her greatest joys is taking to the road to find the fascinating people and places that wait over the hill and around the next bend.

Introduction

My love affair with Louisiana began about five decades ago—and shows no signs of cooling down. During the late '80s, I started in-depth research for this guidebook, now in its eleventh edition. At that time, the state's welcome centers dispensed tourism literature bags touting LOUISIANA—AS AMERICAN AS CRAWFISH PIE. Since then, other slogans have come and gone, but this remains my favorite because it suggests something of the state's uniqueness.

Cultural distinctions jump out at you each time you encounter a word that appears unpronounceable at first (example: Zwolle, a small town near Toledo Bend on the state's western border, rhymes with tamale).

meetthe louisianafamily

Louisiana's residents represent a rich ethnic mix. This includes not only the famous French heritage but also the Scotch–Irish–English background common to many white southerners. Other groups— African American, Hispanic, and Native American, along with Viet- namese, German, Lebanese, and even Hungarian—add to the cul- tural gumbo of the state.

A list of how Louisiana differs from other states could start with the legal system. As Stanley reminds Stella in *A Streetcar Named Desire*, "we have something in Louisiana called the Napoleonic Code." And consider the Long dynasty and that cast of colorful characters associated with past political regimes. Consider too that much of our unique political activity is carried out in what we call parishes, not counties—carryovers from the original divisions drawn by the Roman Catholic Church.

Louisiana dishes up diversity in the arts as well. What other state could possibly serve as a setting for *Divine Secrets of the Ya-Ya Sisterhood*? And where else would you ever see an official portrait of the governor with Blue Dog? It's true. Blue Dog shared the canvas with former Louisiana governor Kathleen Babineaux Blanco.

And who's Blue Dog, you say? Internationally acclaimed Cajun artist George Rodrigue conjured up Blue Dog in 1984, and the image soon grew to pop-icon status. Both Rodrigue and former Governor Blanco hail from New Iberia, and so does novelist James Lee Burke.

Of course, Louisiana's cuisine is as unusual as our other cultural offerings and, as you'll learn, holds a unique importance here.

Research is the heart of writing, especially travel writing, and lucky is the writer whose research leads her through Louisiana. Something about describing this extraordinary state always seems to send me to my kitchen. Many New

Orleanians agree with this famous quote by Ella Brennan: "In some places, they eat to live—in our town, we live to eat."

And it's true. You'll understand why when you travel through our gastronomic wonderland.

Or perhaps you're already familiar with Louisiana's cuisine. Cajun restaurants have proliferated beyond state borders (a friend previously visited one in a remote area of Australia), and packaged Cajun foods, spices, and cookbooks are now readily available to fuel further interest in this celebrated cuisine. Basically French country cooking, Cajun cuisine utilizes fresh indigenous ingredients—rice, peppers, herbs, game, and fish—notably the ubiquitous crustacean called crawfish. Aquaculture, the growing of crawfish and catfish in shallow ponds, plays a significant role in Acadiana's economy.

weatherwise

Given the humid, subtropical (meaning not-quite-tropical) climate of the state, summers can be hot in Louisiana. Winters, blissfully, are mild. Hurricanes can be a coastal-area hazard. Whatever the season, prepare for rain.

The natives will gladly demonstrate the proper way to peel a crawfish and patiently explain it again. If, on the third try, you still don't get the hang of it, they'll probably do it for you. Then, all you have to do is dip it in some delectable sauce. (You might prefer to leave the head-sucking to the locals.)

Louisiana's innovative chefs may tempt you to eat yourself into a coma with pan-seared foie gras, crab and sweet corn bisque, étouffée, jambalaya, soft-shelled crab in sherry sauce, shrimp and artichoke salad, oysters (nude or in sublime sauces), pompano *en papillote*, smoked salmon with tasso, and classic crème brûlée or variations thereof. Menus feature everything from broiled, baked, boiled, blackened, steamed, and fried fish to delectable concoctions of gumbo, shrimp Creole, crabmeat crepes, crawfish bisque, eggplant pirogue, and more. With cuisines ranging from Acadian, Creole, and haute French to Southern—well, what more can be said?

Perhaps only a question—is there a way to take all this home?

For food enthusiasts who want to extend their enjoyment of Louisiana's cooking, this edition contains recipes reflecting the state's varied cuisine. Specialties from Cajun country, Baton Rouge, and New Orleans may inspire you when you're having trouble coming up with ideas for dinner.

If I haven't included that special recipe you're looking for, chances are you'll find it in your travels, at least if you keep your eye out for cookbooks, which abound here. In each region you'll come across excellent cookbooks featuring local specialties, which is not surprising in a state that takes food seriously and regards cooking as an art.

Tasting your way through the state you will probably understand the results of a personal poll I took in my Louisiana travels. Asking residents "What's the best thing about Louisiana," I heard the answer, "the food," as much as I heard, "the people." The other answers described Louisiana amenities you may want to get acquainted with: music, fishing, hunting, the history, the climate, and the "flowers that bloom all year long."

As you plan your itinerary, you'll no doubt first be struck by the state's shape—another example of its uniqueness. Its shape is like a boot or perhaps a Santa Claus stocking, raveling at the toe. We think of it as the natives do, dividing it simply into two parts—North Louisiana and South Louisiana, with New Orleans as a third entity. North and south merge at Alexandria, in the middle of the state.

For the purpose of clustering regional attractions, this book breaks the "boot" into five sections. Starting with the northwestern region, the text moves from west to east in zigzag fashion, culminating in the southeastern area on the doorstep of New Orleans. "The city that care forgot" would serve as a fitting finale for a Louisiana holiday, and several enticements, such as the Garden District and Vieux Carré (French Quarter), are suggested as part of a New Orleans itinerary. As the state's principal tourist magnet, New Orleans hardly qualifies as being off the beaten path; however, it would be a shame to miss some of this grand city's unique attractions.

atleisure

Renowned for its richness of outdoor activities, Louisiana refers to itself as a "Sportsman's Paradise"—as in the longtime state license plate motto. Fishing and hunting are much-favored leisure activities. Among spectator sports, loyalties are divided between professional football's New Orleans Saints and the popular college teams, such as the LSU Tigers and Tulane University's Green Wave.

From blues, jazz, and Cajun to country, swamp rock and pop, and progressive zydeco, music starts with a capital M in Louisiana. Fans flock from afar to Plaisance for the annual Zydeco Festival, where the music's hot and so's the temperature (but the heat doesn't daunt the dancing, clapping throngs).

Because Louisianians love festivals, practically any topic is good enough for a celebration—possums, peaches, pecans, poke salad, pirates, sweet potatoes, frogs, catfish, rice, oil, omelets, crawfish, and the list goes on. (Incidentally, despite what your biology teacher may have told you, the proper term here is crawfish—not crayfish.)

The merrymaking, which always includes good music and great food, can also feature such festivities as frog derbies, crawfish-eating contests, and pirogue races. At Morgan City's long-running Shrimp & Petroleum Festival, two big boats meet in a bow-to-bow "kiss" as the king and queen lean forward from their respective decks for a traditional champagne toast. Of course, all the world knows about the state's biggest festival, Mardi Gras (French for "fat Tuesday"), with its magic, music, and mystique. To enhance your visit to a particular area, find out about any nearby festivals—they fill the calendar.

The state boasts a number of the South's grand plantation manors, and many are mentioned in this guide. If you're a history buff, be sure to check the area through which you're traveling for other showplaces that may be in the same vicinity. Some historic homes, not open on a regular basis, can be visited by appointment. A great number of them, especially along River Road, offer year-round tours. Best of all, many of these mansions now open their doors to travelers, inviting them to sleep in canopied beds, wake up to coffee delivered on a silver platter, and enjoy a full plantation breakfast of grits, ham, eggs, and biscuits or perhaps sugared stacks of French toast with sausages. For a different slant on life along River Road, visit Laura, a Creole plantation and the American home of the legendary Br'er Rabbit tales.

You can also take a look at the lifestyles of early citizens who endured hardship and privation. Their customs and contributions are commemorated in museums across the state—from the Acadian Village and Homer's Ford Museum to Shreveport's Pioneer Heritage Center and Baton Rouge's Rural Life Museum and Lafayette's Vermilionville Living Museum and Folk Life Park.

Some general observations: North Louisiana's culture and topography resemble those of surrounding states—Mississippi, Arkansas, and Texas. This area is primarily Protestant. In contrast, most of South Louisiana's landscape features marshes, swamps, bayous, and bottomlands. Predominantly Catholic, many of its inhabitants descended from the French Acadians, who were forced by England to leave Canada in 1755. *Evangeline*, Longfellow's epic poem, tells their story. In time the pronunciation of "Acadian" was reduced to "Cajun." Known for their *joie de vivre*, or joy of life, Cajuns treasure their ancestry, and many still speak the Cajun-French language.

The state's economy took a big dip during the '80s when gas and oil prices plummeted. Although the financial landscape continues to reflect the ups and downs of the oil industry, the economic sector has broadened considerably during the past two decades. Tourism, for example, generates funds for the state, and its related industries are major sources of employment. The year 2017 was record breaking for tourism in Louisiana. The state welcomed a record 47.1 million visitors in 2017, representing an increase of nearly 500,000 over the 46.7 million visitors in 2016. Those 2017 visitors spent $17.5 billion.

Other areas of diversification include a broader retail base, an expanded health care industry, and an innovative approach to agriculture, reflected in new harvesting techniques, hybridization programs, and state-of-the-art equipment. With sugarcane, rice, and aquaculture (raising crawfish and catfish in shallow ponds) as major industries, agriculture plays a vital role. Alligator ranching certainly qualifies as innovative, and Louisiana leads the world in alligator production—and preservation.

One native recommends "calling any place before you visit, as this is the country, and folks are liable to just leave and go fishin'." When traveling off the beaten path or before driving long distances, take this advice because dates, rates, times, attractions, and facilities *do* change.

For a free Louisiana tour guide or road map of the state, call (800) 677-4082. For more information, check out louisianatravel.com.

For help in planning a visit to the Big Easy, click on NewOrleansOnline .com, the official tourism website of the city of New Orleans. Here, you can book a room in your preferred location and price range, check out restaurants, and order a free guidebook called *New Orleans: The Official Visitors Guide* with money-saving coupons.

Unless otherwise noted, all museums and attractions with admission prices less than $5 per adult will be designated as modest. A restaurant meal (the price of a single entree without beverages) listed as economical costs less than $10, moderate prices range between $10 and $30, and entrees more than $30 are classified as expensive. As for accommodations, those that cost less than $90 per night will be listed as standard, an overnight stay falling in the $90 to $175 range is labeled moderate, and lodging more than $175 is designated deluxe.

Louisiana possesses many wonderful, tucked-away towns and special spots—more than can be included in this volume. If this sampler whets your appetite for a statewide exploration of your own, you'll discover a smorgasbord of tempting offerings. Take along your curiosity and your appetite when you head for Louisiana and let the good times roll! Or, as they put it in Cajun country, "*Laissez les bons temps rouler!*"

FYI

There's plenty to love and learn about the state of Louisiana. Here are some fun-filled facts and practical health notes that will better prepare you for your off-the-beaten-path adventure.

SYMBOLICALLY SPEAKING

Louisiana has a wealth of state symbols. The two state songs are the not-too-well-known "Give Me Louisiana" and the perennial favorite "You Are My

Sunshine," composed by former Louisiana governor Jimmie Davis. The state amphibian is the green tree frog; the state insect, the honeybee; the state fossil, petrified palmwood; the state wildflower, the iris; and the state dog, the Catahoula hog dog (a usually blue-eyed hound with distinctive whorls in its coarse black-and-white or grayish coat, said to be descended from early Spanish dogs).

The official Louisiana state seal shows a pelican feeding three young birds, with the motto "Union, Justice, Confidence" below. Perhaps significantly, the early Louisiana explorer Iberville captained a ship named *Pelikan* in a seventeenth-century victory over the English in Canada.

HEALTH NOTES

Exercise common sense: That's the best health information you need before any vacation. There are, however, a few things to keep in mind.

Because of the weather in Louisiana, pay special attention to temperature changes. Drink lots of water when it's hot. Stay dry and wear warm clothing in the winter—Louisiana duck hunters can be in danger of hypothermia when sudden cold fronts arrive in the marshes. Follow water safety rules and wear your life jacket in any watercraft. Obey all weather warnings from the media— if they say get out, go immediately.

Tuck in your shirt and pull your socks over your pant cuffs when you walk in the woods—Lyme disease ticks are found in the state, mainly in the Florida Parishes. Out in the wild, look where you walk: Snakes and poison ivy are both avoidable hazards. Nature is bountiful in Louisiana, but don't nibble on fruits, berries, or mushrooms in the wilderness unless you are absolutely sure of their identity.

In larger cities practice good sense. Don't walk alone on dark streets. Stay with the lights and the crowds. Obey the laws. And use alcohol in moderation. Even on vacation you still need a designated driver. After all, you're going to want to come back here and fall in love with Louisiana all over again.

Northwest Louisiana

Northwest Louisiana (on a map, the top of the back of the boot) boasts the greatest range of temperatures in the state. The all-time high was 114 degrees in Plain Dealing and the low was minus 16 degrees recorded in 1886 in Minden.

Geologically speaking, this is the oldest part of the state. Louisiana's "hill region" includes the Sabine Uplift, around which curve outcrops of rock strata called "wolds." The Nacogdoches Wold (named for a town in nearby Texas) includes Driskill Mountain, which rises to 535 feet above sea level in Bienville Parish. The Red River and various tributaries and old channels drain the area.

The close proximity of Texas is readily seen not just in the hot weather but also in the local culture, a nice blend of Southwestern and Louisiana Southern that finds chicken-fried steak on the menu as well as shrimp and crawfish, and Wrangler jeans as proper attire for most local events.

Shreveport, the second-largest city in Louisiana, and ***Bossier***, its across-the-Red-River sister city, constitute the commercial center of this section of the state.

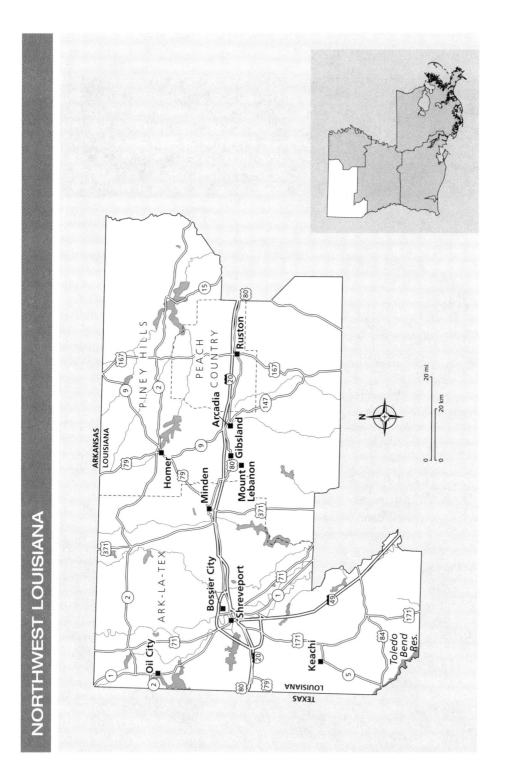

Ark-La-Tex

Entering Louisiana at its northwest corner, a person can stand in three states at the same time. North of Rodessa, the Three States Marker shows where the borders of Louisiana, Texas, and Arkansas all converge. Shreveport and Bossier City, farther south, serve as the hub for a 200-mile radius known as the *Ark-La-Tex*. The Shreveport–Bossier area makes a convenient starting point for exploring other portions of Louisiana. From here you can either proceed eastward or you can angle south into the central section. Both regions provide plenty of off-the-beaten-path attractions.

Named for the Native Americans who once lived here, Caddo Parish was created in 1838. The Caddo (or Kadohadacho) Native Americans who occupied the surrounding forests sold one million acres to the United States government on July 1, 1835.

Afterward, with the discovery of oil, the area turned from happy hunting grounds to hootin' and hollerin' hysteria almost overnight. In one year land values jumped from 50 cents an acre to $500 an acre. Oil City sprang up to become the first wildcat town in the Ark-La-Tex. The resulting large red-light district and influx of rough characters gave the town an unsavory reputation.

When you enter today's Oil City via Route 1 from the state's northwestern corner, you'll find a small, quiet hamlet with few reminders of its brawling boomtown days. To learn more, head for the *Louisiana State Oil and Gas Museum* (318-995-6845; sos.la.gov/historicalresources/visitmuseums/louisiana stateoilandgasmuseum) at 200 South Land Ave. (Oil City's main street). Currently the complex consists of three buildings dating from the early 1900s plus

AUTHOR'S FAVORITES IN NORTHWEST LOUISIANA

American Rose Center, Shreveport

Ford Museum, Homer

Germantown Colony Museum, Minden

Kisatchie National Forest, Homer

Harrah's Louisiana Downs Casino and Racetrack, Bossier City

Louisiana State Oil and Gas Museum, Oil City

Meadows Museum of Art, Shreveport

R. W. Norton Art Gallery, Shreveport

Sci-Port Discovery Center, Shreveport

a museum with galleries highlighting the culture and the role of oil and gas in the area's history.

Start your tour in the new 12,000-square-foot facility. You'll see an adjacent caboose and displays of early oil field equipment, railroad artifacts, old photographs, Native American relics, a collection of pearls found in mussels from Caddo Lake, and other items relating to the area's history.

A ten-minute video presentation acquaints you with North Caddo Parish's history. Take a self-guided tour to learn some of the region's colorful legends, such as the story of an Indian chief who divided his extensive land holdings between his twin sons. Each brave was told to walk for two and a half days—one toward the rising sun and the other toward the setting sun. The eastward-bound son received Louisiana's Natchitoches area as his legacy, and the other's inheritance was the region around Nacogdoches, Texas.

The museum is open Tues through Fri from 10 a.m. until 4 p.m.

After touring the museum, step outside to see the century-old bank and post office, which was moved from nearby Trees City. A security system now protects the small bank, although none was there when the bank did a booming cash business.

Perhaps the closest Oil City comes to its lively past occurs each spring when citizens celebrate the oil industry with their **Gusher Days Festival** (318-470-3446; gusherdaysfestival.com). On tap are such events as arts-and-crafts exhibits, street dancing, parades, and a beard contest. Previous festivals featured a spirited competition in which local businesspeople vied for the dubious distinction of being named Miss Slush Pit.

Not only was the first oil well in Northwest Louisiana drilled in this area, but the world's first marine well was drilled in nearby Caddo Lake. Until May 1911, when this original offshore well was completed, underwater drilling remained in the realm of theory.

Water sports enthusiasts will appreciate Caddo Lake for other reasons. The large cypress-studded lake, which can be reached via Route 1, offers opportunities for boating, skiing, fishing, hunting, and camping. Consulting your map you'll see that the lake also spills over into Texas.

Continue to 8012 Blanchard-Furrh Road, where you'll find the **Walter B. Jacobs Memorial Nature Park** (318-929-2806)—2.9 miles east of Longwood (Route 169) and 2.8 miles west of Blanchard (Route 173). Dedicated to nature's preservation, the park invites those who want to use it for walking, hiking, photography, painting, writing, bird-watching, or simply the pure enjoyment of being outdoors.

At the interpretive building you'll see an exhibit on predators and prey, coiled live snakes in glass cages, and a colony of bees in action. Other displays feature mounted specimens of native wildlife such as a Louisiana black bear, coyotes, and river otters. One of the building's classrooms contains "feel" boxes, helpful for using a hands-on approach with students. Youngsters can reach inside a box, guess what object they're touching, and then describe it for their classmates. This leads to follow-up discussions on different aspects of nature. (I was relieved that my box contained an antler instead of something squirmy.)

Trail and terrain maps are given to visitors who want to hike through the 160-acre park of pine, oak, and hickory forest. Markers identify natural features and animal habitats along the trails. Local woods are populated by deer, snakes, lizards, turtles, rabbits, squirrels, opossums, raccoons, armadillos, and other animals. Plant lovers will want to check out the medicinal and herb garden and the wildflower trail.

The park provides a picnic area with pavilion for people who want to pack a lunch and spend the day. Also two full-time and two part-time naturalists are available to arrange guided tours, present programs, teach sessions, and, in general, share expertise.

You can visit from 8 a.m. to 5 p.m. Wed through Sat and from 1 to 5 p.m. on Sun. The park is closed New Year's Day, Easter, Thanksgiving, and Christmas Day. Admission is free. Check out caddo.org for more information.

Don't miss the ***American Rose Center*** (318-938-5402; rose.org) at 8877 Jefferson-Paige Road, Shreveport. Located just off I-20, the American Rose Center is 5 miles east of the Texas state line and about 10 miles west of downtown Shreveport. Take exit 5 and follow the signs.

Now America's national flower (Congress made it official in 1986), the rose reigns supreme here at America's largest rose garden. The American Rose Society, established in 1892, also makes its headquarters at the center. The center includes Klima Rose Hall, an education and visitor's facility, as well as a gift shop with great items for your favorite gardener. You can stroll along pathways edged by split-rail fences to see more than sixty-five individual gardens spreading over the site's currently developed fifty-seven acres. You don't have to be a rose expert to appreciate the beauty of this place. A label next to each planting provides such pertinent information as the rose's name, type, and heritage. Like the flowers themselves, the names are intriguing: White Masterpiece, New Year, Show Biz, French Lace, Angel Face, Touch of Class, Double Delight, and Sweet Surrender are among the rose varieties you can see here. While sampling this buffet of blossoms, be careful when you sniff—bees like the roses, too.

The Windsounds Carillon Tower rises impressively from plantings of award-winning roses in reds, pinks, yellows, mauves, and a medley of other colors. You'll also find a picturesque log cabin chapel, a gift shop, sundials, gazebos, inviting benches, and picnicking facilities. The gardens and chapel serve as a beautiful backdrop for more than one hundred weddings a year.

Christmas in Roseland makes the place more magical than ever with such entertainment as choral groups, soloists, dancers, and storytellers. Displays include illuminated wire sculptures depicting the Nativity scene, Eiffel Tower, Statue of Liberty, a spotlighted group of large wooden Christmas card panels designed and painted by area students, and other festive displays.

rosamonstrosa

A personal favorite: By far the oddest flower at the American Rose Center is the Rosa monstrosa, an all-green flower with petals the same color as its leaves. It has a certain creepy charm and must look rather like roses do to the color-blind.

You can visit the Rose Center from Apr through Oct between 9 a.m. and 5 p.m. Mon through Sat, and 1 to 5 p.m. Sun. Holiday hours, from Thanksgiving through New Year's Eve (except for Christmas Day), change to 5:30 to 10 p.m. daily. Admission.

Continue into **Shreveport**, now big and bustling. The city truly qualified as an off-the-beaten-path kind of place before Captain Henry Miller Shreve appeared on the scene in 1833 to unclog the Red River. Using snag boats, Shreve and his crews divested the river of a logjam known as the "Great Raft," which extended some 180 miles—a project that took five years and cost $300,000. Later the town that sprang up on the banks of the Red River was named in honor of Captain Shreve. It's a safe bet to say that today the captain would not recognize his riverfront, which has taken on a Las Vegas look with dockside riverboat gaming, specialty shops, lounges, live music, and crowds courting Lady Luck via video poker, blackjack, craps, roulette, slots, and similar pursuits.

The Louisiana legislature officially recognized Shreveport as a town in 1839. During the Civil War Shreveport served as the state's capital for a short time. The last place in Louisiana to concede defeat, its official Confederate flag was not lowered until Federal troops arrived to occupy the city.

Start your visit to Shreveport with a drive through the historical Highland–Fairfield area, a setting for many of the city's elegant mansions. Fairfield Avenue, one of Shreveport's most attractive streets, features grand houses in a diversity of architectural styles.

Afterward, continue your journey by taking in **Spring Street Historical Museum** (318-424-0964; springstreetmuseum.org). Here at 525 Spring Street, you'll get a real feel for the city's history. Built as a bank in 1865 and recently restored, this fine structure with its cast-iron balcony is one of the town's oldest existing buildings. An eight-minute video presentation acquaints you

TOP ANNUAL EVENTS IN NORTHWEST LOUISIANA

Holiday in Dixie
Shreveport, Apr
(318) 865-5555
arklatexambassadors.com

Mayhaw Festival
Marion, Mother's Day weekend
(318) 292-4715
townofmarionla.com/mayhaw-festival

Mudbug Madness
Shreveport, Memorial Day weekend
(318) 225-5641
mudbugmadness.com

Louisiana Peach Festival
Ruston, June
(318) 255-2031
louisianapeachfestival.org

Red River Revel Arts Festival
Shreveport, Oct
(318) 424-4000
redriverrevel.com

Louisiana State Fair
Shreveport, Oct
(318) 635-1361
statefairoflouisiana.com

Christmas in Roseland
Shreveport, Fri after Thanksgiving
through Dec
(318) 938-5402
rose.org/Christmas-in-roseland

with the city's early history. Rotating exhibits allow the museum to showcase its historical collections of furniture, clothing, jewelry, firearms, books, and newspapers.

Don't miss seeing the upstairs with its permanent collection of Victorian furnishings. Beautiful period pieces include American Chippendale chairs that date from 1760 to 1775, paintings from the 1800s, various pieces of carved rosewood furniture, an 1878 cherry and walnut organ that has been restored to playing condition, a child's harp, a melodeon, and a Persian carpet. You'll also see a chair that belonged to Shreveport's famous madam (who received a three-month bank loan for her business and repaid it within two weeks). Hours are from 10 a.m. to 4 p.m. Tues through Sat. Modest admission.

While in the area you can stop for a meal at the ***Blind Tiger*** (318-226-8747) on the corner of Spring and Texas streets at 120 Texas Street in historic Shreve Square. Harking back to the time of Prohibition and speakeasies, when saloons operated behind facades or "blinds" such as museums with wild animal displays to mask back rooms where alcoholic beverages were sold, the restaurant's name serves as a reminder of the town's past.

Erected in 1848, the building burned in 1854 and was rebuilt later to house several businesses, including the Buckelew Hardware Company. The interior

Back to Nature

One pleasant way to dawdle away a Shreveport afternoon is on the paths and by the fountains of Riverview Park (601 Clyde Fant Pkwy.; 318-673-7727). This art gallery and plant-and-flower-exhibit facility is free and open daily. Stroll through the sculpture garden and a specially scented garden, or simply enjoy the quiet greenery you'll find along the walkways. Before some recent landscaping you could find bonus vegetation: Pokeweed growing on the slopes of the nearby Red River levee attracted lots of busy gatherers each spring for poke salad.

echoes the nostalgic theme with stained glass, dark wood paneling, brass rails, and Tiffany chandeliers.

"Our menu offers plenty of variety, although the emphasis is on seafood," says Rick Sloan, who with Glenn Brannan owns the Blind Tiger. Consider an appetizer of tiger wings or pigskins for starters, then try one of the snapper specialties. The restaurant also serves a Cajun sampler of five different entrees as well as great steaks and hamburgers. Prices are moderate. Hours are from 11 a.m. to 9:30 p.m. Mon through Thurs; 11 a.m. to 10:30 Fri and Sat; noon to 8:30 p.m. Sun. The bar is open all night—until 6 a.m. daily, except Sun when it closes at 2 a.m.

Located at 619 Louisiana Avenue in Shreveport, the **Strand Theatre** (318-226-1481; thestrandtheatre.com) is a must-see, although parking can present a problem. Be sure to notice the dome and the exterior's decorative details as you approach. Now restored to its previous grandeur, the neobaroque theater originally opened in 1925 with the operetta *The Chocolate Soldier.* Listed on the National Register of Historic Places, the 1,636-seat theater boasts an organ of 939 pipes, ornate box seats, and gilt-edged mirrors. The interior features a color scheme of rich burgundy with gold accents. Don't forget to look up at the magnificent ceiling and dazzling chandeliers.

Reopened in 1984, this downtown landmark again attracts crowds for performances that range from ballet and musical extravaganzas on ice to touring Broadway hits. The Strand box office is open Mon through Fri from 9 a.m. to 5 p.m. Modest admission.

Continue to the **Meadows Museum of Art** (318-869-5169; themeadows museum.com), located at 2911 Centenary Boulevard in Shreveport on the Centenary College campus. The museum's permanent collection includes works by such artists as Mary Cassatt, Diego Rivera, Alfred Maurer, and George Grosz. Also, you'll see the work of Louisiana artists such as Clyde Connell, John Scott, Maria Lopez, Clementine Hunter, Lucille Reed, Langston McEachern, and Jack

OTHER ATTRACTIONS WORTH SEEING IN NORTHWEST LOUISIANA

Lake Bistineau State Park
Doyline
(318) 745-3503 or (888) 677-2478
crt.state.la.us/Louisiana-state-parks/parks/lake-bistineau-state-park
This park has facilities for camping and cabin and boat rentals. State parks make a welcome break in a driving vacation, even if you don't stay overnight. For information on camping and rentals, write to Lake Bistineau State Park, 103 State Park Rd., Doyline 71023, or call (877) 226-7652, the reservations number for all Louisiana state parks.

Louisiana State Fairgrounds
Shreveport
(318) 635-1361
statefairoflouisiana.com
Even when it's not fair week (last week in Oct) the Louisiana State Fairgrounds are worth visiting for the Louisiana State Exhibit Museum. Inside the marble rotunda, a long, circular corridor leads past dioramas of Louisiana industry and life. You'll find an oil refinery, a sulfur mine, a salt dome, an Indian village . . . in short, a wealth of small tableaux that explain Louisiana, along with murals, other exhibits, and an art gallery.

Sci-Port Discovery Center
Shreveport
(318) 424-3466 or (877) Sci-Port
sciport.org
This hands-on science museum on Shreveport's riverfront offers some 200 programs and interactive exhibits. Here you might lie on a bed of nails and learn why and how you can do this without flinching or screaming. Besides participating in Sci-Port's interactive discovery areas, you can take in an engrossing IMAX production on a 60-foot dome screen. Open Thurs through Sat from 9 a.m. to 5 p.m., and Sun from noon to 5 p.m.

Barham. The museum hosts from three to six temporary exhibitions throughout the year.

The Meadows Museum showcases the work of French academic artist Jean Despujols. On request, visitors can view the museum's award-winning film *Indochina Revisited: A Portrait of Jean Despujols*. This twenty-eight minute documentary will provide some glimpses into the life and work of an extraordinary artist. A seven-minute slide presentation also offers an overview of the Despujols collection.

From December 1936 to August 1938, French artist Jean Despujols made his way through French Indochina's interior, capturing its people and landscapes with pencil, ink, oil, charcoal, and watercolor. This rare collection of 360 works is personalized by excerpts from a diary he kept while traveling through the remote areas of Vietnam, Laos, and Cambodia. Despujols moved to Shreveport in 1941 and became an American citizen in 1945. His collection (hidden at his parents' home in France) survived World War II only to disappear in transit later when the artist requested that it be shipped to him in America. Lost for seven months during the trip from France, the valuable collection surfaced in Guadeloupe, where it had mistakenly been unloaded. The treasure finally arrived in Shreveport in December 1948.

courthouse
copycat

President Harry S. Truman liked Shreveport's Caddo Parish Courthouse (500 Texas Street) so much that he used part of its design for his presidential library in Independence, Missouri.

The Smithsonian Institution exhibited Despujols's works in 1950, and *National Geographic* borrowed twenty-one of his paintings to illustrate a 1951 article on Indochina. Despujols died in 1965, and his works were kept in a Shreveport bank vault. In 1969 Centenary College alumnus Algur H. Meadows purchased the collection, presented it to the college, and also provided funds for a museum to house the rare body of work.

The Meadows Museum is open to the public from 10 a.m. to 6 p.m. Mon through Sat. Admission is free.

Multiple treasures await at the *R. W. Norton Art Gallery* (318-865-4201; rwnaf.org), surrounded by forty landscaped acres that showcase masses of azaleas each spring. Designed in a contemporary style, the gallery at 4747 Creswell Avenue, Shreveport, houses twenty-five exhibition rooms. Here is one of the three largest collections in the country of American Western paintings and sculptures by Frederic Remington and Charles M. Russell, as well as Flemish tapestries (ca. 1540) and works by Corot, Auge Rodin, Sir Joshua Reynolds, and other masters. In addition to its collections of decorative arts, sculptures, and paintings spanning four centuries, the Norton Gallery offers a reference/research library. Except for national holidays, the museum is open from 10 a.m. to 5 p.m. Wed and Thurs; 10 a.m. to 7 p.m. Fri and Sat; and 1 to 5 p.m. Sun. Admission is free.

After a visit to the art gallery, take Route 1 to the campus of Louisiana State University in Shreveport. Near the northeast corner of the campus you'll find the *Pioneer Heritage Center* (318-797-5339; lsus.edu/offices-and-services/community-outreach/pioneer-heritage-center). The complex is composed of several authentic plantation structures that give you a picture—outside the pages of a history book—of how the area's early settlers lived.

The Webb and Webb Commissary serves as a visitor center where you'll get an overview of the operation and an interesting history lesson about the pioneers who settled the northwest corner of Louisiana. The building itself is typical of a company store in an agricultural community, where purchases could be made on credit before a crop was harvested and paid off later when the crop was sold.

You'll come away with a new appreciation for modern dentistry after seeing the dental drill displayed in the doctor's office at the Pioneer Heritage Center. There's also a collection of medical and surgical instruments from the "olden days." One room contains displays of various herbal home remedies.

You'll see the restored 1856 "Big House," a frame antebellum cottage from Caspiana Plantation, and an outside kitchen. A nearby structure, the Thrasher log house, illustrates the dogtrot style. The dogtrot (an open passage supposedly favored by the family dogs) provided a cool covered area for performing household chores during hot weather. The complex also features an equipped blacksmith's shop and a small church.

The Pioneer Heritage Center serves as a "history laboratory" for area schools and visitors. The complex closes for major holidays and from mid-December through February. Admission is modest, and children get in free.

Before continuing east, you may want to sweep south a short distance for a look at a charming little town called **Keachi** (KEY-chi—the second syllable sounds like the *chi* in "child").

To reach Keachi, about 25 miles southwest of Shreveport, take US 171 south (the Mansfield Road), then turn west on Route 5. Incorporated in 1858 as Keachi, the town takes its name from a Native American tribe of Caddo ancestry. You will see a sign that says WELCOME TO HISTORIC KEACHI because members of the local heritage foundation worked hard to get the original spelling restored. At one time, Keachi was known as Keatchie.

Predominantly Greek Revival, described as "kind of a Parthenon temple style," much of the town's architecture dates from the 1840s and 1850s and is on the National Register of Historic Places. A short drive takes visitors by three Greek Revival–style churches, the Masonic Hall, and a Confederate cemetery. On Highway 172 west of downtown stands the 1852 Keachi Baptist Church, originally the chapel for a women's college (no longer in existence). Future plans call for a cultural center on what was once the campus. Another popular event, which takes place the third Sunday of December, features a program of classical and seasonal music performed by a string quartet at the Presbyterian Church with a home tour scheduled afterward.

Next, you can head southeast to historic Natchitoches (described in the section on Central Louisiana) via I-49 or return to Shreveport for an eastward thrust.

Traveling east, Bossier City begins where Shreveport ends. Bossier boasts a well-beaten path, **Harrah's Louisiana Downs**, one of the country's top racetracks for Thoroughbreds. The track is located at 8000 East Texas Street (318-742-5555; caesars.com/harrahs-louisiana-downs).

Also in Bossier City, just across the Red River from downtown Shreveport, you'll find the ***Louisiana Boardwalk*** (318-752-1455; louisianaboardwalk .com), an enticing shopping and entertainment destination. As the state's first lifestyle center, this venue offers outlet shopping, an entertainment district, and riverfront dining. Visitors can hop aboard the Magnolia Belle Trolley, a breezer-style trolley patterned after those of the 1920s and 1930s.

The state's first Bass Pro Shops Outdoor World here lures more than fishermen and hunters. The facility offers equipment for hiking, backpacking, wildlife viewing, camping, outdoor cooking, and more. Look for the Alligator Pit at the front of the store, popular with both tourists and shoppers.

If shopping's not your favorite sport, the Boardwalk offers lots more—a movie theater, bowling alley, carousel rides, live entertainment, riverfront dining, dancing water fountains, and gaming.

The ***Touchstone Wildlife and Art Museum*** (318-949-2323; touchstone museum.com) is located 2.2 miles east of the Louisiana Downs racetrack at 3386 US 80 East, near Bossier City. Founded by professional taxidermists Lura and the late Sam Touchstone, this natural history museum features hand-painted dioramas as backdrops for mounted mammals, birds, and reptiles from all over the world. The collection contains more than 1,000 specimens of wildlife displayed in habitats simulating their natural environments. Sam practiced "taxidermy in action," and all his animals are engaged in lifelike pursuits. Be sure to notice the giraffe and the family of red foxes as well as the 310-pound gorilla that died at age twenty-seven in a zoo.

Also on display are collections of insects, Native American artifacts, war relics, and antique tools. The museum is open Tues through Sat from 10 a.m. to 4:30 p.m. Winter hours from Oct through Feb run Thurs through Sat, 10 a.m. to 4:30 p.m. Parking is free, and admission is modest.

Continue east from Bossier City, by way of either I-20 or U.S. Highways 79–80, and you'll arrive in Minden. Take time to drive along Minden's brick streets to see the downtown area with antiques shops and several homes on the National Register of Historic Places.

Located 7 miles northeast of Minden (and some 30 miles east of Shreveport), you'll find the ***Germantown Colony Museum*** (318-377-6061; sos.la .gov/HistoricalResources/VisitMuseums/GermantownColonyMuseum) at 120 Museum Road off Germantown Road. Watch for signs. Several German families established a village here in 1835, and their furniture, documents, letters, tools, and other artifacts are exhibited both in replica buildings and in original cabins made of hand-hewn logs.

On display is a copy of an 1826 document signed by an archduke ordering Count von Leon (who became the group's leader) to leave Germany. In Pennsylvania the count and his wife met other German families who shared similar religious beliefs. They joined forces and began a journey south to the Minden area, the site they selected to establish a community. During the trip the count died of yellow fever at Grand Encore, Louisiana. Undaunted, the countess carried on and saw the group's goal of establishing a self-sufficient religious colony fulfilled. Germantown functioned as a communal system for more than three and a half decades. The countess earned money by giving music lessons. (Her pupils came from Minden.) Other colonists performed work according to their talents and interests. The group grew grape and mulberry trees for making jellies and wine.

tree*facts*

Forestry is an important factor in Louisiana's economy because paper mills demand vast quantities of wood pulp pine trees. New varieties of the loblolly pine can be brought to market in just nine years.

You'll see the cabin where the countess lived and the kitchen–dining hall where the colonists gathered for meals, as well as reproductions of a smokehouse (on the site of the original), a doctor's cottage, and a blacksmith shop with authentic equipment. All the buildings contain items that the Germantown settlers used, and a map shows where other structures, such as barns and workhouses, once stood.

On the walls of the countess's cabin, you can see remnants of the original wallpaper that she ordered from New Orleans. Among the interesting items on display are the countess's piano, Count von Leon's coronet, the colony's book of laws, German Bibles, ledgers, and slave passes. The museum is open Thurs through Sat from 10 a.m. to 4 p.m. and also by appointment. Admission is modest.

minden's indiana*ties*

Minden's founder, War of 1812 veteran Charles Veeder, purchased 160 acres of land for his new hometown and moved here from Rushville, Indiana, in 1835.

Piney Hills

Travel south on Route 154 for about 3 miles to **Gibsland**. Each year on the weekend closest to May 23, the town stages its ***Authentic Bonnie and Clyde Festival*** with robbery reenactments and more civilized events such as an antique car parade and a street dance. May 23, 1934, is when Bonnie Parker and Clyde Barrow were ambushed in a stolen 1934 Ford by lawmen on Route 154, just a few miles outside Gibsland. The two outlaws were killed in a hail of bullets. Gibsland's *Authentic Bonnie and Clyde Museum* at 1293 S. Second Street contains newspaper accounts and photos relating to the criminal careers of the gun-slinging couple. Check with the town hall at 2463 Main Street (318-843-6141) for more information. For another recounting of the story, visit the *Bonnie & Clyde Ambush Museum* (318-843-1934; bonnieandclydeambush museum.com) at 2419 Main Street in Gibsland. The museum is located in the old Rosa's Café where Bonnie and Clyde dined for the last time before speeding down the road to their deaths.

Afterward, continue south on Route 154 to Mount Lebanon. Located on a downtown corner, the *Stagecoach Museum* (318-286-6926) offers a glimpse of yesteryear; hours vary.

From Mount Lebanon continue south for 5 miles. Here under Ambrose Mountain's shady pines stands a simple marker denoting the *Bonnie and Clyde Ambush Site*. The notorious couple had vowed never to be taken alive. At this spot a surprise attack by Texas Rangers brought the fugitives' spree of bank robberies to a screeching halt. The stone marker, erected by the Bienville Parish Police Jury, reads: "At this site May 23, 1934, Clyde Barrow and Bonnie Parker were killed by law enforcement officials."

One local legend has it that during an attempted robbery of a Ruston bank, the couple took an undertaker as hostage. Clyde's bargain: the man's life for his future services. He was released in Arkansas when Clyde extracted a promise from the mortician to make him "look good" after the inevitable occurred. Later, upon learning the couple had been killed, the undertaker traveled to the Arcadia funeral home (where the bodies had been taken), determined to keep his end of the bargain. Although he found the two corpses beyond salvaging, he was allowed to restore one of Clyde's hands.

After your visit return to Mount Lebanon and continue north to the intersection of US 80. Travel east on this road until you reach *Arcadia*. This small town, along with nearby Homer, Athens, and Sparta, took its name from ancient Greece.

In Arcadia you can stop by the *Bienville Depot Museum* at 2440 Hazel Street to see a permanent exhibit of memorabilia related to Bonnie and Clyde as well as other items of local history. Located downtown, the ca. 1884 depot stands across from City Hall and is also home to the Bienville Chamber of Commerce (318-263-9897; bienvillechamber.org). Arcadia also hosts *Bonnie and Clyde Trade Days* (318-263-2437; bonnieandclydetradedays.com) on Route 9

'Wash Day Meal' Still a Tradition

Before the advent of modern washing machines, many women set aside Monday for the weekly chore of washing and drying the family laundry. At the same time, they would need to plan a hearty supper.

What they did was cook something that wouldn't need a lot of attention, something they could put on the stove and it would be ready at the end of the day.

A favorite washday meal in Louisiana was red beans and rice. It was traditional on Monday and you can still see it being served in homes and restaurants today. Back then, it was also a good way to use pork bones left over from Sunday dinner.

As in many New Orleans recipes, the dish always includes the "holy trinity" of onions, celery, and bell peppers. There are a lot of tomatoes, too, and roux—a mixture of fat and flour that becomes like a paste and is used as a thickening agent.

In addition to being an easy one-pot dinner, red beans and rice was a way of feeding a family economically. Rice and beans is a cheap way to stretch meals, to make the meat go farther. Rice was plentiful in Louisiana so you'll see it in a lot of recipes.

And there are many versions of red beans and rice. Some cooks sauté the celery, bell pepper, and onion before adding it to the beans. Others use more meat. The recipe I'm sharing is basic but you can change it up a bit. A lot of people have their own family recipes for red beans and rice.

Red Beans and Rice

1 pound red beans
3 ribs celery, chopped
1 medium green bell pepper, chopped
1 large onion, chopped
1 clove garlic, minced
1 bay leaf
2 tablespoons dried parsley flakes
12 to 16 ounces smoked sausage, diced
Ham bone or salt pork, optional
Salt and pepper to taste
Boiled white rice

Sort and wash beans. Place beans in 2 quarts of water or chicken stock and soak overnight. Rinse and drain beans. Place in a 5- or 6-quart Dutch oven and add about 6 cups of fresh water or chicken stock. Bring to a boil, then reduce heat to simmer. Cook for about 90 minutes, stirring occasionally. Add remaining ingredients to beans and continue simmering for about an hour. Add additional water if necessary. Serve red beans over cooked white rice. Makes 8 to 10 servings.

about 2.5 miles south of town at 20550 Highway 9. This monthly event takes place the weekend prior to the third Monday.

Homer, located 23 miles north of Arcadia, can be reached by taking Route 9 north, which runs into US 79 just outside town.

Proceed to Homer's town square. On the square's south side, you'll see the *Herbert S. Ford Memorial Museum* (318-927-9190; hfordmuseum.com), located at 519 South Main Street. This museum owes its existence to a German infantry officer's helmet, which inspired the museum's collection. When Herbert S. Ford's sons retrieved the helmet from the town dump, he embarked on a personal campaign to preserve for posterity other items of historical significance.

In 1918 Ford started his collection, and as he accumulated additional artifacts, storage became a problem. At various times the collection occupied a room at the local high school, a railroad car, and the town hall. This remarkable assemblage now has a permanent home in the handsome Hotel Claiborne, a building that dates from 1890.

Downstairs you will see interpretive exhibits for each of the area's major development stages, starting with a dugout canoe and other Native American artifacts. Illustrating Claiborne Parish's pioneer period is an authentic log cabin moved from nearby Haynesville. The structure had to be dismantled and then reassembled inside the museum. Other items of interest at the Ford Museum include a moonshiner's still for making corn whiskey, a scale for weighing cotton bales, an 1830 loom, a collection of handwoven overshot coverlets, and an 1868 Grover and Baker sewing machine. You'll also see a ca. 1832 piano brought by barge and oxcart from New Orleans to nearby Minden. The museum also features a collection of thirty plantation bells, which came from schools and farms throughout the parish.

Don't miss the upstairs area, where individual rooms focus on various themes. You'll see a series of historical settings featuring a doctor's office, chapel, school, general store, hotel room, military room, and the like. Also on display are antique firearms (including Confederate weapons) and a doctor's buggy that was used in a John Wayne movie, *The Horse Soldiers*, filmed in nearby Natchitoches.

Even though the Ford Museum could be considered off the beaten path, about 2,000 persons find their way to this fascinating facility each year. Community volunteers play a major role in the museum's operation. Mon, Wed, and Fri hours are from 9 a.m. to 4 p.m. To see the museum on other days, call for an appointment. There is a modest admission charge.

From the Ford Museum you can walk across the street to the *Claiborne Parish Courthouse*, in the middle of Homer's town square. A classic example of Greek Revival architecture, the structure was completed in 1861 and is still in use. The courthouse served as the departure point for area soldiers mustering for the Confederate cause and remains one of only four pre–Civil War courthouses in Louisiana. Some artifacts from the courthouse are displayed at the Ford Museum.

From Homer, take State Route 2 east to Bernice, a distance of about 25 miles.

You will enjoy a stop at the ***Bernice Depot Museum*** (318-285-2433; tourunionparish.org/destinations/Bernice-depot-museum) and adjacent park. Located at Louisiana and Main streets at 426 E. Fourth Street, the restored 1899 railroad depot features exhibits on railroading, such as its Rock Island memorabilia and a 1938 wooden caboose called The Captain Henderson. You'll also see material on local "Big Woods" history. Open Mon through Fri from 10 a.m. to noon and 1 to 3 p.m., or by appointment.

Afterward, take US 167 to Ruston, about 20 miles south.

Peach Country

You are now in Lincoln Parish, in the heart of peach country. From mid-March through early April, this region becomes a landscape of blooming peach trees. ***Mitcham Farms*** (318-255-3409; michamfarms.com), located just outside Ruston north of I-20 off Highway 544 at 1007 Woods Road, offers fresh peaches for sale from mid-May through mid-August; a retail store with peach products stays open all year.

Ruston hosts the annual ***Louisiana Peach Festival*** (318-255-2031; louisianapeachfestival.org), which has been chosen one of the Southeast Tourism Society's top twenty events for June. Besides eating lots of peach ice cream, festival-goers can enjoy a parade, treasure hunt, cooking contests, craft exhibits, and musical entertainment. The festival is held at 2111 North Trenton Street.

Founded in 1884 as Russ Town, the city of ***Ruston*** was named for Robert E. Russ, who gave the Vicksburg, Shreveport, and Pacific Railroad some acreage to build a railroad and town site on his property. An early center of culture, Ruston was the site of the Louisiana Chautauqua, a summer program providing opportunities for citizens to immerse themselves in music, drama, art, and the like. The parish is now home to two universities, Grambling and Louisiana Tech.

The ***Lincoln Parish Museum*** (318-251-0018; lincolnparishmuseum.org), 609 North Vienna Street, Ruston, serves as a good starting point to begin your exploration of this inviting city. Housed in the lovely Kidd-Davis home, built in 1886, the regional museum features a collection of period furniture, paintings, and other items of historical interest. In the entry hall be sure to notice the hand-painted wall murals that illustrate the Chautauqua and scenes from local history.

You'll see a dollhouse, exquisitely furnished with tiny period pieces, on display downstairs and another on the second floor. The museum's upstairs exhibits feature various collections such as vintage wedding dresses and original textiles designed during the 1930s as part of the government's Works Progress Administration program. Other displays include household items ranging from cornshuck brooms and kitchen utensils to antique radios and tools.

The museum is open Tues through Fri from 10 a.m. to 4 p.m., and on Sat and Sun by appointment.

Jimmie Davis, twice governor of Louisiana (1944–1948 and 1960–1964) and professional country-music artist and composer, started his singing career in 1928. One of his original songs, "You Are My Sunshine," became a hit in 1939 and was later recorded in thirty-four languages. Until his death, Davis paid an annual visit to the Homecoming held at the ***Jimmie Davis Tabernacle***, south of Ruston in Jackson Parish. The revival-style Homecoming, which is held the first Sunday in October, attracts lots of folks. Everyone is invited to bring a dish and enjoy an old-fashioned dinner and a fish fry on the grounds. (At many places in the South, dinner is served at midday, with a lighter supper in the evening.)

Professional gospel groups from across the country join the function held on the site of Davis's parents' home close to the Peckerwood Hill Store. The Tabernacle, built in 1965 by a group of Davis's friends, is located near the junction of Highways 542 and 811 midway between Quitman and Jonesboro at 3185 Highway 542.

At some point during your Ruston visit, plan to stop by the **Log Cabin Grill & Market** (318-255-8023; logcabingrill.com), located a quarter mile north of I-20 at 1906 Farmerville Highway. Housed in an 1886 dogtrot home of hand-hewn logs, the eatery serves barbecue sandwiches or hickory-smoked beef, turkey breast, ham, pork ribs, steaks, burgers, and sausage. Prices are economical to moderate. Open Sun through Thurs from 11 a.m. to 9 p.m., and Fri and Sat 11 a.m. to 9:30 p.m.

Youngsters will enjoy seeing ***Idea Place*** in Woodard Hall on the campus of ***Louisiana Tech University*** (318-257-2866; latech.edu/ideaplace), located on the town's west side. This children's museum features hands-on exhibits designed to encourage both you and the kids to investigate scientific and mathematical concepts and have fun at the same time. Open Mon through Fri 8 a.m. to 5 p.m. or by appointment.

Hot Off the Gridiron

Grambling State University at Grambling, near Ruston, is one of Louisiana's historic African-American colleges. What it is best known for, though, is the large number of its alumni who go on to play pro-football—more than most schools could ever hope for. Drive around the stadium grounds and note the signage directing the media. What the sports reporters know is that if you want to see what the National Football League will look like in the future, go to a Grambling game and read the team roster. And don't miss the halftime show!

Tech is also the place in Ruston to get ice cream—both cones and large containers—filled with such flavors as blueberry cheesecake and the old stand-bys vanilla, strawberry, and chocolate. During summer months you can enjoy peach ice cream, and at Christmastime, peppermint and rum raisin are available. Thanks to the college's cows, you can also purchase other premium dairy products: fresh milk (including chocolate), cheeses, and butter along with rolls and bread—all at extremely reasonable prices. These products are sold daily at the ***Louisiana Tech Farm Salesroom*** (318-257-3550; latech.edu/farm/farm sales) located behind Reese Hall (about 1.5 miles south of the main campus) just off US 80 West at 1306 Clark Drive. You can line up with local students and professors Mon through Fri from 9 a.m. to 5:30 p.m. (With advance notice visitors can tour the nearby dairy plant, which processes these products.)

Places to Stay in Northwest Louisiana

BOSSIER

Hampton by Hilton
1005 Gould Dr.
(318) 752-1112
or (800) HAMPTON
hamptoninn3.hilton.com

Ramada Inn & Conference Center
4000 Industrial Dr.
(318) 747-0711

KEACHI

DeeDee's B&B
422 Church Rd.
(903) 692-0965
deedeebnb.com

MINDEN

Grace Estate B&B
1114 Broadway St.
(318) 639-9595
graceestatemindenla.us

Huffman House Bed and Breakfast
1108 Broadway St.
(866) 925-2912
Huffman.house

RUSTON

Days Inn by Wyndham
1801 North Service Rd.
(318) 251-2360
or (800) DAYS-INN

Hampton Inn
1315 N. Trenton St.
(318) 251-3090
or 800-HAMPTON

Lewis House Victorian Bed & Breakfast
210 E. Alabama Ave.
(318) 255-3848
thevictorianlewishouse.com

SHREVEPORT

2439 Fairfield—A Bed & Breakfast
2439 Fairfield Ave.
(318) 424-2424

Chateau Suite Hotel Downtown Shreveport
201 Lake St.
(318) 222-7620
chateausuitehotel
shreveport.us

Fairfield Place Bed & Breakfast
2221 Fairfield Ave.
(318) 848-7776
thefairfieldplace.com

Knights Inn
4935 West Monkhouse Dr.
(318) 636-0080

Remington Suite Hotel & Spa
220 Travis St.
(318) 425-5000
remingtonsuite.com

Wyndham Garden Shreveport
1419 East Seventieth St.
(318) 797-9900
or (855) 350-4942
wynsp.com

Places to Eat in Northwest Louisiana

BOSSIER

Jack Binion's Steak House
711 Horseshoe Blvd.
(800) 855-0711
caesars.com

Ralph and Kacoo's
1700 Old Minden Rd.
(318) 747-6660
ralphandkacoos.com

Strawn's Eat Shop Also
2335 Airline Dr.
(318) 742-8484
strawnseatshop.com

DOYLINE

Wilson's Steak & Seafood
630 Horseshoe Bend Rd.
(318) 987-2228
wilsonssteakandseafood
.com

RUSTON

Brister's Smokehouse
1420 Cooktown Rd.
(318) 513-9966
bristersbbq.com

Log Cabin Grill & Market
1906 Farmerville Hwy.
(318) 255-8023
logcabingrill.com

Ponchatoulas
109 East Park Ave.
(318) 254-5200
ponchatoulas.com

Roma Italian Bistro
102 N. Monroe St.
(318) 202-3810
myromas.com

Sundown West Tavern Patio & Grill
111 Park Ave.
(318) 255-8028
sundowntavern.biz

SHREVEPORT

Athena Greek and Lebanese Grill
6030 Line Ave.
(318) 869-4260
athenashreveport.com

Blind Tiger
120 Texas St.
(318) 226-8747

Bella Fresca
6307 Line Ave.
(318) 865-6307
bellafresca.com

Chianti
6535 Line Ave.
(318) 868-8866
chiantirestaurant.net

Country Tavern Barbecue
823 Brook Hollow Dr.
(318) 797-4477

Crawdaddy's Kitchen
9370 Mansfield Rd.
(318) 688-7532
crawdaddyskitchen.com

Ernest's Orleans Restaurant and Lounge
1601 South Spring St.
(318) 226-1325
ernestsorleans.com

Herby K's
1833 Pierre Ave.
Shreveport
(318) 424-2724
herbyks.net

FOR MORE INFORMATION

Arcadia/Bienville Parish Chamber of Commerce
2440 Hazel St., Arcadia 71001
(318) 263-9897

Claiborne Chamber of Commerce
519 South Main St., Homer 71040
(318) 927-3271
claibornechamber.org

Kisatchie National Forest
2500 Shreveport Hwy., Pineville 71360
(318) 473-7160 or (318) 927-2061
fs.usda.gov/kisatchie

Ruston-Lincoln Parish Convention & Visitors Bureau
2111 North Trenton St., Ruston 71270
(318) 255-2031 or (800) 392-9032
rustonlincoln.com

Shreveport-Bossier Convention and Tourist Bureau
629 Spring St., Shreveport 71101
(800) 551-8682
shreveport-bossier.org

Webster Parish Convention and Visitors Bureau
P.O. Box 1528, 110 Sibley Rd.,
Minden 71058
(318) 377-4240
visitwebster.net

Area newspapers include the *Minden Press–Herald* in Minden; the *Bienville Democrat–Ringgold Record* in Arcadia; the *Bossier Press–Tribune* in Bossier City; the *Guardian–Journal* in Homer; the *Daily Leader* in Ruston; and the *Shreveport Times* in Shreveport. The *Times* will have the most comprehensive entertainment listings for the area. When near a university, always pick up a copy of the school paper; the local entertainment listings might be useful (and sometimes there are good coupons to clip).

Strawn's Eat Shop
125 Kings Hwy.
(318) 868-0634
strawnseatshop.com

Strawn's Eat Shop Too
7803 Youree Dr.
(318) 798-7117
strawnseatshop.com

Northeast Louisiana

The top northeast corner of Louisiana has some of its richest land along the river bottoms. This is mostly farming country; soybeans predominate, cotton was once king. Settlements grew up along river shipping points.

The area near Monroe has natural gas reserves for mineral wealth. Economically this is a region of sharp contrasts, with a unique cultural blend that affords visitors a pleasant experience among friendly folk.

The upper part of Louisiana is much more akin to nearby Southern states than to the French-Catholic culture near the coast. Notice that older homes look a little different here—the typical saltbox-style Cajun cottage and the New Orleans Victorian shotgun give way to simple farmhouses and the occasional dogtrot (center breezeway) house that derives from log cabin construction.

Cotton Country

After leaving Ruston, travel east on I-20 to **West Monroe**, the first of several stops in Ouachita (*WASH-a-taw*) Parish. You won't find a more inviting place to take a driving break than

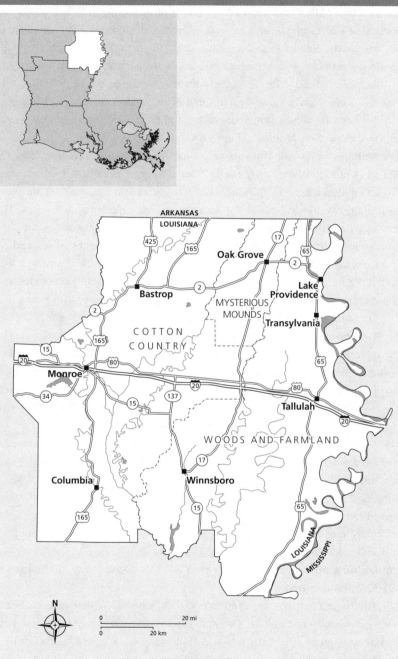

ARKANSAS
LOUISIANA

Oak Grove

Bastrop

MYSTERIOUS
MOUNDS

Lake
Providence

Transylvania

COTTON
COUNTRY

Monroe

Tallulah

WOODS AND FARMLAND

Columbia

Winnsboro

LOUISIANA
MISSISSIPPI

N

0   20 mi
0   20 km

Kiroli Park (318-396-4016; westmonroe.com/resident/kiroli-park/kiroli-park). Located at 820 Kiroli (*ka-ROLL-ee*) Road, the park's entrance is framed by tiers of flowerbeds. Nature trails for hiking and paved paths for jogging provide a pleasant interlude. With a park permit and state license, you can try your luck in the fishing pond. The 150-acre park also features picnic facilities, tennis courts, a lodge, playgrounds, an amphitheater, a conservatory, and restrooms.

Formerly used as a Boy Scout camp, the park is now owned and operated by the City of West Monroe. There's a modest admission fee.

Antiques buffs will want to save time for exploring *Antique Alley* (318-388-3930; antiquealleyshops.org) in West Monroe. Between Trenton Street's 100 and 400 blocks, you'll find a concentration of antiques and gift shops with more than twenty dealers, along with several art galleries and eateries. These renovated shops are housed in downtown buildings dating from the 1880s. Inventories feature American and European antiques, Oriental vases and rugs, silver, crystal, linens, primitives, baskets, railroad and nautical artifacts, quilts, Coca-Cola memorabilia, jewelry, coins, original paintings, and other decorative objects. Most shops are open Tues through Sat from 10 a.m. to 5 p.m.

Continue east until West Monroe merges with *Monroe*. For a fine dinner, try *Warehouse No. 1 Restaurant* (318-322-1340; warehouseno1.com) at 1 Olive Street. The eatery occupies a restored warehouse on the Ouachita River. Featured menu items include Louisiana catfish, blackened jumbo shrimp, red snapper, and rib-eye. Prices are moderate to expensive. Restaurant hours are 11 a.m. to 2 p.m., Tues through Fri for lunch. Dinner hours run from 5 to 9 p.m. Mon through Thurs, and 5 to 9:30 p.m. Fri and Sat; closed Sun.

A world-renowned concert contralto who once performed in Europe, Emy-Lou Biedenharn was forced to return to America when World War II brought her successful operatic career to an abrupt halt. Upon arriving at her Monroe home in 1939, her father, Joseph A. Biedenharn (Coca-Cola's first bottler), presented her with an original John Wycliffe Bible. This gift inspired her to start collecting rare Bibles. She later bought the next-door mansion to contain her vast collection and named it Elsong (for "Emy-Lou's Song"). The result is the *Biedenharn Museum and Gardens* at 2000 Riverside Drive in Monroe (318-387-5281; bmuseum.org).

The theme gardens are gorgeous. You'll see the Garden of Four Seasons with its marble cherubs, an Oriental garden featuring a gazebo and potted bonsai specimens, the Plants of the Bible Garden adjacent to the museum, the Ballet Lawn, and other delightful settings. Except on national holidays, the facility is open Tues through Sat from 10 a.m. to 5 p.m. Modest admission fee.

Take time to drive through Monroe's square-mile *Historic District*, which overlooks the Ouachita River. Founded by Don Juan Filhiol, the original

Car-window Forestry

Driving along I-20 you get a good view of Louisiana forests. Note that the vegetation near the highway is different (and denser) than that back in the woods. More sun, different roadside soils, and mowing by the highway department create a different ecosystem here. Country roadsides are where you find blackberries (late May) and pokeweed (for edible poke salad, late Mar and early Apr).

In the woods the predominant upper-story (tallest) trees are pine (shortleaf and loblolly, some grown from planted seedlings and some natural), plus oak and hickory trees. On the highlands you will see more pines. In the lowlands you will see more hardwoods, which shed leaves in winter.

settlement was known as Fort Miro. Later the town's name was changed to Monroe in honor of the first steamboat to pass that way. Be sure to notice the Ouachita Parish Courthouse. At 520 South Grand Street, near the site of old Fort Miro, stands the frontier-style *Isaiah Garrett House*, a red brick structure that dates from 1840.

Contine to *Masur Museum of Art* (318-329-2237; masurmuseum.org), a modified English Tudor–style building at 1400 South Grand Street. In addition to the museum's permanent collection of paintings, graphics, sculpture, photographs, and other artworks, traveling exhibits are featured throughout the year.

A carriage house serves as an on-premises workshop for art classes. Staff members conduct tours through the museum, which is open Tues through Fri from 9 a.m. to 5 p.m. and Sat from noon to 5 p.m. Admission is free.

At the *Louisiana Purchase Gardens and Zoo* (318-329-2400; monroe zoo.org), 1405 Bernstein Park Drive, Monroe, you can enjoy a delightful outing. Stroll along tree-lined paths and take a leisurely cruise on a canopied pontoon boat along Bayou Safari. The Louisiana Territory's historic events and points

AUTHOR'S FAVORITES IN NORTHEAST LOUISIANA

Louisiana Purchase Gardens and Zoo, Monroe

Masur Museum of Art, Monroe

Poverty Point World Heritage Site, Epps

Tensas River National Wildlife Refuge, Delhi

of interest serve as the park's theme and a backdrop for an animal population that ranges between 450 and 550. The zoo is especially noted for its primate collection; its large group of lemurs (whose forebears came from Madagascar) were all bred on the premises.

In the Louisiana Purchase exhibit, you'll see animals typical of those roaming the region more than two centuries ago—black bears, bison, mountain lions, white-tailed deer, and wild turkeys.

Among lush gardens with live oaks and a host of flowering plants, the zoo offers a gift shop and concessions. Except for Christmas Day, New Year's Day, and Thanksgiving, the facility is open from 10 a.m. to 5 p.m. daily. Admission is modest; children two and under are admitted free.

Continue south on US 165 to **Columbia** in Caldwell Parish. Don't miss the **Martin Home Place** (318-649-6722; caldwellparishla.com/martin-home -place) about a mile north of Columbia off US 165. Watch for the turnoff sign to this historic property, a two-story ca. 1878 farmhouse at 203 Martin Place Road.

The Martin Home Place offers a glimpse of rural life during the early 1900s. Canned jellies from wild fruits make splashes of purple, green, red, and gold on scallop-edged pantry shelves. Martin Home Place is open Thurs and Fri from 10 a.m. to 4 p.m. Donations welcome.

As a result of Columbia's participation in Louisiana's Main Street program (a project of the National Trust for Historic Preservation), many once-forgotten structures have been rescued and restored, such as the unique **Schepis Museum** (318-649-9931; schepismuseum.com). Head for 106 Main Street at the levee, where you'll see this structure topped by life-size statues of George Washington and Christopher Columbus beneath a bald eagle's spread wings.

TOP ANNUAL EVENTS IN NORTHEAST LOUISIANA

Franklin Parish Catfish Festival
Winnsboro, Apr
(318) 435-7607
franklinparishcatfishfestival.com

Deep South PRCA Rodeo
Winnsboro, May & June
(719) 593-8840
rodeousa.com

Louisiana Art and Folk Festival
Columbia, Oct
(318) 649-0726
caldwellparishla.com/
Louisiana-art-and-folk-festival

Built by Italian architect John Schepis, the former mercantile store resembles a Renaissance-style palazzo of the mid-fifteenth century.

The museum, with rotating exhibits every two months, showcases Louisiana artists and offers travel information. One of the museum's past exhibits showcased the 1927 Flood and its devastating impact on eleven states. Other exhibits have featured black-and-white photography depicting rural life in Louisiana from 1939 to 1963 and bayous and wetlands. Hours are Mon through Fri from 10 a.m. to 5 p.m. Free admission.

After strolling along Main Street and browsing for antiques, plan a drive by the nearby **First United Methodist Church**. Ask someone to point you in the direction of this picturesque building, painted dark green with white trim. Constructed from plans brought from Europe by a church member and completed in 1911, the church is listed on the National Register of Historic Places. If time permits, plan a walking tour through the town's hillside cemetery. At this point, you can easily continue south on US 165 to Alexandria and launch an exploration of the state's central section or continue your sightseeing through the state's northeastern corner.

fishyguests

Although catfish farming is more common in the delta area of neighboring Mississippi, there are some commercial catfish ponds in Louisiana. The strangest "tourists" to discover these attractions are the cormorants, fishing birds that come up from their usual haunts on the Gulf to fish in these productive waters. These large black birds with long necks usually perch on utility lines.

Proceed to Bastrop—the seat of Morehouse Parish—north of Monroe. From Bastrop take Route 133 south until you reach Route 134, which leads east to Epps. Located slightly northeast of Epps (and 15 miles north of Delhi) on Route 577 off Route 134, you'll discover Poverty Point World Heritage Site, one of North America's most remarkable archaeological wonders.

Mysterious Mounds

If you happen to fly over Louisiana's northeastern corner during winter months when the earth is not camouflaged by foliage, you can see the outline of a great bird with a wingspan of 640 feet. This bird mound was built some 3,000 years ago by the advanced people of Poverty Point.

The mind boggles to think about the millions of loads of dirt (carried in baskets of animal skin and woven materials and weighing perhaps fifty pounds a load) required to create the site's huge complex of concentric ridges and ceremonial mounds. This tremendous undertaking involved not only tedious labor but also a high degree of engineering expertise. Now known as **Poverty Point World Heritage Site**, this marvel at 6859 Highway 577 (318-926-5492 or 888-926-5492; povertypoint.us) is as archaeologically significant as England's Stonehenge.

In 2014, the site achieved the high honor of being named a World Heritage Site. There are only three other archaeological sites in the U.S. with that distinction.

About 1 percent of Poverty Point has been excavated so far. But that 1 percent tells a remarkable story. When these ridges and mounds were built along Bayou Macon between 1700 and 700 B.C., they were the largest earthworks in the Western Hemisphere. Poverty Point's inhabitants, evidently a bird-revering people, possessed an uncanny degree of astronomical awareness; two of the aisles line up with the summer- and winter-solstice sunsets.

Excavations have uncovered numerous articles of personal adornment, many with bird motifs. Pendants, bangles, and beads of copper, lead, and red jasper appear among the finds. Designs feature various geometric shapes, bird heads, animal claws, locusts, turtles, clam shell replicas, and tiny carved owls. Artifacts also include stone tools, spears, and numerous round earthen balls used for cooking.

You can explore the park on foot—it takes an hour or two to complete the 2.6-mile walking trail—or you can opt for a ride in an open-air tram, which seats forty-four adults. The forty-five-minute tram tour operates from March 1 to October 31 and features stops at Mound A, Mound B, Mound C, and the terrace ridges.

lotsaatl-atls

The Atl-Atl (at-ul at-ul) is a bit of early technology known at Poverty Point in its heyday. It is a spear-throwing aid—a wooden hand-grip supports the spear and enables the thrower to increase range and accuracy. Covering the distance of a football field would be no problem.

The guides at Poverty Point World Heritage Site will demonstrate how one works and let you try your hand. And, you can make your own.

At the visitor center, an audiovisual presentation provides some background on Poverty Point, and you'll see displays of artifacts found on the site. There are also picnic facilities here. If you visit Poverty Point during summer, you may see an archaeological dig in progress. Several state universities schedule digs during this time, and visitors are welcome to watch the excavations.

Poverty Point's hours are from 9 a.m. to 5 p.m. seven days a week year-round, excluding Thanksgiving, Christmas, and New Year's Day. Admission is modest; senior citizens and children three and under are admitted free.

OTHER ATTRACTIONS WORTH SEEING IN NORTHEAST LOUISIANA

Downtown Columbia
Stop and walk about in this pleasant old steamboat stop. Main Street has been revived and focuses on the Ouachita River. Columbia was the hometown of former Louisiana governor John McKeithen.

Lake D'Arbonne State Park
P.O. Box 236
3628 Par Rd. 4410, Farmerville 71241
(318) 368-2086 or (888) 677-5200
crt.state.la.us/Louisiana-state-parks/
parks/lake-darbonne-state-park/
Excellent fishing (buy a license!) and water sports on a man-made lake. Lots of places to picnic.

University of Louisiana at Monroe
700 University Ave.
(318) 342-1000
ulm.edu/
There is always something interesting to see on a university campus. The library will have exhibits, there will be art displays, and you can pick up the campus newspaper for events.

The area surrounding Poverty Point is agricultural country, and the terrain is flat. Along the road you'll see pastureland, crops, cotton gins, and sawmills.

Woods and Farmland

After leaving Poverty Point, head south to Delhi and take US 80 east, watching for a sign to turn right onto a gravel road to reach **Tensas River National Wildlife Refuge** (318-574-2664; fws.gov/refuge/tensas_river). To reach the visitor center, continue south to the end of Quebec Road. (When I entered the refuge via a nearby dirt road, five white-tailed deer leaped across the trail in front of me.)

The Tensas (*TEN-saw*) Refuge's visitor center is a large, rustic building with a rough-cedar exterior. Here you can pick up a refuge map and see dioramas and exhibits of birds, mammals, and reptiles indicative of regional wildlife. The building also houses an auditorium where films and slide shows on the refuge's activities may be viewed. The Hollow Cypress Wildlife Trail, extending about a quarter of a mile, takes you to an observation platform. Along the way you may see birds, squirrels, and, yes, snakes.

As part of the National Refuge System, Tensas serves as a protected habitat for native wildlife such as the Louisiana black bear. According to the Fish and

Wildlife Service, some sixty to one hundred of these bears currently roam the Tensas woods (including the refuge and surrounding forests in Madison Parish).

The Louisiana black bear inspired America's beloved teddy bear. Although the story varies as to locale, it seems that President Theodore Roosevelt, while on a hunting trip to the deep South, wanted to shoot a bear. He once wrote, "I was especially anxious to kill a bear . . . after the fashion of the old Southern planters, who for a century past have followed the bear with horse and hound and horn." Members of Roosevelt's hunting party, knowing of his keen desire to bag a bear, captured a black bear and tied it to a tree—an easy target for the president. Roosevelt's refusal to shoot the helpless animal resulted in much publicity, triggering several editorial cartoons. Soon after the hunting incident, a New York shopkeeper named Morris Michtom came up with the idea of marketing some stuffed toy bears made by his wife, Rose. He called them "Teddy's Bears," and the president gave his approval. The Michtoms' cuddly bears became an instant success, and the rest is history.

Radios have been placed on 200 black bears to monitor their activity in a program aimed at preserving and improving their habitat. The radio collars emit signals, which enable refuge personnel to keep track of the bears' whereabouts.

According to a range technician at the refuge, the small black bears are barely holding their own.

This habitat also provides food and shelter for many other animals, including the bobcat, otter, raccoon, mink, squirrel, woodchuck, wild turkey, barred owl, and pileated woodpecker, as well as thousands of waterfowl and other migratory birds.

In this bottomland forest you'll also see a great variety of trees—several kinds of oak, three or four species of elm, cypress, sweet gum, maple, black locust, honey locust, red haw, and others. Spiky palmetto, muscadine vines, shrubs, and other plants grow here as well.

Deep in the heart of the woods stand the ruins of an old plantation house—about ten handmade-brick pillars (from 10 to 12 feet tall) are all that remain of the former three-story structure. Also hidden in the forest are an old cemetery with eight or nine tombstones and the towering chimney of a pre–Civil War cotton gin.

Primitive canoe launches plus two boat launches allow visitors to explore parts of the refuge by water. Some public hunting is allowed here, but hunters need to familiarize themselves with refuge regulations. Deer hunting permits, which must be requested in advance by writing or phoning, are issued on the basis of drawings. The refuge is open year-round for fishing, but no camping is allowed. If you like the natural things, this is the place to come.

The public is welcome to visit the refuge, which offers an active environmental education program, any time of the year. With the exception of holidays, the visitor center is open Mon through Fri from 8 a.m. to 4 p.m. For further information contact the Refuge Manager, Tensas River National Wildlife Refuge, 2312 Quebec Rd., Tallulah 71282.

After exploring the refuge, head northeast to *Tallulah*. In this area of flat farmland, you'll drive past pecan groves, pastures of grazing cattle, and fields of soybeans, cotton, rice, and wheat.

Tallulah was founded in 1857 and is said to have been named by a traveling railroad engineer in honor of his former sweetheart back home (after he was jilted by a local lady). A bayou winds its way through town and is especially lovely during the holiday season, when lights from a series of Christmas trees placed in the water reflect across its surface.

During the early 1900s Tallulah was the site of a government laboratory where experiments were conducted to find a weapon in the war against the boll weevil. By the 1920s aerial crop-dusting techniques were being developed here. In 1924 Delta Airlines (then called Huff Daland Dusters) entered the picture and established the first commercial crop-dusting company.

Traveling north on US 65 takes you to East Carroll Parish and the town of Transylvania, a tiny community with a spooky name and an unusual white water tower emblazoned with a black bat. The tower has attracted sightseers from England, Italy, Iceland, Japan, and even Romania's Transylvania—including a visitor who identified himself as a descendant of Count Dracula.

After leaving Transylvania, continue north on US 65 (a direct route through the state's northeastern corner to Arkansas) for 10 miles to *Lake Providence*, located on a 6-mile-long oxbow lake that appeared on the local landscape when the Mississippi River couldn't decide which way to go.

According to parish lore, the town of Providence got its name back when Captain Bunch and his band of pirates attacked and robbed travelers on the Mississippi. If settlers got past Bunch's Bend, they thanked Providence for their safe passage. Fortunately, today's visitors don't have to worry about pirates and can stop to enjoy the lake's recreation opportunities.

Afterward, continue to *Byerley House Visitor Center* (318-559-5125; ladelta65.org/places/Byerley.House.htm) at 600 Lake Street (also US 65) in Lake Providence. This restored Victorian structure serves as a visitor and community center. Here you can collect information and maps on local and state attractions, enjoy free coffee (or lemonade during summer months), unpack a picnic lunch in the park across the street, or stroll on the pier over the lake. Byerley House is open from 9 a.m. to 5 p.m. Mon through Fri.

A 500-foot overwater nature walk adjacent to Byerley Park offers a view of **Grant's Canal** through 300-year-old cypress trees. Part of the Civil War Discovery Trail, the channel proved to be a military failure for General Grant in his attempts to find an alternate way to slip Union gunboats past Vicksburg's heavy fortifications during his Southern attack.

Continue to the **Louisiana State Cotton Museum** (318-559-2041; sos.la .gov/historicalresources/visitmuseums/) located a couple of miles or so north of town at 7162 US 65 North, for an overview of the history of cotton and its impact on westward expansion, society, culture, and the economy. Exhibits focusing on the period from 1820 through the 1930s interpret cotton's leading role in the state's heritage and its influence on life in Louisiana and the South as a whole. You'll see a large cotton gin (supposedly the state's first electric version) as well as other museum exhibits and pavilions on the grounds. In early fall, you may get a chance to pick cotton on the premises. The site offers picnic facilities with RV parking nearby. Hours are from 10 a.m. to 4 p.m. Tues through Sat. Admission is free.

thejamesboys

The town of Oak Grove, near Lake Providence, was said to be frequently visited by outlaws Jesse and Frank James, who were such pleasant house guests that they were known to help local kids with their homework.

To see another agricultural product in its various phases, continue north about 8 miles on US 65 to **Panola Pepper Company** (318-559-1774; panola pepper.com) until you see the sign directing you east to Panola, about a quarter of a mile off the highway at 1414 Holland Delta Rd. From planting to pickling peppers, there's always something seasonal and interesting to see at this family cotton plantation, which has diversified into food processing.

The company's country store stocks hot sauces, packaged mixes, gourmet mustards, pepper-stuffed olives, and seasonings. Panola Gourmet Pepper Sauce makes a great souvenir, although hard-core pepper lovers may prefer the Bat's Brew or Vampfire Hot Sauce (inspired by nearby Transylvania). For the undecided, Panola offers a variety pack. The store also carries aprons, T-shirts, and other gift items. Store hours are 8 a.m. to 4 p.m. Mon through Fri. Or you can visit panolapepper.com.

Before leaving the northeast section, consider taking US 65 south toward **Newellton** in Tensas Parish. **Winter Quarters State Historic Site** (888-677-9468), the only plantation home along the banks of Lake St. Joseph that was not torched by Yankee troops during the Vicksburg Campaign, is located at 4929 Highway 608, 6 miles southeast of Newellton (and north of St. Joseph). Ironically, the historic home suffered severe damage during the April 4, 2011, tornado that swept through Tensas Parish. The home was closed for repairs at the time of publication; call the Newellton Chamber of Commerce at (318) 467-5050 for an update on reopening.

The original structure, a three-room hunting lodge, was built in 1805 by Job Routh. The plantation grew to more than 2,000 acres. Later, Routh's heirs added several rooms and a gallery to the lodge. In 1850, Dr. Haller Nutt and his wife, "Miss Julia" (Routh's granddaughter), bought the property and enlarged the house again.

Grant's Vicksburg Campaign brought many changes to Winter Quarters Plantation. The Union army marched south through Tensas during the spring of 1863, carrying out General William Tecumseh Sherman's orders to destroy everything not needed by Union troops. Fifteen plantation homes lined the banks of Lake St. Joseph before the Union troops passed through. When they left, only Winter Quarters remained standing.

According to a letter written by Dr. Nutt and dated October 1863, he and his family were in Natchez, Mississippi, when Union troops tramped through Tensas Parish. His overseer, Hamilton Smith "obtained letters of protection in my [Dr. Nutt's] name from advance officers of this army," Generals McPherson and Smith. Thus, Winter Quarters Plantation was saved. Regrettably, Union army stragglers destroyed all outbuildings, livestock, and crops.

The mansion, which overlooks Lake St. Joseph, features front, back, and side verandas. Furnished with period pieces, the house also contains documents, personal records, copies of diaries, and memorabilia from the Civil War period. Be sure to notice the rare billiard table, ca. 1845. Modest admission.

FOR MORE INFORMATION

Byerley House Visitor Center
600 Lake St., Lake Providence 71254
(318) 559-5125
ladelta65.org/places/Byerley.House.htm

Monroe–West Monroe Convention and Visitors Bureau
601 Constitution Dr., West Monroe 71294
(318) 387-5691 or (800) 843-1872
monroe-westmonroe.org

Winnsboro–Franklin Parish Tourist Center
513 Prairie St., Winnsboro 71295
(318) 435-4488
winnsborochamber.com

Area newspapers include the *News–Star* in Monroe (the largest in the region; should have activities listings weekly), the *Providence-Journal* in Lake Providence, the *Caldwell Watchman* in Columbia, the *Bastrop Daily Enterprise* in Bastrop, the *Franklin Sun* in Winnsboro, and the *Madison Journal* in Tallulah.

Places to Stay in Northeast Louisiana

BASTROP

Preferred Inn & Suites
1220 East Madison Ave.
(318) 281-3621
preferredinns.com

DELHI

Mansion at Red Hill
66 Hwy. 854
(318) 878-5155
mansionatredhill.com

FARMERVILLE

D'Arbonne Lake Motel
101 Dori Dr.
(318) 368-2236

Edgewood Plantation Bed & Breakfast
8876 Hwy. 2
(318) 368-9709
edgewood
plantationlouisiana.com

MONROE

Days Inn by Wyndham
5650 Frontage Rd.
(318) 350-6019

Hampton Inn & Suites
5100 Frontage Rd.
(318) 343-6810

TALLULAH

Super 8 by Wyndham Motel
144 Hwy. 65
(318) 574-2000

WEST MONROE

Hamilton House Inn
318 Trenton St.
(318) 366-2412
hamiltonhouseinn.com

John Thomas Salon Bed and Breakfast
105 North Third St.
(318) 547-3311
johnthomasbandb.com

Motel 6
401 Constitution Dr.
(318) 388-3810
or (800) 228-2800

WINNSBORO

America's Best Value Inn Winnsboro
4198 Front St.
(318) 435-2000

Jackson Street Guest House
803 Jackson St.
(318) 435-4105
jacksonstreetguesthouse
.com

Places to Eat in Northeast Louisiana

COLUMBIA

Mad Jack's Louisiana Kitchen
106 Chase St.
(318) 649-5167

LAKE PROVIDENCE

The Dock
1829 Lake St. (US 65)
(318) 559-3625

MONROE

Copeland's of New Orleans
3851 Pecanland Mall Dr.
(318) 324-1212
copelandsofneworleans
.com

Danken Trail B-B-Q
7702 Desiard St.
(318) 343-0773
dankentrail.com

Genusa's Italian Restaurant
815 Park Ave.
(318) 387-3083

Restaurant Cotton
6745 101 N. Grand St.
(318) 325-0818
restaurantcotton.com

Warehouse No. 1 Restaurant
1 Olive St.
(318) 322-1340
warehouseno1.com

TALLULAH

Country Pride
224 Hwy 65 S
(318) 574-5900

WEST MONROE

Cracker Barrel Old Country Store
309 Constitution Dr.
(318) 325-5505
crackerbarrel.com

La Bella Vita
407 Constitution Dr.
(318) 998-6900

Scott's Catfish & Seafood
2812 Cypress St.
(318) 387-6212

Trapp's
113 S. Riverfront St.
(318) 855-6428
trappsontheriver.com

WINNSBORO

Brown's Landing
120 Brown's Landing Rd.
(318) 435-5291

File Steakhouse and Oyster Bar
3942 Front St.
(318) 367-5190

San Marcos Mexican Restaurant
4198 Front St.
(318) 435-0002

Central Louisiana

Central Louisiana is crossed by rivers and streams, with the old meanders of the Red River and even the Mississippi River still marked in the region's geology. The area around Marksville is on a raised terrace of land, but like most of Louisiana, the general characteristic of the terrain is flat. Rich soil and a long growing season made agriculture, especially of cotton, profitable along the rivers.

Around A.D. 100 the area was home to a Native American culture (named Marksville for its location) of mound building with distinctive pottery. This part of Louisiana was later the gateway to the Spanish colonies of the West, with an early frontier outpost just outside Natchitoches, a city that itself dates to the early eighteenth century.

Woodland and Water

To reach **Fisher**, follow US 171 north and watch for the turn-off sign. Surrounded by a pine forest and off the beaten path, this hamlet could be known as "The Town That Time Forgot." But therein lies its charm—a quaint and quiet place in today's frenetic world.

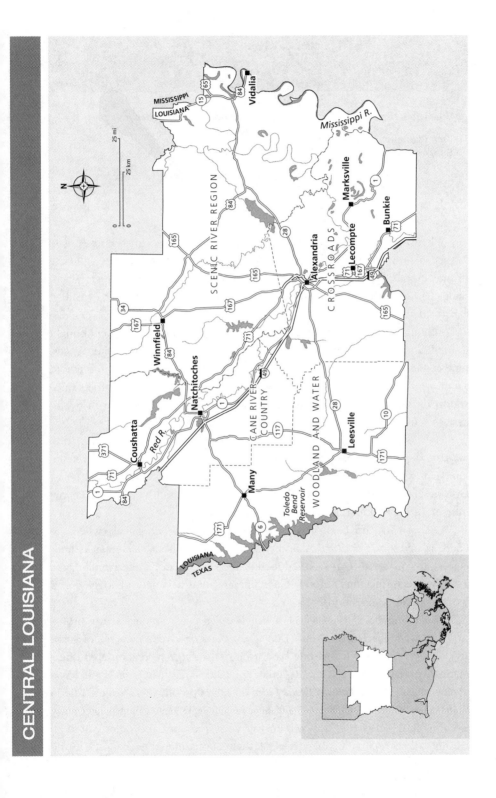

CENTRAL LOUISIANA

AUTHOR'S FAVORITES IN CENTRAL LOUISIANA

Briarwood, Natchitoches

Kent Plantation House State Historic Site, Alexandria

Los Adaes State Commemorative Area, Robeline

Melrose Plantation, Natchitoches

Toledo Bend Lake, Natchitoches

When the Louisiana Long Leaf Lumber Company (also known as Four-L) located here in 1899 to harvest the nearby pine forest, it built Fisher as a base of operations. The town grew into a bustling place with red-dirt streets where mules hauled loads of logs. Fisher was built entirely of local lumber, including board sidewalks.

Although Fisher's sawmill days ended in 1966 when new owners bought the mill and sold the company houses, you can still see white picket fences, pine cottages, a post office, and an opera house where people stood in line to see movies that cost a dime. There's also an old commissary where folks once shopped, standing awhile on the store's long front porch to chat with neighbors. Antiques are now on sale here.

The Fisher Heritage Foundation has received grants to restore the commissary, depot, and opera house. Village residents are working to preserve the lumber town's past, and Fisher has been placed on the National Register of Historic Places. Other sites include a caboose painted red with canary yellow trim, an office building, and the Old Fisher Church.

Visitors can step back into the village's history at Christmas, when the entire village glows with lights, and each May, when Fisher celebrates its heritage with **Sawmill Days** (toledobendlakecountry.com/fisher-sawmill-days), a festival featuring music, food, entertainment, and a variety of logging and woodworking competitions.

Continuing north on US 171 about 6 miles takes you to **Many** (*MAN-ee*). Westward lies Toledo Bend country, an outdoor lover's paradise of some 185,000 acres. Famed for its fine bass fishing, this large recreation area offers marinas, public parks, restaurants, boating facilities, and camping. Should you decide to go fishing, **Toledo Bend Lake** promises prolific possibilities. Toledo Bend Lake Country (318-256-5880 or 800-358-7802, toledobendlakecountry .com) at 1601 Texas Highway will answer your questions and point you in all the right directions on this big lake. Ask them about annual events such as the nearby *Zwolle Tamale Fiesta* held the second weekend in October (zwolle tamalefiesta.com).

Leaving Many, take Route 6 northeast to Natchitoches Parish.

Cane River Country

The lovely town of *Natchitoches* (pronounced *NAK-a-tush*), which sprang up on the Red River, is now located on the Cane River (actually a lake). The town didn't move—the river did. But perhaps that's why the place retains its historical charm. As Louisiana's oldest town, Natchitoches was a thriving steamboat port that showed promise of growing into a major metropolis, second in size only to New Orleans, until destiny, in the guise of a spring flood, deemed otherwise. When the Red River carved a new course, Natchitoches was separated from the main body of water and lost its strategic location as a trade center. The shrunken stream left flowing through the old channel was renamed the Cane River. A dam constructed in 1917 created Cane River Lake, which drifts through the city's heart.

Natchitoches also holds the distinction of being the oldest permanent European settlement in the entire Louisiana Purchase Territory, a vast acreage from which all or parts of fifteen states were carved.

When French Canadian Louis Juchereau de St. Denis (de-NEE) docked here in 1714, he found the Native American Natchitoches (a Caddo tribe) living along the north bank of the Red River. The town takes its name from this tribe, and various translations of the word include "place of chinquapin eaters," "chestnut eaters," and "pawpaw eaters." St. Denis chose this spot to found Natchitoches, which evolved from a trading post with both the Native Americans (the French exchanged guns, knives, and trinkets for furs, bear oil, salt, and such) and the Spanish. To thwart Spanish advances *Fort St. Jean Baptiste* (318-357-3101; crt.state.la.us/ Louisiana-state-parks/historic-sites/fort

losadaes

Natchitoches was once an outpost on the frontier. Los Adaes, near Robeline and Many on Louisiana Highway 6 at Highway 485, is where a mission was built by the Spanish in 1717 and a fort was established in 1721 to guard this section of the Camino Real (royal road).

Until 1773 this was the capital of the Spanish Province of Texas. Los Adaes today is a state historic site where visitors will find reconstructions of buildings and evidence of archaeological explorations of the setting. *Los Adaes State Historic Site* is located at 6354 Highway 485, Robeline; (318) 356-5555; crt.state.la.us/ Louisiana-state-parks/historic-sites/ los-adaes-state-historic-site.

-st-jean-baptiste-state-historic-site/index) was established here in 1716. Located at 155 Jefferson Street, the fort boasts a lovely entrance and attractive and inviting museum. The site is open Wed through Sun from 9 a.m. to 5 p.m. Modest admission. Free for senior citizens and children age 3 and under.

You can see a replica of the old French fort with its walls of sharpened logs on the riverfront. The compound, which contains the commandant's house, a small warehouse, a chapel, barracks, and three huts, is not far from the American Cemetery (where some historians surmise St. Denis and his wife are buried).

If you happen to drive through Natchitoches during December, you'll see why it's called the City of Lights. Some 170,000 multicolored lights glow along the downtown riverbank during the Christmas Festival of Lights (318-652-7078; natchitocheschristmas.com), an annual event that attracts thousands of sightseers. The movie *Steel Magnolias,* which was filmed in Natchitoches, features some night scenes showing this glittering spectacle. You may want to take a Steel Magnolias tour to see some of the locations used in the movie. For more information and a local map, stop by the Natchitoches Convention & Visitors Bureau (318-352-8072 or 800-259-1714; natchitoches.com) at 780 Front Street.

Along the town's picturesque brick-paved Front Street, you'll pass many antebellum structures in the original downtown area. At the 1843 **Hughes Building**, be sure to notice the courtyard with its ornate spiral staircase of cast iron.

To continue your exploration you can park down by the riverside, just below Front Street, to see the **Roque House and Gardens**. Located on the bank of Cane River Lake at 760 Front Street, the Roque (*rock*) House dates from the 1790s. Originally built as a residence at nearby Isle Brevelle, the French colonial structure of hand-hewn cypress was moved to its present site during the 1960s. The restored wood-shingled cottage is especially noted for its *bousillage* (*BOO-see-ahj*) construction. Bousillage, which was used in a number of the state's French colonial buildings, was made by boiling Spanish moss and combining it with mud and hair scraped from animal hides. When packed between wooden wall posts, the procedure was known as *bousillage entre poteaux.* Covered with plaster (sometimes made with lime and deer hair), this mixture provided good insulation.

Natchitoches offers a number of other attractions such as the **Old Courthouse** and the **Immaculate Conception Catholic Church**, both located on Second and Church streets, and also the **Trinity Parish Church** at Second and Trudeau streets.

Don't leave Natchitoches without stopping by **Lasyone's Meat Pie Restaurant** (318-352-3353; lasyones.com), located at 622 Second Street. Meat pies,

TOP ANNUAL EVENTS IN CENTRAL LOUISIANA

Alexandria/Pineville's Mardi Gras Weekend
Alexandria, Feb
(318) 473-9501 or (800) 551-9546
alexmardigras.net

Choctaw-Apache Powwow
Ebarb, Apr & May
(318) 645-2588
Choctaw-apache.org

Sawmill Days
Fisher, May
(318) 256-5880
toledobendlakecountry.com

Melrose Plantation Arts and Crafts Festival
Melrose, Apr
(318) 379-0055
Melroseplantation.org

Natchitoches-Northwestern Folk Festival
Northwestern State University, July
(318) 357-4332
Natchitoches.com/events

Zwolle Tamale Fiesta
Many, Oct
(318) 645-2334
zwolletamalefiesta.com

Natchitoches Pilgrimage
Natchitoches, Oct
(800) 259-1714
Natchitoches.com/
fall-pilgrimagetour-homes

Louisiana Pecan Festival
Colfax, Nov
(318) 627-5196
lapecanfest.com

Christmas Festival of Lights
Natchitoches, Dec
(318) 652-7078 or (800) 259-1714
natchitocheschristmas.com

the featured specialty, resemble fried fruit pies except for the filling. For these tasty items, the staff uses a combination of pork and ground beef with onions and spices. The slowly cooked meat is later thickened with a roux (flour sautéed in oil as a thickening agent) and chilled overnight. At serving time a dollop of the mixture is dropped on a circle of dough; after the crust is folded over and crimped on the edges, the pie is ready to fry.

A former grocer, Jamel Lasyone (*lassie-OWN*) started the business in 1967. Angela Lasyone and Tina Lasyone Smith continue to carry on family tradition at this restaurant, established by their father.

Order a meat pie with dirty rice (the name given to the dark-stained version cooked with chicken giblets) and a green salad. For dessert you'll want to try another house specialty, Cane River cream pie. The restaurant offers a complete menu and features daily luncheon specials, such as red beans and rice with sausage, veal cutlets, catfish, or chicken breast. Prices are economical.

Hours are Mon through Sat from 7 a.m. to 3 p.m. You can also order meat pies at lasyones.com.

Allow some time for driving through the fertile plantation country surrounding Natchitoches, where you'll see pecan groves and fields of soybeans and cotton. You'll also want to visit one or more of the many nearby plantation homes for which Cane River Country is famous, but be sure to call before you go because operating hours change.

Don't miss ***Melrose Plantation*** (318-379-0055; melroseplantation.org), 2 miles east of Route 1 at the junction of Routes 493 and 119 at 3533 Route 119. Your guide will tell you the legend of the remarkable Marie Thérèse Coincoin, a freed slave who obtained a land grant from the Spanish colonial authorities and, with the help of her sons, established and operated what is now Melrose Plantation.

You'll see the Yucca House, Marie Thérèse's original two-room cypress-timbered home built in 1796, and the African House, supposedly the only original Congo-like architecture still standing in the United States. Other plantation buildings include the white clapboard Big House built in 1833 by Marie Thérèse's grandson, the Weaving House, the Bindery, Ghana House, and the Writer's Cabin. Also on the grounds is the cabin home of former Melrose cook Clementine Hunter, whose colorful and charming murals cover the upstairs walls of the African House.

At one time Melrose was one of the country's largest pecan orchards. John Henry and his wife, fondly known as Miss Cammie, restored the plantation's buildings and turned Melrose into a renowned retreat for artists and writers. Among the many writers who accepted their hospitality were François Mignon, Erskine Caldwell, Lyle Saxon, and Caroline Dormon.

Melrose, which closes on Christmas and New Year's Day, is open Tues through Sun from 10 a.m. to 5 p.m., and the last tour starts at 4:15 p.m. Admission is charged.

Afterward, continue to ***Magnolia Plantation Home*** (318-356-8441) at 5487 Highway 119 in the town of Natchez near Derry. Surrounded by stately oaks and magnolias (which inspired the home's name), the large manor house replaces one built in the 1830s. During the Civil War, General Nathaniel Banks's Union forces burned the original home. The family restored it in 1896, using the same foundation and floor plan with fourteen fireplaces and twenty-seven rooms, including a Catholic chapel still used for Mass. Throughout the house, you'll see Louisiana-crafted and Southern Empire furnishings such as the parlor's square grand piano made of rosewood.

A working plantation of 2,192 acres, Magnolia has been in the same family since 1753, when Jean Baptiste LeComte II acquired it through an original

French land grant. The property also features several dependencies and a massive mule-drawn cotton press. Once known for its racing stables, this National Bicentennial Farm is open for tours Tues through Sun 10 a.m. to 5 p.m.; the last tour starts at 4:15 p.m. Admission is charged.

If time permits, drive south along Route 1, where you'll see acres of pecan groves. Several pecan processing plants dot the roadside in this area. In season you can stop and buy whole or shelled pecans, roasted pecans, candies made with pecans, and other nutty delights.

Afterward you can either drive on to Alexandria, the state's crossroads, or head north of Natchitoches to take in some interesting sites in that direction.

Taking the northern option, you can retrace your route to Natchitoches or get on US 71 north for a visit to **_Briarwood_** (318-576-3379; briarwoodnp.org) at 216 Dormon Road in the northwest corner of Natchitoches Parish. This wonderful wooded area, some 19 miles north of Campti, is located just off Route 9, north of Readhimer and 2 miles south of Saline. (Saline is especially noted for its fine watermelons, so you may want to stop and buy one if you pass this way during summer months.) Briarwood, a wild garden definitely off the beaten path, will especially delight botanists and bird-watchers. A rustic sign suspended over a wooden gate marks the entrance to this 154-acre nature preserve, once the home of Caroline Dormon, America's first woman to be employed in forestry.

scrapbook heaven

Cammie Henry, longtime owner of Melrose, was renowned for her extensive collection of clippings and scrapbooks on Louisiana history. Everything is now in the Cammie Henry Collection at the Watson Library at Northwestern State University in Natchitoches. To learn more about "Miss Cammie" and her collections, tap into nsula.edu.

A pioneer conservationist, Dormon played a major role in establishing Louisiana's Kisatchie National Forest, which extends over seven parishes and covers 600,000 acres. Also known internationally for her work as a naturalist, Dormon described and painted rare native species of plants. Her books _Flowers Native to the Deep South_ and _Wild Flowers of Louisiana_ are both botany classics.

Briarwood boasts Louisiana's largest collection of plants native to the southeast, where spring might bring spectacular shows of pink dogwoods, white pompons, crabapples, pale pink native azaleas, and mottled-green trilliums. The nature preserve is also home to a woodland iris garden and six different species of pitcher plants.

This serene retreat can be explored on foot or aboard a shuttle. Located deep in the wood, Miss Carrie's former log cabin home is now a museum. The house contains furniture, household items, and original illustrations from one of the naturalist's books. Be sure to spend a few minutes looking through the scrapbooks, where you'll see some of Miss Carrie's correspondence. One note to a friend reads: "That everlastin' bird book is out at last! I'm bound to say I think it's a darlin'—even if I am its mama!"

Surrounding the cabin you'll see many giant trees, including a longleaf pine possibly three centuries old, known as Grandpappy. Nearby are tulip and sourwood trees, big-leafed magnolias, and native sasanquas—fall-blooming camellias with delicate blossoms and handsome dark foliage.

A trail winds past a pond and through tall pines, mountain laurel, and wild ginger to a one-room cabin on a gentle knoll even farther back in the forest. The simply furnished log house, called Three Pines Cabin, served as Miss Carrie's retreat for writing and painting when too many visitors found their way to Briarwood. It was her hideaway when the world beat a path to her door. Even though Briarwood does not advertise, some 2,000 visitors discover it each year. The nature preserve is open to the public every weekend in Mar, Apr, May, Oct, and Nov. Hours are from 9 a.m. to 5 p.m. on Sat, and from noon to 5 p.m. on Sun. Tours at other times may be arranged by appointment. Admission is charged.

corduroyroads

At Briarwood the vegetation is not the only authentic Louisiana object underfoot. On the grounds is a segment of what was a "corduroy road." These old carriage roads were made of logs laid sideways along the roadbed, providing nineteenth-century riders with a jolting journey.

Scenic River Region

After exploring and savoring Briarwood, head for neighboring Winn Parish, the home of Winnfield and the birthplace of Huey P. Long, O. K. Allen, and Earl K. Long—all former governors of Louisiana. Both Routes 126 and 156 east will take you to Highway 167, where you'll turn south to reach Winnfield (less than an hour's drive from Briarwood).

Downtown, you'll see a statue of Huey Long on the courthouse lawn. Nearby, the ***Louisiana Political Museum and Hall of Fame*** (318-628-5928; lapoliticalmuseum.com), housed in a ca. 1908 train depot at 499 East Main Street, offers a look at the lives and times of Louisiana's prominent politicians. You'll see life-size wax figures of brothers Huey P. and Earl K. Long.

Other exhibits include photos, campaign memorabilia, and audio and video excerpts from political speeches and public appearances. The museum is open Mon through Fri from 9 a.m. to 5 p.m., and Sat by appointment. Free admission.

Stop by the **Earl K. Long State Commemorative Area**. Established in honor of Louisiana's first three-term governor, the one-acre park features a symmetrical design and lovely landscaping. An 8-foot bronze statue, dedicated on July 4, 1963, stands as a memorial to Earl Kemp Long, younger brother of Huey Long. A hedged circular sidewalk leads to a pavilion, a pleasant spot for a picnic.

From Winnfield, take US 167 south via Pineville to Alexandria.

Crossroads

Arriving in Pineville, you'll cross the Red River via the O. K. Allen Bridge to reach Alexandria. Known as a crossroads city, **Alexandria** marks the state's geographic center. The parish seat of Rapides (*ra-PEEDS*), Alexandria lost most of its buildings and records in 1864 when the Yankees set fire to the city during the Civil War. Another disaster occurred with the flood of 1866. The Red River separates Alexandria from its sister city, Pineville.

Soon after your arrival, stop by **Kent Plantation House** (318-487-5998; kenthouse.org) at 3601 Bayou Rapides Road, Alexandria. Believed to be Central Louisiana's oldest existing building (one of a few area structures to survive the Civil War), the home was completed in 1800. Kent House, which stands on brick pillars, exemplifies the classic Louisiana style of French and Spanish colonial architecture. An elevated construction protected buildings from floods and dampness.

Now restored, the house was moved to its present location from the original site, 2 blocks away. **Kent House** serves as a museum where visitors may see eight rooms filled with Empire, Sheraton, and Federal furniture, authentic documents dealing with land transfers, and many interesting decorative items.

The four-acre complex also contains slave quarters, a notched-log carriage house, a barn, a blacksmith shop, a sugar mill, and gardens. You'll see a detached kitchen and milk house along with a collection of early nineteenth-century cooking utensils. From Oct through Apr open-hearth cooking demonstrations are given each Wed between 9 a.m. and noon. Prepared foods might include corn bread, chicken, corn soup, lima beans, and cakes. Admission. Kent House is open from 9 a.m. to 5 p.m. every day except Sun, when the house is open by appointment only. Tours begin on the hour from 9 a.m. to 3 p.m. Admission is charged.

Museum Honors Three Cousins Who Became World Famous

Three little boys growing up in small town Louisiana showed early musical talents. But the three cousins probably had no idea that their names would one day be known worldwide.

The three youngsters from Ferriday were Jerry Lee Lewis, Jimmy Swaggart, and Mickey Gilley—sometimes known as the Killer, the Preacher, and the Cowboy.

"We're proud of all of them," says Linda Gardner, director of the **Delta Music Museum & Arcade Theater**. "We have so much talent in the Mississippi Delta and it includes every genre of music."

Located just 15 minutes from Natchez, this Ferriday museum is a hidden gem along the Mississippi Blues Trail. Opened in 2002, the museum is housed in a historic post office building and filled with musical treasures.

The first exhibit in the museum shows mannequins of the three cousins at the piano—Jerry Lee playing while Mickey and Jimmy sing along. Born within 12 months of each other—Jerry and Jimmy in 1935, Mickey in 1936—during the Great Depression, the cousins grew up poor and were raised in the Pentecostal Church. All three were interested in music.

The boys also played a dangerous game called "Unconquered," Gardner says. The three would dare each other to do some death-defying feat such as jumping from boxcar to boxcar or attempting crazy tricks on their bicycles.

"One of them would do a stunt and the others would have to do it, too, or be 'Conquered.' It's a wonder they weren't killed," she says.

Instead, Jerry Lee grew up to be a piano-thumping rock-and-roll pioneer; Jimmy gained fame as a televangelist; and Mickey became a county music legend best known for

Don't miss the ***Alexandria Museum of Art*** (318-443-3458; themuseum .org) at 933 Second Street, Alexandria. The museum occupies the original Rapides Bank building, which dates from 1898, the first major building to appear after twin disasters of fire and flood in the 1860s. The facility features a fine collection of modern and contemporary works as well as Louisiana folk arts, traveling exhibits, and a gift shop. The museum, which also sponsors educational and interpretive programs, is open Tues through Fri from 10 a.m. to 5 p.m., and Sat from 10 a.m. to 4 p.m. The admission fee is nominal.

Continue to nearby ***River Oaks Square Arts Center*** (318-473-2670; riveroaksartscenter.com) at 1330 Main Street, Alexandria. This lovely Queen Anne–style house was given to the city by the Bolton family to be used for opening Gilley's, the world's biggest honky-tonk in Texas and model for the dance hall in the 1980 John Travolta movie *Urban Cowboy*.

On display are Mickey Gilley's stage outfit, Jimmy Swaggart's Bible and religious album covers, and photos of Jerry Lee including one of his young wife. The 22-year-old singer married his 13-year-old cousin in 1957. The marriage caused Jerry Lee's career to crash when radio stations refused to play his music, fans turned against him, and concerts were cancelled. It took years for Jerry Lee to regain his musical following.

Wall exhibits and films showcase other talents from the Mississippi River Delta country like Aaron Neville, Irma Thomas, Conway Twitty, Fats Domino, Pete Fountain, Tony Joe White, "Pee Wee" Whittaker, Percy Sledge, Johnny Horton, Clarence "Frogman" Henry, Johnny Rivers, James Burton, the Ealey Brothers, and many more.

Performances of the stars can be watched in the video room. Visitors also can learn how Conway Twitty got his unusual name and almost became a baseball star and why Aaron Neville wears a St. Jude earring.

Born Harold Lloyd Jenkins, Conway Twitty was a baseball standout in high school and on semi-pro teams and was offered a contract with the Philadelphia Phillies. But, before he could sign, the young man was drafted into the Army. When he returned from the Korean War, the soldier decided to focus on his second love—music.

As for that name, Gardner says he picked it from a road map because Harold Lloyd Jenkins didn't seem a fitting entertainer's name. "He got the Conway from Conway, Arkansas, and the Twitty from Twitty, Texas," she says.

The story about the St. Jude earring that Aaron Neville wears is that he honors St. Jude with helping him kick drugs. "Aaron's mother told him about St. Jude," Gardner says. "St. Jude is the patron saint of hopeless cases."

For more information: Contact the Delta Music Museum, 218 Louisiana Avenue, Ferriday 71334; (318) 757-9999; deltamusicmuseum.com. Hours are from 9 a.m. to 4 p.m. Mon through Fri. Free admission.

the arts. Adjacent to the home stands a new structure housing studios and galleries. About forty local artists now work at the center, and you can watch creativity in action as painters, weavers, and sculptors practice their callings. Browse through individual studios and enjoy Preston Gilchrist's wax encaustic creations, Joseph Pearson's portraits, and Debra Smith Barnes's works in mixed media. In addition to showcasing artists at work, the center sometimes offers classes and workshops in drawing, watercolor, printmaking, sculpture, and collage for both children and adults. River Oaks Square, which features more than twenty exhibits a year, is open from 10 a.m. to 4 p.m. Tues through Fri, and from 10 a.m. to 2 p.m. on Sat. Besides browsing, you can also buy unique works of art. Modest admission.

Challenge awaits at ***Oakwing Golf Club*** (318-561-0260; oakwinggolf.com). Located at 2345 Vandenburg Drive, 1 mile off I-49, the Jim Lipe–designed course features tree-lined fairways and undulating greens along with a series of Scottish links–style holes that require your attention. But you can take the guesswork out of your game because the golf carts come equipped with global positioning systems that let you know exactly how far you are from the pin.

This course ranks as a prime example of how a property can be recycled. Now England Industrial Airpark, the airport area had its beginning as an emergency airstrip to Esler Field Airport. In 1939, the Army Air Corps leased it to use as a training facility for B-17 and later B-29 crews during World War II. The site served as home for the Twenty-third Fighter Wing, the successor to the Flying Tigers of Claire Chennault in China.

We Want Beads!

Unless you've done it, it's hard to imagine the thrill of catching a string of beads flung in your direction by Mardi Gras revelers on passing floats. It's absolutely heady—the more you snatch, the more you want. And the number of necklaces you wear reveals the level of your greed (though many of the athletically inclined pass their loot on to others whose catching skills have not evolved to such a high level).

Nearby, a man not only gets beads—the strand lands around his neck. Now that's what I call precision pitching. Between passing floats, kids play around with a basketball, doing tricks on the sidelines. The excitement is contagious, and you get totally caught up in the carnival atmosphere with uplifted arms as far as you can see.

Standing beside me, a woman instructs her two granddaughters: "It's not 'give me something—it's throw me something, mister or please.' Wave your arms and yell, or you won't get anything." The girls follow her advice as festive floats pass with masked riders tossing shiny beads, plastic cups, doubloons, candy, and other treats. Then comes a beauty queen, seated atop a convertible. "Oh, don't waste your breath on her," my parade neighbor says. "She can't throw this far, but she's certainly got that pageant wave down pat."

For a fun-filled, family-oriented Mardi Gras celebration, including a chance to catch those beads, head to the Alexandria/Pineville area in Louisiana's Crossroads. The festival features a full weekend of entertainment. Friday night arrivals can enjoy specialties from the area's best restaurants at booths set up in the Alexandria Riverfront Center. Saturday events include a children's parade, a 5K run, and another run for fun. Parades on both Saturday and Sunday start with policemen on motorcycles, their sirens going full blast, performing figure eights. Then come the marching bands and flamboyant floats. The annual Krewe Parade draws some 150,000 attendees from as far away as East Texas, South Louisiana, and Mississippi, and an evening post-parade party follows at Convention Hall. For more information, call (318) 442-9546 or (800) 551-9546, or check out alexandriapinevillela.com.

ANOTHER ATTRACTION WORTH SEEING IN CENTRAL LOUISIANA

Alexandria Zoological Park
3016 Masonic Dr., Alexandria
(318) 473-1143
thealexandriazoo.com
This pleasant zoo features a miniature train to ride and more than 500 animals. In the award-winning habitat exhibit, which showcases the state's wildlife, architecture, industry, and culture, you'll see alligators, otters, snapping turtles, and more. Open daily from 9 a.m. to 5 p.m.; closed Thanksgiving, Christmas, and New Year's Day. Small admission fee.

In 1946, the base was gradually turned over to the city of Alexandria to be used as a municipal airport, but with the outbreak of hostilities, it was reactivated as Alexandria Air Force Base and assigned to the Tactical Air Command. Then, in 1955, the property became England Air Force Base until another base closing in 1992. It now serves as Alexandria International Airport.

Along with the airport and related facilities came a nine-hole base golf course, the nucleus of today's Oakwing Golf Club. While playing a round, you can enjoy the setting with lakes, bayous, and wildlife, and even dip into some history. You'll see an old cemetery and a cluster of five mounted military aircraft from World War II through the Gulf War at Heritage Park, which honors the Flying Tigers.

Oakwing Golf Club made the cut as one of the state's fifteen courses included in the Audubon Golf Trail, named for renowned naturalist and artist John James Audubon.

Afterward, head back downtown and cross the Jackson Street Bridge to Pineville's Main Street. You'll soon see a cemetery on the left and then *Mount Olivet Chapel*. Built in 1854, the church was dedicated by Bishop Leonidas Polk, who later "buckled sword over gown" to become a Confederate general. The picturesque chapel survived the Civil War, probably because it served as a headquarters for the Union Army.

The Gothic Revival structure, which features some Tiffany windows, was designed by Richard Upjohn, the architect of New York's Trinity Church. Except for its oak floor, the chapel is constructed entirely of native pinewood. Take some time to explore the surrounding cemetery with tombstone dates as early as 1824 still discernible. For a cemetery tour or information about the chapel, call (318) 473-8787.

Ya-Yas

What other state could possibly serve as a setting for *Divine Secrets of the Ya-Ya Sisterhood*? Alexandria native Rebecca Wells uses central Louisiana as a backdrop for her Southern novel based on a group of friends who remain close through the years and through life's changing circumstances. In Alexandria, you can experience the charm and southern hospitality of Louisiana's Crossroads as you visit sites that inspired Wells's bestseller.

Military buffs may want to visit the ***Alexandria National Cemetery*** at 209 East Shamrock Avenue, also in Pineville. This cemetery, an art gallery in stone, contains graves from the Civil War, Spanish-American War, and both World Wars.

Central Louisiana's role in supporting the nation's armed forces goes back a long way. In Pineville at 623 G Street, the ***Louisiana Maneuvers & Military Museum*** (318-641-5733; geauxguardmuseums.com) depicts the history of the region's commitment with Maneuvers-era arms, uniforms, and equipment at Camp Beauregard. This facility honors soldiers and civilians of the Louisiana Maneuvers. On the grounds, you'll see a Sherman tank, Patton tank, F-100 Super Saber aircraft, and more.

The re-created World War II barracks museum, which even includes a latrine "living room," houses sergeants' quarters and illustrates how the troops were bunked—head to foot—to help prevent spread of contagious diseases.

Exhibits showcase main players in the Maneuvers—Generals Marshall, Eisenhower, Patton, and Bradley. You'll see a rare and battered Japanese war flag from a ship in Hiroshima Harbor when the atomic bomb was dropped. Other displays of uniforms, and photographs of women at work doing "men's jobs," interpret the female contribution to the war effort.

Upstairs, a home front display shows a family living room with period furnishings, sweetheart pillows, ration cards, and blue stars (in service) and gold stars (killed in service), which were placed on the windows of family dwellings.

Currently a Louisiana Army and Air National Guard training facility, the camp served as an induction center during World War II. Have a photo ID ready as you approach the post. The museum is open Tues through Fri from 9 a.m. to 5 p.m. Free admission.

After visiting Pineville take US 71 south to ***Lecompte***, about 12 miles south of Alexandria to 1810 US 71. Here you'll find ***Lea's Lunchroom*** (318-776-5178;

Dip into Nostalgia at Lea's Lunchroom

Established in 1928, **Lea's Lunchroom** in Lecompte attracts the locals as well as visitors from all over the world. Lea's has been featured on numerous TV shows and in magazines, newspapers, and tour guides throughout the country. Toby Traylor, grandson of the late Mr. Lea Johnson who founded this popular restaurant, now serves as manager. Here he shares the recipe for a perennial favorite:

Chicken and Dumpling

1 stewing chicken
1½ to 2 teaspoons salt
1 onion, chopped
1 red bell pepper, chopped
2 cups flour
2 teaspoons baking powder
1 teaspoon salt
⅓ cup shortening
½ cup milk

Cut up chicken; place in deep pot and barely cover with water. Add salt and simmer until meat is tender.

Debone chicken and set aside, reserving the broth. Add chopped onion and bell pepper to broth, and cook down until soft.

Sift together the flour, baking powder, and salt; cut in shortening. Add milk to make a stiff dough. (Note: If you don't want to make your own dough, use biscuit mix.) Roll out to ¼-inch thickness on floured board. Cut into 1-inch squares, and sprinkle with flour. Drop into briskly boiling chicken stock. Cover tightly and simmer for about 40 minutes. Add meat last and serve. Yields 6 to 8 servings.

leaslunchroom.com), a country-style cafe that dishes up hearty Southern cooking. Lea Johnson established this popular eatery in 1928.

The staff believes in fast service and objects to written menus because "they take too much time." At Lea's the server recites the menu, which might feature red beans and sausage with rice and crackling corn bread or a choice of fried fish, beef tips, or ham along with turnip greens and sweet potatoes. Prices are economical. Milk is served in chilled glasses, and you can have a demitasse of coffee after your meal. The restaurant is famous for its hams baked in dough and homemade pies made from secret family recipes. The staff makes about 65,000 pies a year, including apple, pecan, banana cream, cherry, blueberry, blackberry, lemon, chocolate, and coconut. In fact, the Louisiana senate named Lecompte the Pie Capital of the state as a tribute to Lea's seven-plus decades of service.

Cotton: Then and Now

While in this area, consider an eastward excursion to *Frogmore Plantation and Gins* (318-757-2453; frogmoreplantation.com), where owners Lynette and George Tanner offer a contrast between the old and the new. "Even if you grew up on a cotton plantation, you're going to learn history and trivia at Frogmore that no one else tells. For instance, most of us eat cotton every day," says Lynette. Find out more at 11656 Highway 84 in Frogmore near the Mississippi border. This 1,800-acre working cotton plantation features eighteen antebellum structures, including authentically furnished slave row cabins dating from 1810. Besides touring the buildings, you'll see a film on cotton's role in history, an 1884 antique steam gin, and today's computerized version. You may also get a chance to pick cotton here. Call ahead for hours, which vary by season. Admission charged. From time to time, Lynette schedules gospel music tours.

The restaurant also offers a large selection of regional cookbooks and purchases much of its produce from local growers. Lea's is closed on Mon, but open 7 a.m. to 4 p.m. every other day.

Lecompte (*le-COUNT*) was named after an 1850s record-breaking racehorse from a local plantation. Before a sign painter inadvertently inserted a *P,* the place was Lecomte. Before leaving this area you may want to drive through the surrounding countryside. Some 300 nurseries are located in the nearby Lecompte–Forest Hill area. Along ***Nursery Row*** you'll find landscaping bargains in a variety of shrubs, trees, and plants, including ornamental and exotic plants. Although the nurseries supply commercial markets, most will accommodate drop-in retail customers.

Consider a trip to the town of ***Marksville***. About a mile or so from a 1,000-acre Indian reservation, you'll find the ***Marksville State Historic Site*** (318-484-2390; crt.state.la.us/Louisiana-state-parks/historic-sites/Marksville-state-historic-site/index) at 837 Martin Luther King Drive, Marksville. Marksville's Indian civilization flourished here some 2,000 years ago, and museum exhibits interpret that culture. Situated on a bluff overlooking Old River, the Marksville site encompasses six prehistoric Indian mounds as well as encircling earthworks ranging from 4 to 6 feet tall. Open by appointment only. Call to schedule a visit.

Places to Stay in Central Louisiana

ALEXANDRIA

Baymont by Wyndham
2301 North MacArthur Dr.
(318) 619-3300

Best Western of Alexandria Inn and Suites & Conference Center
2720 North MacArthur Dr.
(318) 445-5530
or (800) 528-1234

Hotel Bentley of Alexandria
200 Desoto St.
(318) 442-2226
hotelbentleyandcondos
.com

Parc England—A Boutique Hotel
1321 Chappie James Ave.
(318) 445-7574
parcengland.com

Motel 6
742 MacArthur Dr.
(318) 448-1611

MARKSVILLE

Paragon Casino Resort
711 Paragon Pl.
(318) 253-1946
paragoncasinoresort.com

NATCHITOCHES

Andrew Morris House Bed and Breakfast
422 Second St.
(800) 441-8343
andrewmorrishouse.com

Best Western of Natchitoches
5131 University Pkwy.
(318) 352-6655
or (800) 528-1234

Hampton Inn
5300 University Pkwy.
(318) 354-0010
or (800) HAMPTON

Holiday Inn Express
5137 University Pkwy.
(318) 354-9911
or (800) HOLIDAY

Jefferson House Bed and Breakfast
229 Rue Jefferson
(318) 352-5834
jefferson
housebedandbreakfast
.com

Judge Porter House
321 Second St.
(800) 441-8343
judgeporterhouse.com

Queen Ann Bed and Breakfast
125 Pine St.
(800) 441-8343
queenannbandb.com

Steel Magnolia House LLC
320 Jefferson St.
(318) 238-2585

Violet Hill Bed and Breakfast
917 Washington St.
(866) 357-0858
violethillbandb.com

Places to Eat in Central Louisiana

ALEXANDRIA

Cajun Landing
2728 MacArthur Dr.
(318) 487-4912
cajunlanding.com

Critic's Choice
5208 Rue Verdon
(318) 445-1680
criticschoicecenla.com

El Reparo Mexican Restaurant & Grill
550 MacArthur Dr.
(318) 487-0207

BOYCE

Tunk's Cypress Inn
9507 Hwy. 28 W
(318) 487-4014
tunkscypressinn.com

LECOMPTE

Lea's Lunchroom
1810 Hwy. 71 S
(318) 776-5178
leaslunchroom.com

MANY

Bayou Crawfish
650 San Antonio Ave.
(318) 451-1503

Country Boy Restaurant
105 North Highland St.
(318) 256-3953

MARKSVILLE

Brown Bag Gourmet
310 Acton Rd.
(318) 240-8211
brownbaggourmet.online

FOR MORE INFORMATION

Alexandria/Pineville Area Convention and Visitors Bureau
707 Second Ave., Alexandria 71301
(318) 442-9546 or (800) 551-9546
Alexandriapinevillela.com

Avoyelles Commission of Tourism
8592 Hwy. 1, Mansura 71350
(318) 964-2025 or (800) 833-4195
Travelavoyelles.com

Natchitoches Convention and Visitors Bureau
780 Front St., Ste. 100, Natchitoches 71457
(318) 352-8072 or (800) 259-1714
Natchitoches.com

Sabine Parish Tourist and Recreation Commission
1601 Texas Hwy., Many 71449
(318) 256-5880
Toledobendlakecountry.com

Vernon Parish Tourism Commission
201 S. Third St., Leesville 71496
(318) 238-0783 or (800) 349-6287
vernonparish.org

Winn Parish Tourist Commission
499 E. Main St., Winnfield 71483
(318) 628-5928

Area newspapers include the *Town Talk* in Alexandria (the largest paper in the area; should have weekly entertainment listings), the *Sabine Index* in Many, the *Natchitoches Times* in Natchitoches, the *Winn Parish Enterprise* in Winnfield, *Avoyelles Today* in Marksville, the *Record* in Bunkie, and the *Weekly News* in Marksville.

Fresh Catch Bistreaux/ Broken Wheel Brewery
109 E. Tunica Dr.
(318) 253-6543
brokenwheelbrew.com

Legends Steakhouse at Paragon Casino Resort
711 Paragon Pl.
(800) 946-1946
paragoncasinoresort.com

NATCHITOCHES

The Landing
530 Front St.
(318) 352-1579
thelandingnatchitoches.com

Lasyone's Meat Pie Restaurant
622 Second St.
(318) 352-3353
lasyones.com

Maglieaux's Riverfront Restaurant
805 Washington St.
(318) 354-7767
maglieauxs.com

Mama's Oyster House
608 Front St.
(318) 356-7874
mamasandpapas natchitoches.com

Mariner's
5948 LA 1
(318) 357-1220
marinersrestaurant.com

Merci Beaucoup Restaurant
127 Church St.
(318) 352-6634
mercibeaucouprestaurant.com

Papa's Bar and Grill
604 Front St.
(318) 356-5850
mamasandpapas natchitoches.com

PINEVILLE

Paradise Catfish Kitchen
4820 Monroe Hwy.
(318) 640-5032

Southwest Louisiana

The southwest portion of Louisiana includes coastal marshes with oak ridges along their edges. Inland are found prairie lands. The prairies are cut by several watercourses, including the Calcasieu and the Vermilion Rivers. The low meandering ridges of the prairies are also marked by intermittent, slow-moving streams called coulees. Rice cultivation (which necessitates seasonal irrigation and is often rotated with crawfish farming), along with petroleum, cattle, and seafood industries, makes up a large portion of the regional economy.

Imperial Calcasieu

Forming the heel of the Louisiana boot, the parishes of Cameron, Calcasieu (*KAL-ka-shoe*), Beauregard, Allen, and Jefferson Davis compose what was once called Imperial Calcasieu.

Made up mostly of marshlands and bayous, Cameron is the state's largest parish and home to Louisiana's outback. Its ***Creole Nature Trail All-American Road*** affords close-up views of the wetlands and wildlife along with myriad birding opportunities. Before planning your visit, check creolenaturetrail.org for the latest updates and openings.

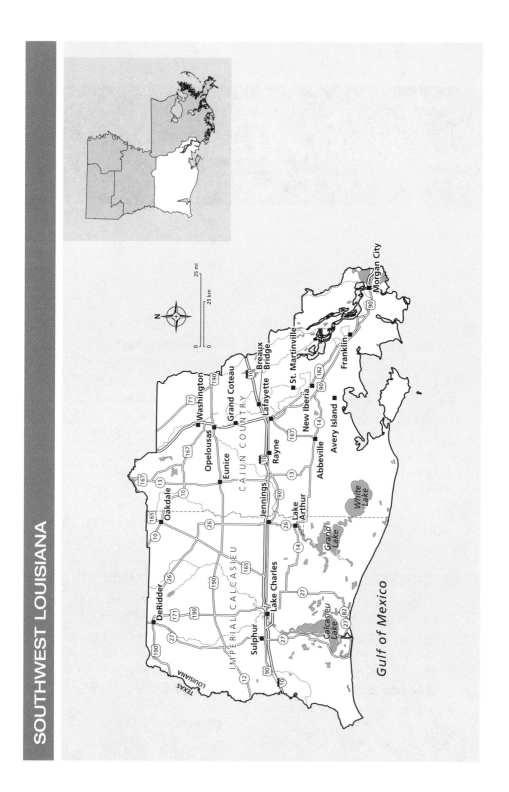

SOUTHWEST LOUISIANA

AUTHOR'S FAVORITES IN SOUTHWEST LOUISIANA

Acadian Village, Lafayette

Atchafalaya Basin, near Henderson

Longfellow-Evangeline State Historic Site, St. Martinville

Mardi Gras Museum of Imperial Calcasieu, Lake Charles

Shadows-on-the-Teche, New Iberia

Vermilionville Living History Museum and Folk Life Park, Lafayette

The Cameron Ferry runs daily every 15 minutes from 5 a.m. to 9 p.m. This fifty-car ferry transports travelers across the Calcasieu Ship Channel. For eastward-bound passengers the trip is free, but those heading west pay a toll of $1 per car and 50 cents for pedestrians who walk onto the ferry. If you step to the rail, you might catch a special performance by porpoises, who frequently put on a free show for ferry passengers.

The fishing in Calcasieu Lake will make anglers smile, but accommodations remain few and far between for now. Still, if you're determined to go fishing, birding, or hunting in this area, give Capt'n Sammie Faulk a call at (337) 540-2050. He knows the territory and can guide you past obstacles.

Railroad buffs might like to start exploring the state's southwestern portion at DeQuincy, reached by taking Route 27 north. Once a rowdy frontier town with eight saloons to serve a transient population of some 200 persons, DeQuincy managed to live down its early reputation after the railroad's arrival, when it began attracting more serious settlers.

The *DeQuincy Railroad Museum* (337-786-2823; dequincyrailroadmuseum .com) occupies the Kansas City Southern Railroad's original depot at 400 Lake Charles Avenue. Museum exhibits include a 1913 steam locomotive, a coal car, a vintage caboose, and several restored railcars. You'll also see telegraph and railroad equipment, local historical memorabilia such as tickets and timetables dating from the early 1900s, uniforms, and an old mail pouch. You may admire the dispatcher's ability to concentrate as he sits before an antique typewriter absorbed by his work and apparently oblivious to all activity around him . . . until you realize that he's a mannequin. Museum hours are Tues through Sat 10 a.m. to 5 p.m. Admission is free, but donations are appreciated.

After leaving DeQuincy take Route 27 south to *Sulphur*. The *Brimstone Museum* (337-527-0357; brimstonemuseum.org), located at 900 South Huntington Street, Sulphur, is housed in the Southern Pacific Railway Depot. You'll

TOP ANNUAL EVENTS IN SOUTHWEST LOUISIANA

Mardi Gras of Southwest Louisiana
Lake Charles, Feb
(337) 436-9588
visitlakecharles.org

Louisiana Railroad Days Festival
DeQuincy, Apr
(337) 786-8241
Larailroaddaysfestival.com

Festival International de Louisiane
Lafayette, Apr
(337) 232-8086
festivalinternational.org

Breaux Bridge Crawfish Festival
Breaux Bridge, May
(337) 332-6655
Bbcrawfest.com

Louisiana Pirate Festival
Lake Charles, May
(337) 436-5508
louisianapiratefestival.com

Frog Festival
Rayne, May
(337) 334-2332
raynefrogfestival.com

Cajun Food & Music Festival
Lake Charles, July
(800) 456-7952
visitlakecharles.org

Shrimp Festival
Delcambre, Aug
(337) 685-2653
shrimpfestival.net

The Original Southwest Louisiana Zydeco Music Festival
Plaisance, Aug
(337) 290-6048
Zydeco.org

Louisiana Shrimp and Petroleum Festival
Morgan City, Labor Day weekend
(985) 385-0703
shrimpandpetroleum.org

Louisiana Sugar Cane Festival
New Iberia, Sept
(337) 369-9323
hisugar.org

Festivals Acadiens
Lafayette, Oct
(800) 346-1958
festivalsacadiens.com

International Rice Festival
Crowley, Oct
(337) 783-3067
ricefestival.com

see a wildlife diorama, an antique medical instrument collection, photos of the town during its sulfur-mining heyday, and other exhibits related to the southwestern region.

The museum's focus concerns the history of the American sulfur industry, which started here, thanks to the ingenuity of Herman Frasch. Although it was no secret that sulfur deposits existed in the area, nobody knew how to tap this wealth. Extracting the yellow mineral from its underground home remained in the realm of the impossible until scientist-inventor Frasch solved the problem.

He came up with a superheating water process that led to the commercial production of sulfur in the United States. (Prior to 1900 almost all sulfur came from Sicily.) The Brimstone Museum, established in 1976, commemorates Frasch's contribution. Among other things, sulfur is used in making medicines, rayon, fertilizers, insecticides, paper pulp, matches, and gunpowder.

The museum is open Mon through Fri, from 10 a.m. to noon and 1 to 5 p.m., and Sat 10 a.m. to 2 p.m. Admission is free.

After browsing through the Brimstone Museum, proceed to the adjacent historic home that houses the **Henning Cultural Center** (337-527-0357; brim stonemuseum.org). Here, you'll see the work of local artists as well as traveling exhibits from around the country. Hours are 10 a.m. to noon and 1 to 5 p.m. Mon through Fri, and Sat 10 a.m. to 2 p.m. Free admission.

After visiting Sulphur, continue to nearby Lake Charles. For a relaxing base in this vicinity, consider making reservations at **A River's Edge Bed and Breakfast** (337-497-1525 or 337-540-3813), only seven minutes from downtown Lake Charles. Located at 2035 Gus Street in Westlake, the property offers a private cottage.

Savor the serene bayou setting with wildlife and beautiful sunsets from the porch swing, rockers, or patio furniture. Owners Wanda and Billy Traweek encourage guests to enjoy the pool in warm weather months, the fireplace when temperatures turn cool, and Southern hospitality around the calendar. Moderate rates. Preview the property at lakecharlesbedbreakfast.com.

When you arrive in **Lake Charles**, you may think that the sandy beach studded with palm trees is a mirage. But the artificially created North Beach is indeed real—and the only inland white-sand beach on the entire Gulf Coast. A drive over the I-10 Bridge affords a panoramic view of the beach, which borders the highway.

While driving across the I-10 Bridge, be sure to notice the railing with its design featuring pirate pistols. This area was once **Jean Lafitte**'s stomping ground. The "Gentleman Pirate" was a poetic sort who allegedly stashed some of his treasure in nearby watery mazes. To this day Lake Charles still plays host to pirates. Just visit in the spring when the city celebrates Louisiana Pirate Festival, starting with "Lafitte's invasion." The pirate's swashbuckling arrival sets off a jolly two-week round of parades, parties, pageants, boat races, and other festivities. In true buccaneering tradition, one event features the mayor "walking the plank."

Lafitte's loot may be hopelessly hidden, but you'll discover treasure aplenty at the **Cottage Shops**, clustered around Hodges, Alamo, and Common Streets. Some dozen downtown specialty shops offer items ranging from antique armoires and handmade quilts to Cajun upside-down pickles and stained glass.

For those who would like to chance finding their own treasure, Lake Charles offers two popular casinos: L'Auberge and Golden Nugget.

Inspired by the Texas Hill Country, ***L'Auberge Casino Resort*** (337-395-7777; llakecharles.com) at 777 Avenue L'Auberge offers non-stop Vegas-style gaming action with about 1,600 slots and 70 table games. L'Auberge features a 26-story hotel with 1,000 rooms and suites, Contraband Bayou Golf Club, eight restaurants, world-class spa, shops, and top name entertainment.

Opened in 2014, the ***Golden Nugget Lake Charles*** (2550 Golden Nugget Blvd.; 337-508-7777; goldennugget.com/lake-charles) offers Vegas-style gaming, 740 guest rooms, an 18-hole golf course, multiple restaurants, shops, meeting space, marina, private beach, top-notch entertainment, and more. A complimentary shuttle runs between Golden Nugget and L'Auberge.

At 2801 Ryan St., you'll find ***Catina Couture*** (337-433-5220; catinacouture .com), brimming over with lovely fashions and accessories. Continue to ***A Piece of Cake*** (337-437-9884; apieceofcake-lc.com) at 2711 Hodges Street for some sweet treats. Among the shop's taste tempters are cakes, pies, cookies and cupcakes. You're sure to discover something that speaks to you.

Hackberry, the Crab Capital of the World

One of the simplest outdoor pastimes Louisiana folks enjoy is crabbing.

Because hard-shell blue crabs are so plentiful in the Hackberry area, many people enjoy crabbing, so you might like to try your luck, too. The basic equipment boils down to two pieces: a net to scoop up the crabs and a bucket to hold them. You can buy crabbing supplies at one of the area bait shops. With net in hand you can walk along a pier and capture any crabs you see on pilings, or you can wade in shallow water and scoop them up before they scurry away. Then there's the string-and-bait method. It entails attaching a one-ounce fishing weight plus a chunk of meat or fish to a string about 20 feet long. Toss the loaded line into the water, preferably near rocks or a dock. When you feel a slight tug, slowly pull the string toward you, keeping the net submerged and as still as possible so that it will look like part of the underwater scenery. As long as it's in the water, the crab will cling to the line. When it gets close enough, sweep it into your net. You have to be swift and synchronized, or the crab will win. After you collect enough crabs to constitute a meal, you can trade your bucket for a cookbook.

Buy some crab-boil mix (a bag of spices; Zatarain's brand is good). Boil a huge pot of water, steep the mix plus salt and lemon, and add crabs. Twenty minutes later you have a free feast (not counting your net and seasoning costs).

To acquaint yourself with the history of Lake Charles, you can visit the **Imperial Calcasieu Museum** (337-439-3797; imperialcalcasieumuseum.org), located at 204 West Sallier Street. The museum stands on the site of a cabin built by early settler Charles Sallier (*sal-YAY*), for whom the city was named.

Look left as you enter, and you'll see the steering wheel from the paddle wheeler *Borealis Rex*. In earlier days this ship served as the only link between Lake Charles and Cameron, located on Calcasieu Lake's southern side. Each Wednesday a crowd gathered to welcome the steamer bringing mail, freight, and passengers.

Along the museum's right aisle, you'll pass a furnished parlor, kitchen, and bedroom, all depicting scenes from yesteryear.

A collection of personalized shaving mugs adds to the decor in the museum's Gay Nineties barbershop, and a re-created country store nearby features nostalgic merchandise. A mannequin pharmacist stands ready to dispense remedies in his apothecary, an original section from a downtown drugstore. You'll see a physician's travel kit and a glass-cased display of bottles in a rainbow of colors. Be sure to notice the ornate set of ironstone apothecary jars made in France during the early sixteenth century.

A Civil War flag from the Battle of Mobile Bay is on display in the War Room. You'll also see a uniform worn by General Claire Chennault, who led the famed Flying Tigers. This exhibit includes Mrs. Chennault's wedding gown and going-away costume, books, and various items of historical significance.

A Geneva Bible, an Edison phonograph, and a stereopticon are all treasures you won't want to overlook. The museum features a fine collection of bird and animal prints by John James Audubon as well as excerpts from the diary he kept while working in Louisiana. There's an exhibit of Lafitte memorabilia with a copy of the privateer's journal, published more than a century after his death. (Maybe it contains a clue as to where he concealed his contraband.) Admission fee is modest. Be sure to take in the current offerings in the nearby **Gibson-Barham Gallery**, which features ever-changing exhibits of both contemporary and traditional work. In the gift shop, you'll find some unique handcrafted items.

Don't leave without stepping out to the museum's backyard for a view of the venerable **Sallier Oak**. Some tree experts estimate this magnificent live oak to be more than 300 years old. Whether or not the tree has weathered three centuries, it carries its age well, and its credentials include membership in the Live Oak Society. With branches dipping almost to the ground, this inviting oak would fulfill any child's tree-climbing fantasies. Although the Sallier Oak may be visited at any time, the museum's hours are Tues through Fri from 10 a.m. to 5 p.m., Sat 10 a.m. to 3 p.m.

A walking or driving tour of the city's historic *Charpentier Historic District* takes you through some twenty square blocks of homes dating from the Victorian era. Because many of the houses in this area were constructed before professional architects arrived on the scene, they express the individuality of their various builders. Area carpenters created their own patterns by changing rooflines, porch placements, and other exterior features. Sometimes they combined traditional design elements in new ways. A typical house constructed of native cypress and longleaf yellow pine might feature an odd number of columns with a bay on one side and a porch on the other. This distinctive look now commands an architectural category all its own—Lake Charles style.

For a fun photo opportunity and a chance to admire even more Mardi Gras paraphernalia, stop by the *Mardi Gras Museum* (337-430-0043) at 809 Kirby Street in the Central School Arts & Humanities Center.

The six-room museum has the largest Mardi Gras costume display in the world. Rooms feature the history of the festival, the Captains' Den, costume design, king cakes, and the marvel of 12th Night. Also featured is a Mardi Gras parade display, including a parade float you can climb aboard for a hand-waving photo. The museum is open Tues through Fri from 1 to 5 p.m.

The Lake Charles Convention and Visitors Bureau produces an illustrated brochure that outlines a walking/driving route through the historic district. You can request one by calling (337) 436-9588 or (800) 456-7952 or check their website at visitlakecharles.org.

Better yet, you can stay overnight in one of the lovely historic homes in the Lake Charles Charpentier (French for "carpenter") Historic District, such as *Aunt Ruby's Bed & Breakfast* (504 Pujo St.; 337-430-0603; auntrubys.com), the city's first boardinghouse. Now owned by the proprietor of Pujo Street Cafe (only 2 blocks away), Aunt Ruby's offers six rooms with charming period furnishings. This ca. 1911 home provides private baths, private phone lines, cable TV, a meeting room, and full breakfast. Moderate rates.

If you have offspring in tow, consider stopping by the *Children's Museum* (327 Broad St.; 337-433-9420; swlakids.org) while in this area. Youngsters can indulge their curiosity and creative instincts through various participatory programs. They can don uniforms and pretend to fight fires or

hurricane audrey memorial

On June 27, 1957, Hurricane Audrey hit Cameron Parish, leaving 525 dead. There is a monument in front of Our Lady Star of the Sea Church, 4 miles east of Cameron on Highway 82.

A Howling Good Mardi Gras Parade

Rosie proudly struts down the street, her long slender legs clad in gold boots. Peacock feathers atop her head sway in the breeze as parade watchers cheer and clap when she passes by.

Accepting the adulation with calm poise, she seems to know she is top dog.

In fact, the beautiful Rosie is a Rhodesian Ridgeback and she will be crowned the grand winner Mystical Dog in the Mystical Krewe of Barkus Parade in Lake Charles. Held along Lakeshore Drive, the annual event is a family-friendly Mardi Gras celebration featuring costumed human companions with their dressed-up doggies.

"I used to go to the parade when I was a child but this is the first time we ever entered the contest. We were shocked when we won," said Rosie's human companion, Jacey Broussard. "We put a lot of effort into our costumes, but so did many other people and their dogs looked amazing."

Not only did Broussard craft Rosie's showgirl attire by hand, she also turned the family's small Schnauzer/Yorkie mix named Diesel into a gold nugget.

"You wouldn't believe how I did it," Broussard said. "I used cans of expanding foam and I carved the foam down to look like a gold nugget. Then I sprayed it gold and fixed it so it would fit over Diesel."

When she emailed some photos to her parents, however, Broussard said she got a different response. "They said Diesel looked like a baked potato."

Tiny Diesel had the easy job. All he had to do was rest comfortably in a wagon pulled by Rosie along the parade route. To complete the trio's look, Broussard cut out some gold letters and pasted them onto a black T-shirt she wore proclaiming herself Nugget Security.

"I actually had a few people approach me and ask how long I had been working for Golden Nugget," said Broussard, who is not a Golden Nugget employee but a farrier—a person who specializes in equine hoof care and puts horseshoes on horses.

The Golden Nugget parade getup, of course, is a nod to the $600 million Golden Nugget Casino Resort that opened in Lake Charles in December 2014. "They actually have a real gold nugget on display there. That's what gave me the idea to make Diesel a little nugget," Broussard said.

More than 100 costumed dogs paraded in the hour-long procession to the delight of about 1,000 viewers lining both sides of the riverfront road. Sponsored by the local Cumulus Broadcasting, the Barkus Parade was started in 1995.

Not only is the parade a fun celebration, it is also a fundraiser for local animals. Parade participants pay a $10 pre-registration fee or $15 the day of the parade to enter a dog. The money is given to a local animal shelter.

broadcast their own news from a television-studio setting. Visit swlakids.org for more information.

Changing exhibits explore areas of natural and physical science, history, art, crafts, and geography. Except for major holidays, hours are from 10 a.m. to 5 p.m. Mon through Sat, 1 to 5 p.m. on Sun. Admission charged; kids under two get in free.

Traveling east from Lake Charles, most drivers take I-10. Route 14, however, runs south of the interstate (more in a meandering fashion than parallel) and offers some scenic vistas denied interstate travelers (albeit periodic road signs caution motorists about speeding on a substandard highway). If you do opt for Route 14, keep in mind that it takes longer, but you might see such striking vistas as entire fields white with egrets.

croprotation

When the people of Lake Charles wanted to do something with the land that used to serve as the town poor farm (where people went in the days before government aid), they put McNeese State University's campus on it.

Some travelers bypass highways entirely and simply fly in. An airport adjacent to the interstate attracts all sorts of "fly people"—from Cessna owners to Stearman pilots—who migrate to Jennings during a designated weekend for the annual end-of-the-season fly-in. Pilots practice formation flying in pairs and in groups because the airport allows "free flight" if sessions are performed by seasoned veterans. Pilots can taxi right up to the door of the local Holiday Inn. (From cockpit to motel room might mean a hop, skip, and jump of some 50 yards.)

Whether your visit in *Jennings* results from coercion or choice, all sorts of delights await you off the beaten path. Start with the *Louisiana Oil and Gas Park*, just north of town (and visible from I-10) at 100 Rue de l'Acadie (337-821-5521). Louisiana's first oil well produced "black gold" on September 21, 1901, just 5 miles northeast of town in a rice field that belonged to farmer Jules Clement. The park, which commemorates that significant event, contains a replica of the small wooden oil rig used to drill the first well. Next to the derrick stands an early Acadian-style house where the visitor information center is located.

An ideal place to take a driving break, the public recreation area includes a jogging trail, picnic facilities, playground equipment, a lake, and flocks of ducks and geese that act as a welcoming committee. You also can see *Château des Cocodries* (800-264-5521; 337-821-5521), a live alligator exhibit.

Select a table and spread a picnic, but save some sandwich crusts for the ducks—they consider it their duty to dispose of any leftovers. Maybe the ducks

Mardi Gras is Contagious

Momus, king of Mardi Gras, stepped from his royal yacht at the foot of Pujo Street in Lake Charles at 4 p.m. on Tuesday, February 21, 1882. He boarded a chariot waiting on shore, and the parade began. So it was in the beginning when some 2,000 people lined the parade route. Today's Mardi Gras parades attract some 150,000 spectators annually.

The Royal Gala features a colorful promenade of more than forty-two krewes (social clubs) in glittering costumes. Thousands of residents and visitors watch kings and queens, dukes and duchesses, captains, courtesans, and jesters in an evening of merrymaking at the Lake Charles Civic Center Coliseum.

should be thanked for the trophy designating Jennings as Louisiana's cleanest city. After winning the Cleanest City Award three years in a row, Jennings received the trophy for its permanent collection.

Jennings celebrated its centennial in 1988. The town was named for a railroad contractor, Jennings McComb. When the railroad came through this section in 1880, McComb erected most of the depots, so railroad officials honored him by giving his first name to the unpopulated area around one of the depots. (A town in Mississippi had already claimed his last name.) Sure enough, the blank spot on the prairie began to attract settlers, mostly from the Midwest. Farmers did not have to first clear the land of trees—there were none. Homesteaders received extra land for planting trees on their property. They also planted crops they had raised in their home states of Iowa, Illinois, Indiana, and Missouri, and began to experiment with rice-farming techniques. By 1894 more than 1,000 acres of rice grew on the Cajun prairie surrounding Jennings.

Later a number of Yankees who had fought in the area during the Civil War returned to settle here. The local cemetery contains quite a few more graves for the Blue than the Gray. Consequently Jennings came to be known as a "northern town on Southern soil."

Don't leave Jennings without visiting the ***Zigler Art Museum*** (337-824-0114; ziglerartmuseum.org), acclaimed for its outstanding fine arts collection representing five centuries of European and American art. At 154 North Main St., the museum is located in the renovated City Hall building.

The galleries host ever-changing exhibits of works by both state and national artists. The museum also has a permanent collection and features such artists as Rembrandt, Whistler, VanDyke, Durer, Pissaro, and Constable. The museum's Louisiana artists collection includes the works of Ellsworth

Vive la Louisiane

In Lafayette there are large parades celebrating Mardi Gras, rather like the New Orleans version. In the country you will find the Courir du Mardi Gras, or Mardi Gras Run, which is a wild trail ride by costumed horseback riders (sometimes with homemade masks of screen wire) who go from house to house collecting ("stealing") chickens and supplies for a giant gumbo. The riders are well fueled, the routes (complete with pickup trucks, beer, and a band) and the gumbo are all planned, and there is a big fais-do-do, or dance, at the end. You will find this sort of event either on Mardi Gras Day or during the weekend immediately preceding it in Mamou, Iota, Church Point, and Eunice.

Woodward, Knute Heldner, A. J. Drysdale, Robert Rucker, Muriel Butler, William Tolliver, and others.

The Zigler Art Museum is open Mon through Sat from 10 a.m. to 4 p.m. Closed holidays. Admission is modest.

Continue to the end of Clara Street, which runs into Cary Avenue. Next, turn on Second Street and go to State Street. At 710 North State Street stands *Our Lady Help of Christians Catholic Church*, one of the town's historic buildings. Step inside for a view of the windows in glowing stained glass, made in Germany. In designing the church, Father Joseph Peeters, a native of Belgium, was inspired by Notre Dame in Paris. You'll recognize some of the great Gothic cathedral's characteristics, such as the three arched entrances, in this smaller, plainer version. Constructed of homemade concrete blocks that were cast on the building site, the church was dedicated in 1916 after a building period of several years.

A short walk takes you to the *Marian Prayer Park*, located adjacent to the church on the rectory's south side. From here you'll do a bit of backtracking. While retracing your drive, you might want to take a ride along Cary Avenue for a look at the lovely old homes. Architectural features, reflecting a midwestern influence, include turrets, balconies, porches, and gables accented with gingerbread woodwork and fish-scale shingles.

Take a sentimental journey to the *W. H. Tupper General Merchandise Museum* (337-821-5532; tuppermuseum.com) at 311 North Main Street, Jennings. The museum's stock came from a store built near Elton in 1910 by Mary and W. H. Tupper for their farm workers. Although the store closed in 1949, the contents remained intact—frozen in time for more than seven decades. The store's original inventory consisted of toys, cosmetics, dishes, drugs, cooking utensils, seeds, fans, jewelry, denim overalls, and other items that bring back memories.

You'll also see a large selection of baskets made by members of the Chitimacha and Coushatta tribes. The Coushattas live 3 miles northwest of Elton on the northern edge of the parish. Museum hours are Mon through Fri from 9 a.m. to 5 p.m. Admission is modest.

Also sharing the Tupper building, the ***Telephone Pioneer Museum of Louisiana*** features displays of phones from past to present with exhibits going back to switchboards and party lines. The Children's Telephone Museum addition offers an educational experience.

Before leaving the area, stroll along the brick sidewalks of nearby ***Founder's Park*** with its fountains, landscaped patios, wrought-iron benches and

OTHER ATTRACTIONS WORTH SEEING IN SOUTHWEST LOUISIANA

Cypremort Point State Park
Franklin
(337) 867-4510 or (888) 867-4510
Crt.state.la.us/Louisiana-state-parks/
parks/cypremort-point-state-park
Manmade beach in the marshland on the shores of Vermilion Bay.

Cypress Island Preserve
St. Martinsville
(337) 342-2475
Nature.org/en-us/get-involved/how-to-help/places-we-protect/cypress-island
Off Louisiana Highway 353 between Lafayette and Breaux Bridge. Go to Lake Martin and look for the Nature Conservancy signs. Park at the yellow gates on the levee. You can see virgin cypress swamp; old-growth, live-oak ridges (chenieres); and a huge rookery of birds, including white ibis.

Delta Downs
Vinton
(800) 589-7441
Deltadowns.com
This track offers Thoroughbred and Quarter-Horse races from January into August. Quarter-Horse racing is quick and the betting is lively. Even the food is pretty good in the clubhouse—try the gumbo. A good place to wear your Wranglers and your old Tony Lama boots.

The Jeanerette Museum
Jeanerette
(337) 276-4408
Jeanerettemuseum.com
Sugarcane history with wildlife and Mardi Gras thrown in.

Sam Houston Jones State Park
Lake Charles
(337) 855-2665 or (888) 677-7264
Crt.state.la.us/Louisiana-state-parks/
parks/sam-houston-jones-state-park/
index
At the confluence of three rivers, this woodsy park offers boating, hiking trails, camping, and even cabins for rent (call far in advance).

chairs, and antique clock. This public park features a large hand-painted mural depicting the history of Jennings.

Afterward, stop by **_Boudin King_** (906 West Division St.; 337-824-6593). No trip to this area would be complete without sampling boudin (_BOO-dan_). The state legislature passed an act declaring Jennings the Boudin Capital of the Universe, and you would be hard-pressed to find a better place for trying this specialty. The late restaurant owner Ellis Cormier, whose customers called him the Boudin King, defined his boudin as a mixture of pork, spices, and long-grain rice. Louisiana French people have been partial to boudin for more than two centuries, and Cormier's Acadian recipe passed down in the family for generations. Parsley, peppers, green onions, and rice (cooked separately) are added to the prime pork. The resulting mixture is stuffed into a sausage casing, then steamed and served warm.

A great appetizer, boudin comes in links, both mild and hot. If you can't decide which to try, you may sample each. Start with mild and work your way up to hot (my favorite).

Although boudin gets star billing here, the menu offers other items such as chicken-and-sausage gumbo, fried crawfish, catfish, chicken, and red beans and rice with smoked sausage. You also can buy hogshead cheese, a sort of pâté especially good when spread on crackers.

Prices are economical to moderate. Boudin King, which closes on Sun, operates from 9 a.m. to 8 p.m. Mon through Thurs, and until 8:30 p.m. on Fri and Sat.

Before leaving Jefferson Davis Parish, take Route 26 down to Lake Arthur, 9 miles south of Jennings. For some picturesque scenery, drive along the edge of the lake, lined with lovely old homes. Cypress trees, with swaying Spanish moss trailing from their branches, stand knee-deep in Lake Arthur. In this laid-back resort area, you can fish, hunt, or watch the cranes, egrets, herons, and other birds.

Lake Arthur Park offers a bandstand, pavilions, picnic facilities, and an enclosed swimming area. Throughout the year the town stages events at the park. The park is also the setting for a star-spangled Fourth of July Celebration and a Christmas Festival with thousands of lights. For more information on Lake Arthur events, call the Town Hall at (337) 774-2211.

After enjoying Lake Arthur Park, drive back to Route 26 and travel north until the road intersects US 90. You'll then go east, passing by acres of rice fields on your way to Crowley, the Rice Center of America.

Cajun Country

As home of the International Rice Festival, **Crowley** promises plenty of good food along with rice-eating contests, fiddling and accordion competitions, parades, a street fair, a livestock show, and other events.

While you're in Crowley, go by the courthouse square. Starting on Main Street you can drive through the downtown historic district, which features some 8 blocks of lovely Victorian homes. From here take US 90 east to reach Rayne, about 7 miles from Crowley and 13 miles west of Lafayette.

If you didn't realize that **Rayne** is the Frog Capital of the World, you will before you depart. The first clue might be big colorful murals on the sides of old buildings—all depicting frogs in one fashion or another. On your driving tour be sure to notice the interesting aboveground cemetery.

Mark Twain's jumping frog of Calaveras County would have been in his element here, happy among his peers. This town is filled not only with bona fide frogs but also with pictures of frogs, statues of frogs, literature about frogs, and even frog factories. What do frog factories export? Frog legs for restaurant menus and specimens for scientific purposes, of course. Besides being the center of Louisiana's frog industry, Rayne also ranks as one of the world's largest shippers of frogs.

For fifty-one weeks of the year, Rayne could be considered off the beaten path. During a May weekend, however, the world beats a path to its door for a fun-filled Frog Festival, which features fireworks, frog-cooking contests, frog derbies, and frog beauty contests.

Soon after arriving in town, search out **Chef Roy's Frog City Cafe** (337-334-7913; chefroy.com) at 1131 Church Point Hwy., a quarter of a mile north of I-10, exit 87. Here, you'll find even more frogs—both in the cafe's frog boutique and on the menu.

Chef Roy Lyons, former owner, instructed chefs in Canada, Mexico, France, Belgium, Turkey, Holland, the Netherlands, and elsewhere on the preparation of Cajun cuisine. In fact, Chef Roy sold his cafe in 2005 to concentrate on his travels. "We haven't changed a thing," said owners Robert Credeur and Chef Benoit Morel.

Start with an appetizer of seafood gumbo or a crab cake, grilled and served with crawfish cream sauce. Blackened chicken salad features mixed greens, juicy blackened chicken strips, and the chef's fig vinaigrette dressing. Popular entrees include shrimp or crawfish enchiladas, seafood platters, and Catfish Willie, grilled and topped with crawfish herb cream sauce. And yes, you can get a fried frog leg platter or a combination with frog leg étouffée. As for dessert, popular choices include peach bread pudding with rum sauce, crème

Blue Stories

At **Crystal Rice Plantation Heritage Farm** (337-783-6417; crystalrice.com) you'll find the Blue Rose Museum, located at 6428 Airport Road in Crowley. The museum's name came from a variety of rice that was developed locally. Rice is the main crop in this area, and the Blue Rose Museum covers the development of the rice industry. (Also on the premises, you can tour a rice farm and see crawfish ponds and an antique automobile collection.) Admission. Find out more about the site's tours by appointment only.

The fictionalized version of the search for a hybrid rice (which the Blue Rose Museum commemorates) is told in the late Frances Parkinson Keyes's 1956 novel *Blue Camellia*. Keyes, a New Englander who lived from 1896 to 1970, spent years in Louisiana churning out big-selling historical novels. Her research is good, and her stories are usually long, family sagas. If you like romance novels or historical fiction, you'll enjoy her books.

River Road covers the sugar industry; *Crescent Carnival* describes New Orleans old-line Mardi Gras krewes (the carnival organizations that sponsor balls and parades), and dishes out generations-old gossip. Look for Keyes's books in your public library—they are mostly out of print.

brûlée, or the turtle specialty combining chocolate cake and vanilla ice cream served in a pool of caramel.

The cafe opens Tues through Thurs at 11 a.m. to 9 p.m. (Fri 'til 10 p.m.), Sat 4 p.m. to 10 p.m., and Sun 11 a.m. to 2 p.m. Closed Mon. Prices are moderate.

After leaving Rayne, return to Crowley and take State Route 13 north. Consider a short trip on the **Acadiana Trail** (also US 190), which runs through a number of interesting towns such as **Eunice**, the state's crawfish-processing center. Depending on the season you'll see acres of rice growing or thousands of crawfish traps in this area where fields do double duty. Now a major agricultural industry, crawfish farming utilizes flooded rice fields during winter and early spring.

Complement your trip to Cajun country by taking in a performance at the **Liberty Center for the Performing Arts** (337-457-1776; eccbc.org/liberty -center) on the corner of South Second Street and Park Avenue in downtown Eunice. Every Sat night from 6 to 7:30 p.m., *Rendezvous des Cajuns,* a live radio show, features a lineup of musicians and entertainers. Don't miss the outstanding exhibits at neighboring **Jean Lafitte National Historical Park and Preserve/Prairie Acadian Cultural Center** (337-457-8499; nps.gov/ jela/prairie-acadian-cultural-center-eunice.html), open Tues through Fri from 9 a.m. to 4:30 p.m., and Sat 8:30 a.m. to noon. Closed Christmas Day.

Continue to Ville Platte. About 6 miles north of Ville Platte, you'll find **Chicot State Park** (3469 Chicot State Park Rd.; 888-677-2442 or 337-363-2403; crt.state.la.us/Louisiana-state-parks/parks/chicot-state-park/index). With 6,500 acres of rolling hills and a 2,000-acre lake, the park offers plenty of recreation opportunities. Modest admission. Just beyond at 1300 Sudie Lawron Lane, you can visit **Louisiana State Arboretum** (888-677-6100 or 337-363-6289; crt.state .la.us/Louisiana-state-parks/parks/Louisiana-state-arboretum-state-preservation -area/index) with inviting nature trails and footbridges interspersed among labeled specimens of native plants. Rambling through the forest and across hills, ravines, and creeks, you'll see birds, deer, and local flora such as pine, oak, magnolia, beech, dogwood, and paw-paw. The arboretum is open daily from 9 a.m. to 5 p.m.; modest admission fee.

Afterward, continue to **Washington**, one of the state's oldest permanent settlements. Located on Bayou Courtableau, Washington once bustled as a steamboat town, and you can glimpse a bit of local history at **Steamboat Warehouse Restaurant** (337-826-7227; steamboatware house.com) at 525 North Main Street, Washington, and enjoy a good meal at the same time. The large brick warehouse, built between 1819 and 1823 and restored as a restaurant in 1976, specializes in steaks and seafood. After dipping into Catfish Lizzy topped with crawfish étouffée, or a rib-eye, take time to look at lading bills and other documents displayed here. An 1870 shipment, for instance, included candles, claret, coffee, tea, table salt, pickles, apples, and nails. Except for Christmas Day and New Year's Day, the restaurant is open Tues through Sat from 5 to 10 p.m., and Sun from 11 a.m. to 2 p.m.

theloneprairie

In Eunice, back by the old railroad tracks, there is a preserved area of prairie that encompasses several city blocks. Although Louisiana once had miles of prairie, civilization and the plow removed most of the deep-rooted grasses and fragile wildflowers that form the typical prairie ecosystem. Here, where some untouched land was found, grasses and plants that are original to this soil have been replanted and a true prairie has been growing. Future plans call for an interpretive center, but the sweet smell of prairie grasses is already here. Ask for directions at the Jean Lafitte Park offices; (337) 457-8499.

Many of Washington's historic homes, plantations, and buildings were constructed between 1780 and 1835, and some are open for tours or as bed-and-breakfasts. For more information, contact the Washington Museum and Tourist Center at 404 Main St.; (337) 826-3627. The museum is open Mon through Fri from 8 a.m. to 4 p.m., and on weekends from 9 a.m. to 4 p.m.

After exploring Washington, head south to **Opelousas**. On US 190 East at 828 East Landry, you'll find the tourist information center (337-948-6263;

cityofopelousas.com). You'll see exhibits on Acadian culture along with old documents, photographs, farm equipment, and firearms.

Another interesting display showcases Jim Bowie's contributions. During his boyhood, Bowie lived in Opelousas. After serving for a while in the Louisiana legislature, Bowie moved to Texas, where he fought and died at the Alamo. While legend credits him with the invention of the Bowie knife, some historians contend that this is not a fact, although Bowie may have contributed to the knife's design. The center is open weekdays from 8 a.m. to 4:30 p.m., Sat from 9 a.m. to 4 p.m., and there's no admission charge.

The **Opelousas Museum and Interpretive Center** (337-948-2589; cityof opelousas.com/Opelousas-museum-interpretive-center) at 315 North Main Street, Opelousas, presents a fascinating overview of local culture back to prehistoric times. The area can be described as a melting pot or "cultural gumbo" because the settlers came from many ethnic backgrounds. Named for a Native American tribe that occupied the site earlier, Opelousas became a bayou trading post for French and Indian interchange in 1720. This fertile area also attracted the Spanish around the same time. Displays in the main exhibit room spotlight the people—their agriculture, home and family, business and professions, music, and food.

Among other things, the town pays tribute to the sweet potato's cousin, the yam, with an annual Yambilee Festival the last weekend in October. Spring and fall Folklife Festivals focus on the "olden days." A **Zydeco Festival** (337-942-2392, zydeco.org) is staged in nearby Plaisance each September, and you'll see a presentation on zydeco (*ZI-da-ko*), which might be described as a musical merger of such sounds as rhythm and blues, jazz, rock and roll, gospel, and Cajun music. Opelousas, the birthplace of this unique style, was the home of "Zydeco King," the late Clifton Chenier. Also, before leaving the main room, be sure to notice the exhibits on Mardi Gras and the 1914 Dunbar kidnapping case.

Another section contains the Geraldine Smith Welch doll collection. You'll see more than 400 dolls, grouped in categories from antiques and miniatures to pop culture.

The center also houses the Louisiana Video Collection Library, a valuable resource for delving into state history, and a section on the Civil War when Opelousas served as the state's capital for a brief period. You can visit the center (which is fully wheelchair accessible) Mon through Fri between 8 a.m. and 4:30 p.m. Admission is free, but donations are accepted.

Before leaving town, stop by the **Palace Cafe** (337-942-2142) at 135 West Landry Street (Hwy 190 W). Try the fried chicken salad, Grecian salad, or house specialty—baked eggplant stuffed with crab. Top off your meal with the restaurant's famous baklava, a Greek pastry made with pecan butter and honey. Prices are moderate. The cafe is open Mon through Sat from 6 a.m. to 8 p.m., and Sun from 6 a.m. to 2 p.m.

As you drive through this part of the country, tune in to local radio stations, where you'll hear the unique sounds of Cajun music and dialect. Sometimes the news is broadcast in French and sometimes in English.

For a special treat, take Route 93 (designated a Louisiana State Scenic Byway) and go back across I-49 to the little town of *Grand Coteau*. This was the center for early-nineteenth-century religious education in Acadian Louisiana, with both males and females being accommodated. *St. Charles College*, now a Jesuit seminary, began in 1837 and serves as a center for religious retreats.

The *Academy of the Sacred Heart* (1821 Academy Rd.; 337-662-5275) began in 1821 and is still operated by the Religious of the Sacred Heart, known worldwide for their elite girls' schools. The convent and grounds are open for free tours Mon through Fri by appointment only. The main school building was erected in 1831; fluted iron columns support its 300-foot-long galleries. Stroll in the pleasant gardens, and be sure to notice the century-old camellia plants.

The convent also has strong Catholic religious associations: One of the miracles attributed to St. John Berchmans at his canonization occurred here when a young postulant was miraculously cured.

On a secular note, the village of Grand Coteau is a good place for visitors to spend time: You can shop diligently, eat well, and browse through antiques shops along the way.

Oldest of the upscale stores is *The Kitchen Shop* (296 E. Martin Luther King Dr.; 337-662-3500), which offers interesting cookware and gadgets, scrumptious lunches, delicious desserts, and so much more. Step next door to *Pistache* (294 E. Martin Luther King Dr.; 337-662-3599) for some unique jewelry and clothing designs.

Continue south to reach *Lafayette*, the hub city of Acadiana. The Acadiana area, which comprises nearly one-third of Louisiana's sixty-four parishes, was settled by French Acadians who were ousted from Nova Scotia and New Brunswick by the British in 1755. Forced to leave their homes and property, families were broken up and sent to various destinations. Many eventually made their way to South Louisiana, where Acadians came to be known as "Cajuns."

Make the *Jean Lafitte National Historical Park and Preserve/ Acadian Cultural Center* (501 Fisher Rd.; 337-232-0789; nps.gov/jela/new -acadian-cultural-center.htm) one of your first sight-seeing stops. A free thirty-five-minute film chronicles the Cajun experience, tracing the exile from Nova

Cajun/Creole Heritage Preserved at Vermilionville

The tempting aroma of sweet dough pies wafts through the kitchen and out the doorway. Made of simple ingredients, the treats were a favorite of early settlers and are now popular with visitors to Vermilionville in Lafayette.

"It was basically ingredients you usually had in the kitchen with a bit of fruit preserves added," a costumed interpreter says. "My favorite was peach because my aunt had a peach tree and my mama would can the peaches and make preserves."

Today, Vermilionville is helping share the joys of cooking at the **Living History Museum & Folk Life Park** in Lafayette. Cooking demonstrations highlight Cajun and Creole cooking.

"I try to keep the menu very simple and teach people how to make dishes they would like to have at home," the guide says. "You would be surprised how many people can't make a roux, and that's an important thing to know in Cajun and Creole cooking."

The demonstrations and cooking classes are popular with men and women of all ages.

"I think people are wanting to cook more now, to spend time with their families," the guide says. "Cajuns and Creoles learned to live off the land, to create with what you had. Many people are looking for simple things like that now."

Created in 1990, Vermilionville seeks to preserve the area's natural and cultural resources. Nestled along Bayou Vermilion, the beautiful center is laid out as a historic village containing 19 structures, including seven restored original homes.

In most of the structures, costumed interpreters demonstrate traditional crafts and musical styles. A full-service restaurant, art gallery, and gift shop filled with Cajun and Creole items are also available and a boat tour of the bayou is a leisurely way to enjoy the water and landscape.

Structures include a Creole plantation house, a plantation overseer's house, cooking school, watershed exhibit, performance center, 1840s Acadian style home, Native

Scotia to settlement in the state's Southern landscape of bayous, swamps, and prairies. Another sixteen-minute film revisits the Atchafalaya Basin. Exhibits highlight Acadiana's contemporary culture. Except for Mardi Gras and federal holidays, the park is open Tues through Fri from 9 a.m. to 4:30 p.m., and Sat from 8:30 a.m. to noon.

During the 1770s a large number of Acadians settled in Lafayette (then called Vermilionville because of the nearby bayou's reddish color). In 1884 the town was renamed to honor Lafayette, the French general of American Revolutionary War fame. Now ***Vermilionville Living History Museum & Folk Life Park*** (337-233-4077 or 866-992-2968; vermilionville.org) has been reincarnated as a twenty-three-acre living-history attraction focusing on Cajun and Creole

American dwelling, Acadian trapper's hut, boat shed, 1890s schoolhouse, 1810 Acadian house, blacksmith shop, 1803 Creole home, chapel, barn, and La Maison Broussard— the 1790 home of Amand Broussard.

Broussard arrived in Louisiana from Canada at the age of 11. His father was the famous Acadian resistance fighter, Joseph "Beausoleil" Broussard, who died only months after bringing 250 Acadians to Louisiana after the time of exile from their homeland.

Amand Broussard became a patriot of the American Revolution and fought in the Battle of New Orleans during the War of 1812 when he was 58 years old. He died six years later.

Dealing with exile, hurricanes, floods, oil spills, and other disasters, the folks of Louisiana have learned to survive and thrive. Vermilionville proudly honors their heritage.

Sweet Dough Pies

½ cup shortening or ¼ cup vegetable oil
¾ cup sugar
1 egg
¼ cup milk
1 teaspoon vanilla
2 cups flour
½ teaspoon nutmeg
pinch of salt
2 teaspoons baking powder

Preheat oven to 350 degrees. Cream shortening and sugar. Add egg and milk. Mix well. Add vanilla. Mix in dry ingredients and mix until smooth—should be the consistency of biscuit dough. If necessary, add more flour. Divide dough into 12 pieces. Roll dough about ⅛-inch thick. Put one tablespoon fig or other fruit preserves on top of dough and fold in half. Seal edges with fork. Place on cookie sheet and bake about 25 minutes or until brown. Makes 12 pies about the size of a cookie or biscuit.

culture. The complex, located at 300 Fisher Road across from the airport, features entertainment, craft demonstrations, and an operating farm typical of those in the eighteenth century. Also, a cooking school staff demonstrates Creole and Cajun methods of food preparation.

Geese strut about, and costumed storytellers, musicians, and craftspeople re-create the folk life of bayou settlers from 1765 to 1890. As Acadian descendants, many staffers switch easily from speaking English to Cajun French. A hand-pulled ferry takes you across Petit Bayou to Fausse Pointe, where you'll meet Broussard family members such as Camille and Eliza. The couple speak and behave as people did in the 1840s and may inquire about your strange apparatus called a camera, your attire, or some unfamiliar expression. Except major holidays, Vermilionville is open Tues through Sun from 10 a.m. to 4 p.m. Admissions stop at 3 p.m. There is an admission fee.

Basically French country cooking, Cajun cooking utilizes fresh indigenous ingredients such as rice, peppers, herbs, game, and fish—notably the ubiquitous crustacean called crawfish—and Lafayette boasts some great places to sample traditional specialties.

For classic Cajun and Creole cuisine, stop by **Cafe Vermilionville** (1304 West Pinhook Rd.; 337-237-0100; cafev.com) housed in a ca. 1818 Acadian inn. For lunch, try the bronzed shrimp and artichoke salad or crab cakes Vermilion. Dinner selections might include such specialties as smoked salmon and tasso, pecan tilapia, or tuna steak topped with seared foie gras.

Because music plays a primary role in Acadiana's culture, you might enjoy "two-stepping" to the sounds of Cajun triangles, fiddles, and accordions at one of the local Cajun dance hall/restaurants. Both **Randol's Restaurant and Cajun Dancehall** (2320 Kaliste Saloom Rd.; 337-981-7080; randols.com) and **Prejean's Restaurant** (3480 Northeast Evangeline Thwy; 337-896-3247; prejeans.com) specialize in Cajun cooking and feature live music.

Save plenty of time to explore downtown Lafayette, and consider starting your tour at the **Acadiana Center for the Arts** (101 West Vermilion St.; 337-233-7060; acadianacenterforthearts.org). This multifaceted arts and cultural facility features worldwide traveling exhibits and the work of local artists. Many artists maintain studios in the Lafayette area, and you can spend a couple of days gallery hopping. The center's hours are Mon through Sat from 10 a.m. to 5 p.m. If a special exhibition is in progress, the facility also opens on Sat from 10 a.m. to 6 p.m. Admission. For a coffee break, visit **AcAfe: A Reve Coffee Stop** (acadianacenterforthearts.org) serving Reve Coffee from local crafters.

Afterward, head to nearby Jefferson Street. While strolling around, be sure to look for the fascinating outdoor murals painted by Robert Dafford. One intriguing creation, "'Til All That's Left Is a Postcard," can be viewed at 407 Jefferson Street.

Other great downtown stops include **Teche Drugs & Gifts** (509 Jefferson St.; 337-235-4578), which offers much more than sundries and gifts, and **Sans Souci Fine Crafts Gallery** (219 East Vermilion St.; 337-266-7999; louisiana crafts.org). Here, you'll find creations by Louisiana Crafts Guild members in both traditional and contemporary pottery, blown glass, wood and metal sculptures, jewelry, furniture, and more.

The **Lafayette Science Museum** (433 Jefferson St.; 337-291-5544; lafayette sciencemuseum.org) offers educational fun. You'll view interesting exhibitions, a state-of-the-art planetarium, discovery room, and museum store. Kids especially find it intriguing to investigate a crime scene in the forensic lab. Museum hours are Tues through Fri from 9 a.m. to 5 p.m., Sat from 10 a.m. to 6 p.m., and Sun from 1 to 6 p.m. Admission.

Don't miss the **Lafayette Museum–Alexander Mouton House** (1122 Lafayette St.; 337-234-2208; lafayettemuseum.com). The home of Louisiana's first Democratic governor, this antebellum town house contains antiques, Civil War relics, and historic documents. Go upstairs and see the lavish hand-beaded Mardi Gras costumes and other glittering regalia. The museum's hours are Tues through Sat from 10 a.m. to 4 p.m. Admission is modest.

A walking tour from this point will take you past some of the city's landmark buildings, including the **Cathedral of St. John the Evangelist**, an interesting structure of German-Romanesque design.

Either University Avenue or St. Mary Avenue, both of which turn off Lafayette Street, will lead you to the University of Louisiana at Lafayette. Look for a parking place somewhere near the student union, then head for the tall cypress trees. Right in the middle of campus, you'll see an honest-to-goodness swamp studded with cypress trees trailing their streamers of Spanish moss. Called **Cypress Lake**, the natural swamp (about the size of a city block) comes complete with native vegetation, waterfowl, migratory birds, fish, and even alligators.

Because this is a miniature swamp, you get a sense of the mysteries such an environment conceals—without the threat of danger. Visitors are welcome to stroll along the water's edge and feed the ducks. Small signs placed at intervals in the murky water invite you to please feed the fish and inform you that this is an alligator habitat. (You're not supposed to feed the alligators, but if you toss half a hot dog to the fish and it's intercepted by an alligator, it's best to let him have his way.)

While on campus, be sure to visit the **Paul and Lulu Hilliard University Art Museum** (710 East St. Mary Blvd.; 337-482-2278; hilliardmuseum.org) a handsome reflecting structure. After taking in the current exhibitions, you can check out the great titles at the James W. Bean Bookstore on the second floor. Museum hours are Tues 9 a.m. to 5 p.m., Wed 9 a.m. to 8 p.m., Thurs and Fri 9 a.m. to 5 p.m., Sat 10 a.m. to 5 p.m.; admission charged.

Night owls will want to take in some lively music and dancing at the **Blue Moon Saloon** (337-234-2422 or 877-766-2583; bluemoonpresents.com), a venue for Cajun, country, and zydeco music. Join the honky-tonk troubadours at 215 East Convent Street and kick up

ilssontparti!

In south Louisiana even the horses might speak French. At the start of each race at Evangeline Downs, the announcer does not shout "They're off!" but rather "Ils sont parti!"

your heels. Check out the in-house hostel, an economical place to hang your hat while visiting Cajun country and in walking distance of both the bus and train stations.

A must-see in Lafayette is *LARC's Acadian Village* (337-981-2364 or 800-962-9133; acadianvillage.org), located on the southwest edge of town. After leaving the campus take Route 167 south until you reach Ridge Road, where you'll turn right. Next take a left on West Broussard Road. Then you'll follow the signs to Acadian Village at 200 Greenleaf Drive. By the time you reach this cluster of buildings situated on a bayou and surrounded by gardens and woodlands, you'll agree it's definitely off the beaten path.

When you step through the gate, you may feel as if someone turned the calendar back about 200 years. With its general store, schoolhouse, chapel, and original steep-roofed houses, the folk life museum replicates a nineteenth-century Acadian settlement.

Stop at the general store to buy a ticket and pick up a guide sheet describing the individual buildings. Strolling along a brick pathway and crossing wooden footbridges, you'll wend your way in and out of the various vintage structures. Although the blacksmith shop, chapel, and general store are reproductions, all other structures are authentic, most dating from the early 1800s. Transported from various locations throughout Acadiana, they were restored and furnished with native Cajun household items, clothing, photographs, books, and tools. The charming village captures the spirit of early Acadiana, and commercialism is noticeably absent.

The *LeBlanc House*, birthplace of Acadian state senator Dudley J. LeBlanc, contains a display featuring the tonic Hadacol. An early elixir touted to cure all ailments, this vitamin tonic concocted by LeBlanc, fondly known as "Couzan Dud," contained 12 percent alcohol. During the early 1950s George Burns, Bob Hope, Jack Benny, Mickey Rooney, Jimmy Durante, and other entertainers performed in Hadacol caravans, updated versions of the old-time traveling medicine shows.

The *Billeaud House*'s exhibits focus on spinning and weaving. You'll see looms, spinning wheels, and a display of homespun coverlets and clothes. Take a look at the cotton patch, planted behind the cottage. If you packed a picnic, this peaceful setting is the perfect spot to enjoy it as you watch villagers (wearing the traditional clothing of their ancestors) spin wool on a porch or chat by the bayou.

Acadian Village is open Mon through Sat from 10 a.m. to 4 p.m. except for major holidays. Admission is charged.

From Lafayette's outskirts it's only a fifteen-minute drive northeast via Route 94 to *Breaux Bridge*, also known as the Crawfish Capital of the World.

Only a few miles east of Breaux Bridge lies one of this country's great untamed regions, the **Atchafalaya Basin** (that large uncluttered area west of Baton Rouge on your state map). In this vast wilderness swamp, an overflow area for the Atchafalaya (*a-CHAFF-a-lie-a*) River, you can step back into a pristine world, but don't venture into its depths on your own. If you're game for a guided safari, take Route 347 northeast from Breaux Bridge, then pick up Route 352 to reach Henderson, the gateway to the Atchafalaya Basin. This area features a number of boat tours designed to introduce visitors to the Atchafalaya Basin's mysteries.

Driving through various portions of South Louisiana in the spring, you sometimes see people wading in ditches of water near the roadside. They are crawfishing—capturing those tasty little lobster look-alikes. Now that commercially grown crawfish is so readily available, this practice is not as common as it once was. Crawfishing is still great sport, however, and if you feel the urge to engage in this activity (children especially find it fascinating), it's a simple matter to buy some set nets at a local hardware store. Next, find a nearby grocery store and buy some beef spleen, known as "melt." Then search out a deep ditch or swampy area. In this area of the state, you don't have to be a super sleuth to find one. Cut the meat into small pieces, and tie them to the centers of the nets. Spacing the nets several yards apart, place them in the water. After a few minutes grab a stick and start yanking the nets up, and presto!—dinner.

If you prefer someone else to snare and prepare your crawfish, head for Henderson and **Pat's Fisherman's Wharf Restaurant** (337-228-7512; pats fishermanswharf.com), located on Route 352 across the bridge at 1008 Henderson Levee Road. Request to be seated on the porch, and you can look directly down into Bayou Amy.

Restaurant owner Pat Huval helped put Henderson on the map. After buying the restaurant in 1954, he added crawfish to the menu. (At that time, restaurants seldom served crawfish.) The specialty proved so popular that it created a new industry for the town—raising, processing, and selling crawfish.

Here is the place to sample Hank Williams's famed "jambalaya, crawfish pie, and filet gumbo," while a Cajun band provides listening entertainment. Be sure you're hungry because the meal starts with a salad and a cup of delicious gumbo (probably the state's most famous dish and often served with a dollop of rice). If you don't want crawfish for dinner, a delicious alternative is Pat Huval's seafood platter, a house specialty featuring a green salad, seafood gumbo, fried shrimp, oysters, catfish, French fries, and hush puppies. "Our food is so fresh," says Huval, "the catfish slept in the river last night." The restaurant is noted for its dirty rice (so called because it's cooked with chopped chicken giblets). In season you can also order turtle soup. Rates are moderate.

The restaurant is open Sun through Thurs from 11 a.m. to 9:30 p.m., and until 10:30 p.m. on Fri and Sat.

For your excursion into the Atchafalaya, you can catch a boat tour (airboat and swamp tours are also available) at *McGee's Louisiana Swamp Tours & Adventures* (1337 Henderson Levee Rd.; 337-228-2384). To get there, turn left at the fourth exit. Just past Whiskey River landing, you'll see McGee's.

The ninety-minute tour takes you into a different world—a jungle of plants such as wild hibiscus, lotus, and elephant ears. Lots of trees also grow here—cypress, hackberry, willow, and oak, to name a few. The swamp serves as home to alligators, nutrias, muskrats, minks, opossums, otters, ducks, turkeys, wading birds, and other wildlife. You'll glide under the Swampland Expressway, the 18-mile span on I-10, which opened up Cajun Country to the rest of the world. Building this bridge, once considered impossible because of the basin's boggy bottom, required considerable engineering ingenuity. If you encounter fog when driving on this stretch of interstate over the swamp, please exercise extreme caution. Heavy mists come with the terrain, and being suspended over a swamp magnifies the hazard. Tours are offered daily, starting at 10 a.m. If you arrive before or after a tour begins, you can grab a sandwich or full meal at McGee's Atchafalaya Café. Hours are 10 a.m. to

Marked Routes

Out from St. Martinville on Louisiana Highway 96 there are small hand-painted wooden shrines, commemorating the fourteen Stations of the Cross, affixed to trees along the highway. Catholics from the church at the Isle L'Abbe community walk this route annually during Lent.

You can see one shrine next to the historic marker at the beginning of Oak and Pine Alley. The marker signals the starting point of the fabulous pre–Civil War wedding procession for a bride of the locally prominent Durand family. During her wedding, the bride passed under trees that were decorated for the occasion with gold dust sprinkled on webs spun by imported spiders.

While driving along Highway 90, watch for the Cade/St. Martinville exit and follow Louisiana Highway 182 to enjoy a picturesque drive. Along the way you'll see an old dance hall that dates back more than forty years, now renamed The Stockyard Saloon, plus inviting golf courses.

Other roadside landmarks include Bruce Foods, where authentic Cajun seasoning and food are prepared for distribution, and Camp Pratt, a prisoner-of-war camp for German soldiers during World War II. Spanish Lake, a natural refuge for wildlife and waterfowl, lies adjacent to Camp Pratt. The Jean Lafitte Scenic Byway follows State Route 182 to Highway 14 in New Iberia and then continues to Holmwood.

5 p.m. Mon through Thurs, until 10 p.m. Fri and Sat, and until 7 p.m. Sun or 8 p.m. during summer.

From here head south toward **St. Martinville**. You can either return to Breaux Bridge by way of Route 347, which continues to St. Martinville, or follow Route 31 south from Breaux Bridge. Another option is Route 96, an off-the-beaten-path road by way of Catahoula.

Only a few minutes from downtown St. Martinville in a serene park setting at 1200 North Main Street, you'll find the **Longfellow-Evangeline State Historic Site** (337-394-3754 or 888-677-2900; crt.state.la.us/Louisiana-state-parks/historic-sites/Longfellow-evangeline-state-historic-site/) on the banks of Bayou Teche. (The word *teche,* pronounced "tesh," comes from a Native American word meaning "snake" and refers to the bayou's serpentine path.)

This large complex offers a museum and visitor center and an Acadian farmstead and facilities for picnicking. The park's main thrust, however, is to preserve and interpret the history of its early French settlers. Many Acadians who were forced by Britain to leave their Canadian "Acadie" in 1755 later made their way to South Louisiana. Henry Wadsworth Longfellow's epic poem *Evangeline,* the symbol of all Acadiana, tells the story of their long struggle to find a new home.

On the **Olivier Plantation**, an 1815 Creole raised cottage serves as the park's focal point and contains furnishings typical of that period. This plantation house and its detached kitchen and herb garden, in a setting of ancient live oaks for which Cajun country is famous, present a living history lesson. Stop by the visitor center for a look at the variety of exhibits related to early Acadian and Creole lifestyles. Except for Thanksgiving, Christmas, and New Year's Day, the park is open Tues through Sat from 9 a.m. to 5 p.m. Tours take place on the hour with the day's last one starting at 4 p.m. Plan to arrive fifteen minutes early to watch the video site introduction. Admission is modest.

Continue to the charming downtown area of "Le Petit Paris," as St. Martinville was once known. The town became a haven for aristocrats escaping the French Revolution's horrors during "the worst of times." Slave rebellions in the Caribbean sent other French planters here, and French Creoles from New Orleans joined them. With a patrician population prone to staging courtly ceremonies, elaborate balls, concerts, and operas, St. Martinville developed into a cultural mecca.

The mother church of the Acadians occupies a place of prominence on the **St. Martin de Tours Church Square**. Dating from 1832, the current structure contains some original sections from its 1765 predecessor—an altar, box pews, and a chapel. Inside St. Martin de Tours Catholic Church are a silver and gold sanctuary light and carved marble baptismal font, said to be gifts from Louis

XVI and Marie Antoinette. Somewhat to the side and rear of the church, you'll see a statue of Evangeline, for which actress Dolores del Rio posed when she portrayed the heroine in an early movie filmed here. Movie cast members later presented the bronze monument to the townspeople.

Within easy walking distance (a block or so) from Church Square, you'll see the **Evangeline Oak** on Bayou Teche's bank. Like Evangeline, many Acadian refugees in pursuit of their dreams stepped ashore at this spot. According to legend, Evangeline's boat docked under the large old tree when she arrived from Nova Scotia searching for her lover. Local lore differs from Longfellow's tale, but both stories portray the heartbreak of a forced exodus. Emmeline Labiche (Evangeline's real-life counterpart), after a ten-year search, discovered her true love, Louis Arceneaux (Gabriel in Longfellow's poem), here under the Evangeline Oak, only to learn that he had since married another. (If oak trees could talk, this one might say that another tree actually witnessed the sad scene because *which* live oak is the authentic Evangeline Oak remains a topic of debate. This massive specimen nevertheless serves as a stately symbol.)

maraisand platins

On the southwestern prairies of Louisiana you'll find two distinct types of ponds that are referred to by terms that are French in origin. "Marais" are irregular-shaped marshy spots that fill seasonally. "Platins" are on higher ground and are circular. Both occur naturally and are useful to the region's cattle ranchers.

The adjacent **Museum of the Acadian Memorial** (121 South New Market St.; 337-394-2258; acadianmemorial .org) pays tribute to the memory of individual women, men, and children who came to Louisiana during the 1760s after the harsh exile from their Canadian homeland. A mural portrays the Acadians' arrival, and in several cases, direct descendants posed for this group portrait. The Wall of Names lists some 3,000 refugees identified using early state documents. Visitors can step out back to the garden, which features an eternal flame as its focal point and overlooks Bayou Teche. This facility also serves as a genealogy and media center and is open Tues through Sat from 10 a.m. until 4 p.m.

Only a few steps from the memorial and the Evangeline Oak's spreading branches, the **Old Castillo Bed and Breakfast** (337-394-4010 or 800-621-3017; oldcastillo.com) beckons travelers. Located at 220 Evangeline Boulevard, the galleried two-story brick structure with French doors features large rooms furnished with antiques and reproductions. Some rooms overlook Bayou Teche and the celebrated Evangeline Oak, and others offer a view of St. Martin de Tours Church Square. Owner Peggy Hulin encourages guests to enjoy beignets

Look Around You . . .

English architect Christopher Wren's burial marker in St. Paul's Church advises those who seek a monument to "look around you." Likewise, visitors to Abbeville can look around them for "monuments" to the work of contemporary Louisiana architect A. Hays Town.

Town, who has achieved fame for his architectural restorations, began his work here in Southwest Louisiana.

For instance, St. Mary Magdalen Church is a restoration for which Town can claim credit. Among the thousands of homes he has restored, you'll find some along the river here in Abbeville.

Town works to achieve the look of Louisiana's heritage in his restorations: warm brick, aged wood, pleasant vistas, gentle living spaces. He does so by using recycled building components: wood, shutters, doors, windows, and bricks. Town's patrons collect these items themselves, and it can take years to gather enough for a single home.

So anyone with a Hays Town house has personally put in long hours of effort to assist Town in achieving the level of perfection you'll see in Abbeville.

or French toast with cafe au lait prepared the traditional way but also offers full Cajun breakfasts. Standard to moderate rates.

After exploring "Evangeline country," follow Route 31 south toward New Iberia, into Vermilion Parish. To see why Vermilion Parish has been called the most "Cajun place" on earth, head southwest on State Route 14 to **Delcambre Shrimp Boat Landing**. Known as the Shrimp Capital of Louisiana, the picturesque Acadian town of **Delcambre** stands with one foot in Vermilion Parish and the other in Iberia Parish.

At the fisherman's wharf you can hear Cajun French spoken and watch the day's catch being unloaded. You can also buy shrimp—fresh, frozen, cleaned, or the do-it-yourself kind—at any of the several seafood shops here and indulge in a shrimp feast at the covered picnic area nearby.

Delcambre hosts a four-day shrimp festival in August (shrimpfestival.net), which includes a blessing of the fleet. During shrimping season, generally from April through June and again from August through October, you'll see shrimp boats departing from Delcambre on their way to Vermilion Bay or the Gulf of Mexico. After harvesting their bounty the shrimp trawlers return to home port, their hulls filled with iced-down shrimp to be sorted, packed, and frozen. From this small inland port, millions of pounds of shrimp are shipped annually to both American and international markets.

Afterward, continue west to nearby Erath, a sleepy French village and home of the **Acadian Museum**, also known as Musée Acadien (337-937-5468 or 337-233-5832; acadianmuseum.com). "Probably more French is still spoken in business and on the streets of Erath than anywhere in South Louisiana," says attorney Warren Perrin, who founded the museum. Housed at 203 South Broadway in the "Old Bank of Erath," exhibits offer both French and English interpretations and focus on the Prairie Bayou Acadians. Some 2,000 artifacts, books, drawings, photos, maps, and models pertaining to Cajun culture back to the Acadian expulsion from Nova Scotia fill three rooms. Open Mon through Fri 1 to 4 p.m. Admission is free.

Be sure not to miss **Abbeville**, Vermilion's parish seat. This charming French-flavored town, which served as the setting for several movies, lies west of Erath on Route 14. You'll find the beautiful St. Mary Magdalen Church built in 1910, lovely homes, and outstanding eateries such as **Black's Oyster Bar** (319 Père-Megret; 337-898-2597), which specializes in fresh shellfish.

The town is also home to the **Abbey Players**, a local theater group that has a reputation for presenting polished performances and producing professional actors. You'll find the **Abbey Theater**, which is on the National Register of Historic Places, at the corner of Lafayette and State streets. For information on performances, call the Vermilion Parish Tourist Commission (337-898-6600; vermilion.org) or the Abbey Players (337-893-2442; abbeyplayers.com).

Steen's Syrup Mill, located in Abbeville, is one of the nation's largest open-kettle syrup mills. Here, from mid-October through December, you can smell the sweet boiling cane syrup as raw sugarcane is converted into an amber-colored substance almost as thick as taffy. For more information on the area, call the Vermilion Parish Tourist Commission at (337) 898-6600 or visit vermilion.org.

Abbeville also is home to the **Depot at Magdalen Place** (201 West Lafayette St.; 337-740-2112; vermilion.org/activities/depot-magdalen-place), with two restored cabooses nearby (one is wooden with a cupola, the other is steel with a bay window). You will also find

herecomes the . . .

Daytime weddings in Abbeville at **St. Mary Magdalen Church** provide a spectacular entrance for the bride. As the last of the wedding party, the bride and her father come in from outside the church, with the door being held open so that light streams into the dim interior and forms a halo around her.

At the wedding reception (perhaps just down the street at Magdalen Place, a recently restored building on the town square) you'll witness an old Cajun custom as the occasional guest pins money to the bride's veil for the privilege of a dance.

a museum with local artifacts (ask about alligator products) and an assortment of regional gifts for sale. Also ask here about taking a walking tour with a local costumed tour guide—or use a handy brochure to guide yourself. Hours run 10 a.m. to 5 p.m. Tues through Sat.

Afterward, return to Delcambre and take Route 675 to Jefferson Island, about 10 miles west of New Iberia. *Jefferson Island*, the setting for *Cottages at Rip Van Winkle Gardens* (337-359-8525; ripvanwinklegardens.com), sits atop a salt dome (the tip of a huge mountain of salt forced to the surface from deep within the earth). Located at 5505 Rip Van Winkle Road, the site boasts a rich history, which guests will enjoy delving into.

You approach the property along a 2-mile drive lined with live oak trees. And you'll check in at the opulent home that stage actor Joseph Jefferson designed and had built in 1870. Guests can stroll through twenty-five acres of lovely landscaped gardens.

Jefferson, one of America's most famous nineteenth-century actors, made a name for himself portraying Rip Van Winkle. He bought Jefferson Island to use as a winter retreat and hired French craftsmen from New Orleans to build the unique house with its elements of Moorish, Victorian, gingerbread, and Steamboat Gothic architecture.

Never Too Late for an Apology

In 1755, the British forced French Acadians to leave their homes in Nova Scotia. In 2003, the Queen of England signed a Royal Proclamation addressing this injustice to an entire culture. How did this expression of royal regret come about? Louisiana attorney Warren A. Perrin embarked on a long crusade for an apology from the British Crown regarding the Acadian deportations. Here's what he has to say about the matter:

"Without the support of the two million Acadians in the world, the apology would not have been possible. My goal was to make the effort one of reconciliation rather than confrontation, and results speak for themselves: the Proclamation has become a rallying point of both the Acadians and the descendants of the settlers who took over their lands after the diaspora. Further, it is on display in the church at Grande Pre in Nova Scotia, acknowledged to be the most-visited and revered place for Acadians in the world today."

Look for Perrin's historical biography, *Acadian Redemption: From Beausoleil Broussard to the Queen's Royal Proclamation*, available at bookstores, the Acadian Museum in Erath, and online at acadianmuseum.com (where you can also read the Queen's Proclamation). The Louisiana Press Women's Association chose it as Best History Book for 2004.

It is said that Jefferson Island was one of pirate Jean Lafitte's hideouts, and the three pots of gold and silver coins discovered here in 1923 lend credibility to the rumor; the Lafitte Oaks mark the spot where the treasure was found.

Wandering about, you can enjoy views of peaceful Lake Peigneur. Tranquility, however, has not always been part of the picture. In 1980, a freak mining disaster violently rearranged the island's geography when a drilling rig punctured the salt dome under Lake Peigneur. The resulting maelstrom swallowed up the lake's contents—crewboats, barges, and all. Visitors can view a ten-minute film on this strange episode and take a house and garden tour. Admission. Moderate to deluxe rates.

From Jefferson Island, continue on Route 675 into **New Iberia**. The Spanish-influenced town takes its name from Europe's Iberian peninsula. Many of James Lee Burke's novels take place in this setting, which he calls "one of the most beautiful places in America." For a map detailing a walking/driving tour of sites that figure prominently in several of Burke's famed Dave Robicheaux novels, stop by the Iberia Parish Convention and Visitors Bureau at 2513 Highway 14. Also, check out iberiatravel.com or call (337) 365-1540 or (888) 942-3742 for more information on the local scene.

Don't miss **Shadows-on-the-Teche** (337-369-6446; shadowsontheteche .org), a white-pillared plantation house located at 317 East Main Street. Start your tour at the new Shadows Visitors Center, located directly across the street from the mansion, and view the orientation video.

Statuary, camellias, wisteria, magnolia trees, and magnificent live oaks festooned with Spanish moss form a serene backdrop for Shadows-on-the-Teche. The mansion's name was inspired by the interplay of lights and darks across the lawn, created by sunlight filtering through the trees.

Built in 1834 for sugar planter David Weeks, the manor house stands on Bayou Teche's bank. (You don't see the bayou until you step into the backyard.) Slaves collected mud from the bayou's banks to make the house's coral-colored bricks. All the Shadows' main rooms open onto galleries, and there is no central hall. An exterior flight of stairs in front of the house, concealed by a lattice, leads to the second floor.

When William Weeks Hall (the original owner's great-grandson) took over the mansion during the early 1920s, he found it in an advanced state of deterioration. An artist, Hall lived in Paris before relocating to New Iberia to accept his lifetime challenge of restoring the Shadows to its former grandeur. Throwing himself into the restoration project, he also threw open his doors to extend Southern hospitality to such celebrities as Mae West, Henry Miller, W. C. Fields, and H. L. Mencken. In the studio you'll see a door covered with signatures scribbled by Hall's houseguests—Cecil B. DeMille, Arleigh Burke, Tex Ritter,

Walt Disney (along with his alter ego, Mickey Mouse), and others. Hall's friends referred to him as "the last of the Southern gentlemen."

Hall, who died in 1958, willed Shadows-on-the-Teche to the National Trust for Historic Preservation. When researchers discovered the mansion's original inventory of furnishings filed in an adjoining parish, they used it as a mandate to furnish the house as authentically as possible. The mansion's accessories include everything from indigo-dyed trousers and pier tables to finger bowls and foot warmers.

Except for major holidays, the mansion is open Mon through Sat from 10 a.m. to 4 p.m. Last tour begins at 3:15 p.m. Admission is charged.

Take an after-dinner stroll to the nearby Iberia Bank and see the spotlighted statue of **Hadrian**, the only full-length rendering that dates from the Roman emperor's lifetime. Created by an unknown Roman sculptor around AD 130, the statue of white marble stands 7 feet tall and weighs about 3,000 pounds. After departing Italy, the statue commanded a post at an English castle prior to its arrival in New Iberia.

The **Estorge-Norton House** (337-365-7603; estorgenortonhouse.com), a charming three-story structure of cypress that dates from about 1912, offers bed-and-breakfast accommodations. Located at 446 East Main Street in the heart of New Iberia's historic district, the home makes an ideal place to headquarter while taking in the local attractions, which should definitely include a walking tour of the historic district.

On the second floor a variety of accommodations is offered. A suite on the third floor sleeps four. Guests can enjoy a full breakfast in the sunroom or dining room. Maybe a Creole specialty, grits and grillades, will be on the menu. Standard to moderate rates.

At 309 Ann Street, you'll find the **Konriko Rice Mill and Company Store** (337-364-7242 or 800-551-3245), offering tasty treats and an interesting tour. Sip a cup of coffee while you watch a twenty-minute slide presentation on Cajun culture and the history of rice harvesting and milling. Afterward you can tour America's oldest working rice mill and browse in the Konriko Company Store (a replica of an actual company store). You might be given a rice cake to munch on and a sample of artichoke rice or other Konriko specialty. The store, which carries local foods, craft items, and gifts, is open Mon through Sat from 9 a.m. until 5 p.m. Modest tour charge. See conradricemill.com.

Before leaving town, plan an outing to **Antique Rose Ville** (2007 Freyou Rd.; 337-367-3000) where you'll find a ca. 1830 antebellum cottage with a backdrop of lovely gardens. Guests can stroll the grounds, smell the roses, and enjoy a meal or high tea. Call first for a reservation. You can view the property at antiqueroseville.com.

Learn the History, Taste the Spice at New Tabasco Facilities

Back in the 1860s, Edmund McIlhenny was a prosperous Louisiana banker. He also was a food lover and an avid gardener.

When he was given some pepper seeds from Mexico or Central America, McIlhenny sowed the gift at his Avery Island property. He had no idea that what would sprout would change his future—and spice up cuisine for generations to come.

What McIlhenny did with his peppers was invent a popular hot sauce that he named Tabasco, a Mexican Indian word meaning "land where the soil is hot and humid." Today, McIlhenny's descendants still create Tabasco on Avery Island and visitors now have even more reasons to visit the historic home place. A new Tabasco visitors center, museum, plant tour, and restaurant were recently unveiled to the delight of pepper sauce devotees.

Crushing the reddest peppers from his blooming plants, McIlhenny mixed them with Avery Island salt and aged the mixture for 30 days in crocks and barrels. He then blended in some French white wine vinegar and aged another 30 days.

After straining the mixture, he put it in small cast-off cologne bottles with sprinkler tops. McIlhenny didn't want his special sauce poured on food. He wanted it sprinkled for maximum appreciation. Then he corked the bottles, sealed them with green wax, and gave his creation to family and friends. Back then, food was rather bland and folks were quite happy to have McIlhenny's sauce to jazz it up.

After the Civil War, McIlhenny needed a new job in the Reconstruction South. Seeing that his Capsicum peppers were thriving, he decided to sell his sauce. Ordering thousands of new cologne bottles from a New Orleans glassworks, McIlhenny was soon in business. To this day, the company is still a fifth-generation, family-owned company operated on the very same site.

After visiting the museum to learn the history of Tabasco, visitors can take a factory tour. Large windows let visitors see Tabasco being made and bottled. Walk through the greenhouse to see peppers growing on small plants. Peek in the mixing area and barrel warehouse where pepper mash is aged three years. A favorite photo spot is a row of huge Tabasco bottles where even tall visitors seem dwarfed.

Stop by the Country Store for all things Tabasco, including complimentary taste samples like Tabasco ice cream, which is surprisingly good. Many items are exclusively sold in the Country Store, from fun Tabasco ties and boxer shorts to branded cookware.

With all that walking and shopping, a welcome spot is the new Restaurant 1868—so named for Tabasco's founding year. Big wooden trays on each table hold bottles of Tabasco for diners to spice to their hearts' content. With its lengthy menu (unsurprisingly, every dish contains Tabasco) printed on signs over the serving line, 1868 offers a chance to enjoy the mouth-watering sauce on authentic regional Louisiana favorites, including crawfish étouffée, red beans and rice, crawfish corn maque choux, and boudin.

From New Iberia it's only about 6 miles south on Route 329 to ***Avery Island*** (800-634-9599). Chances are your kitchen cabinet already contains the island's famous export, Tabasco sauce. The red sauce comes in a small bottle for a very good reason: It is meant to be used sparingly, unless Cajun blood runs in your veins.

While here, take time to explore the island's 250-acre bird and animal sanctuary, ***Jungle Gardens*** (either by car or on foot). If you packed a lunch, head for the picnic tables under massive bearded live oak trees. You'll be entertained by prancing peacocks and nesting egrets against a backdrop of exotic vegetation from all over the world. Wasi orange trees, Chinese bamboo, South American papaya trees, and Egyptian papyrus all grow here as well as a profusion of other trees, shrubs, and blooming plants. Don't miss the ancient statue of Buddha, originally commissioned for a Chinese temple, sitting atop a lotus throne in a glass pagoda overlooking a lagoon.

Another must in this wildlife paradise is ***Bird City***, one of the country's largest egret rookeries. During the latter part of the nineteenth century when the great demand for feathers to adorn women's hats almost led to the egret's extinction, conservationist Edward Avery McIlhenny (son of Tabasco's creator, Edmund McIlhenny) caught seven young egrets and raised them in a flying cage that he built on the island. The snowy egrets were later released to fly south for the winter, but they returned to Avery Island the next spring. Their descendants continue the practice—to the tune of some 20,000 birds each year.

Proceed on your safari with caution. Alligators slither all around. (How close they get is up to you.) Jungle Gardens (337-369-6243; junglegardens.org) can be visited seven days a week; hours are from 9 a.m. to 5 p.m. Admission is charged.

While in this area, consider a visit to ***Franklin***. A lovely town founded in 1808, Franklin features several plantation homes as well as the nearby ***Chitimacha Tribal Museum*** (3289 Chitimacha Trl.; 337-923-4830; Chitimacha.gov) in ***Charenton***. Here, you'll see authentic clothing, dugouts, and other exhibits pertaining to the tribe's history. Hours run Mon through Fri from 9 a.m. to 4:30 p.m., Sat by appointments only. Admission is free.

Settled mainly by the English, the town (said to be the only one in the state that sided with the North during the Civil War) was named for Benjamin Franklin.

Located off Irish Bend Road, ***Oaklawn Manor*** (3296 East Oaklawn Dr.; 337-828-0434; oaklawnmanor.com) makes an interesting stop. The home was built in 1837 by Judge Alexander Porter, an Irish merchant who founded the state's Whig Party and also served as a United States senator.

Once the center of a large sugar plantation, the three-story Greek Revival house, which faces Bayou Teche, is splendidly furnished and contains many European antiques and extensive collections of Audubon prints and hand-carved game birds of Louisiana. The house's bricks were made from clay on the premises. Magnificent live oaks and lovely gardens provide a perfect setting for the mansion, now owned by former Louisiana governor Mike Foster.

You'll see an aviary, a gift from Warner Brothers following the filming of a movie here. Be sure to visit the mansion's original milk and butter house on the grounds.

Except for major holidays, Oaklawn is open daily (except on Mon, when the plantation is closed) from 10 a.m. to 4 p.m. Admission is charged.

Continuing south on US 90 takes you to **Morgan City**, a commercial fishing center and home of the **Louisiana Shrimp and Petroleum Festival**, shrimpandpetroleum.org. This annual Labor Day weekend celebration features a Blessing of the Fleet ceremony on Berwick Bay and a water parade of shrimp boats, pleasure craft, and the king's and queen's big vessels. With much music and merriment, the boats bearing royalty meet and greet in a bow-to-bow "kiss" (a feat requiring skillful navigation), and the king and queen lean forward from their respective decks for the traditional champagne toast. Along with shrimp eating, other events include a Cajun cook-off, a gala street parade, fireworks, arts and crafts, and children's activities. In the downtown Historic District, festival-goers can enjoy music under the oaks at **Lawrence Park**.

Before leaving Morgan City, consider taking a guided walking tour through the **Swamp Gardens** (725 Myrtle St.; 985-384-3343), and visiting a cypress home called **Cypress Manor and Mardi Gras Museum** (715 Second St.; 985-380-4651). Tours take place Tues through Sat from 10 a.m. to 4:30 p.m., and Sun from 1 to 5 p.m.

About 3 miles north of town on Route 70 at Lake Palourde, you'll find **Brownell Memorial Park & Carillon Tower** (985-384-2283), a pleasant place to take a driving break. The Brownell Carillon Tower houses sixty-one bronze bells, which chime on the hour and half hour. The park offers picnicking facilities and is open Wed through Sun from 10 a.m. to 4 p.m. Admission is free.

If you continue traveling southeast on US 90, you'll arrive in Houma, a perfect place to begin exploring the toe portion of Louisiana's boot.

Places to Stay in Southwest Louisiana

BREAUX BRIDGE

Maison Madeleine B&B at Lake Martin
1015 John D. Hebert Dr.
(337) 332-4555
maisonmadeleine.com

CROWLEY

Days Inn by Wyndham
9571 Egan Hwy.
(337) 514-0093

LAFAYETTE

Days Inn by Wyndham
1620 North University Ave.
(337) 237-8880

DoubleTree by Hilton Lafayette
1521 West Pinhook Rd.
(337) 235-6111

Hilton Garden Inn Lafayette/Cajundome
2350 West Congress St.
(337) 291-1977

La Quinta Inn
2100 Northeast Evangeline Thwy.
(337) 233-5610
or (800) 531-5900

Moulton Plantation
338 N. Sterling St.
(337) 233-7816
moultonplantation.com

T'Frere's House Bed & Breakfast
1905 Verot School Rd.
(337) 984-9347
tfrereshouse.com

LAKE CHARLES

Aunt Ruby's Bed & Breakfast
504 Pujo St.
(337) 430-0603
auntrubys.com

Days Inn by Wyndham
1212 North Lakeshore Dr.
(337) 240-9945

Golden Nugget Hotel & Casino
2550 Golden Nugget Blvd.
(337) 508-7777
goldennugget.com

Grosse Savanne Lodge
1730 Big Pasture Rd.
(337) 598-2357
grossesavanne.com

L'Auberge Casino Resort
777 Avenue L'Auberge
(337) 395-7777
llakecharles.com

Motel 6 on the Bayou
1101 West Prien Lake Rd.
(337) 474-5151

Richmond Suites Hotel
2600 Moeling St.
(337) 433-5213

NEW IBERIA

Estorge-Norton House
446 East Main St.
(337) 365-7603
estorge-nortonhouse.com

ST. MARTINVILLE

Old Castillo Bed and Breakfast
220 Evangeline Blvd.
(337) 394-4010
or (800) 621-3017
oldcastillo.com

SULPHUR

Hampton Inn
210 Henning Dr.
(337) 527-0000
or (800) 426-7866

Places to Eat in Southwest Louisiana

ABBEVILLE

Dupuy's Oyster Shop
108 S. Main St.
(337) 893-2336
dupuys.com

BREAUX BRIDGE

Buck & Johnny's
100 Berard St.
(337) 442-6630
buckandjohnnys.com

Poche's
3015-A Main Hwy.
(337) 332-2108
poches.com

BROUSSARD

Riverside Inn
240 Tubing Rd.
(337) 837-4011
poorboysriversideinn.com

CROWLEY

Rice Palace
2015 North Cherokee Dr.
(337) 783-3001
Ricepalace.com

HENDERSON

Pat's Fisherman's Wharf Restaurant
1008 Henderson Levee Rd.
(337) 228-7512
patsfishermanswharf.com

JENNINGS

Boudin King
906 West Division St.
(337) 824-6593

LAFAYETTE

Blue Dog Cafe
1211 West Pinhook Rd.
(337) 237-0005
bluedogcafe.com

Cafe Vermilionville
1304 West Pinhook Rd.
(337) 237-0100
cafev.com

Charley G's
3809 Ambassador Caffery Pkwy.
(337) 981-0108
Charleygs.com

Don's Seafood and Steak House
301 East Vermilion St.
(337) 235-3551
donsdowntown.com

Judice Inn Restaurant
3134 Johnston St.
(337) 984-5614
Judiceinn.com

LaFonda Restaurant
3809 Johnston St.
(337) 984-5630
Lafonda1957.com

Prejean's Restaurant
3480 Northeast Evangeline Thwy.
(337) 896-3247
prejeans.com

Randol's Restaurant and Cajun Dancehall
2320 Kaliste Saloom Rd.
(337) 981-7080
randols.com

LAKE CHARLES

Big Daddy's Sports Grill
1737 West Sale Rd.
(337) 477-9033
Bigdaddyssportsgrill.com

Blue Dog Café
609 Ryan St.
(337) 491-8880
lakecharles.bluedogcafe.com

Ember Grill at L'Auberge Casino Resort
777 Avenue L'Auberge
(337) 395-7777
or (866) 580-7444

La Truffe Sauvage
815 W. Bayou Pines Dr.
(337) 439-8364
thewildtruffle.com

Luna Bar and Grill
719 Ryan St.
(337) 494-5862
lunabarandgrill.com

Mazen's
217 W. College St.
(337) 477-8207
mazens.com

Pujo Street Café
901 Ryan St.
(337) 439-2054
pujostreet.com

Rikenjaks Brewing Company
3726 Ryan St.
(337) 602-6635
rikenjaks.com

Seafood Palace
2218 Enterprise Blvd.
(337) 433-9293

Steamboat Bill's
732 Martin Luther King Dr.
(337) 494-1700
Steamboatbills.com

Steamboat Bill's on the Lake
1004 North Lakeshore Dr.
(337) 494-1070
Steamboatbills.com

Stellar Beans Coffee House Café
319 Broad St.
(337) 602-8441
stellarbeanscafe.com

Vic & Anthony's Steakhouse
2550 Golden Nugget Blvd.
(337) 508-4103
vicandanthonys.com

NEW IBERIA

Antique Rose Ville Tea Room
2007 Freyou Rd.
(337) 367-3000
antiqueroseville.com

Bon Creole
1409 East St. Peter St.
(337) 367-6181
bon-creole.com

Acadia Parish Tourist Commission
401 Tower Rd., Crowley 70526
(337) 783-2108
Acadiatourism.org

Allen Parish Tourist Commission
8904 Hwy. 165, Oberlin 70655
(337) 639-4868 or (888) 639-4868
Allenparish.com

Beauregard Parish Tourist Commission
204 West First St., DeRidder 70634
(337) 463-5534
Beauregardtourism.com

Breaux Bridge Bayou Teche Visitor Center
314 East Bridge St., Breaux Bridge 70517
(337) 332-8500
breauxbridgela.net

Cajun Coast Visitors & Convention Bureau
900 Dr. Martin Luther King Blvd., Morgan City 70380
(800) 256-2931
Cajuncoast.com

Cameron Parish Tourist Commission
P.O. Box 388, Cameron 70631
(337) 775-5718
cameronparishtouristcommission.org

Iberia Parish Convention & Visitors Bureau
2513 Hwy. 14, New Iberia 70560
(888) 942-3742
iberiatravel.com

Jefferson Davis Parish Tourist Commission
100 Rue de l'Acadie, Jennings 70546
(337) 821-5521 or (800) 264-5521
jeffdavis.org

Lafayette Convention and Visitors Commission
P.O. Box 52066
1400 Northwest Evangeline Thwy., Lafayette 70505
(800) 346-1958
lafayettetravel.com

Southwest Louisiana Lake Charles Convention and Visitors Bureau
1205 North Lakeshore Dr., Lake Charles 70601
(337) 436-9588 or (800) 456-7952
visitlakecharles.org

St. Landry Parish Tourist Commission
978 Kennerson Rd., Opelousas 70570
(337) 948-8004 or (877) 948-8004
Cajuntravel.com

Area newspapers include the *Daily Advertiser* and *Times of Acadiana* in Lafayette. Both will have entertainment listings. The weekly *Times of Acadiana* will be trendier and also covers Cajun music venues well. Other local newspapers are the *Lake Charles American Press* in Lake Charles (which has a very good website: americanpress.com), the *Breaux Bridge Banner* in Breaux Bridge, the *Cameron Parish Pilot* in Cameron, the *Crowley Post Signal* in Crowley, and the *Daily World* in Opelousas.

Put your radio on in Cajun country—in Ville Platte you can catch the music show from Fred's on Saturday morning from 9 to 11 on KVPI at 1250 AM. KRVS at 88.7 FM in Lafayette will have Cajun music on the early show every morning and zydeco on Sunday. You will also hear newscasts in French on AM stations throughout the area from time to time. Also, if you want to really hear the local accent, just listen to the TV spots in Lafayette.

Little River Inn
833 East Main St.
(337) 367-7466
poorboysriversideinn.com

Victor's Cafeteria
109 West Main St.
(337) 369-9924

RAYNE

Chef Roy's Frog City Cafe
1131 Church Point Hwy.
(337) 334-7913
chefroy.com

ST. MARTINVILLE

Clambeaugh's
111 North Main St.
(337) 394-3949

WASHINGTON

Steamboat Warehouse Restaurant
525 North Main St.
(337) 826-7227
steamboatwarehouse.com

Southeast Louisiana

Southeast Louisiana—the toe of the boot—boasts incredibly diverse landscapes to charm any traveler. And there have been many visitors, from the early Europeans who marveled at the almost bank-to-bank alligators in the rivers to the stars of the 1967 film *Easy Rider* on their high-flying quest for the perfect Mardi Gras.

North of Lake Pontchartrain lie the piney Florida Parishes, where local heritage is more likely English than French. This area was not part of the 1803 Louisiana Purchase but was a section of Spanish, then English, west Florida, hence the name.

Plantation homes can be found along the River Road between New Orleans and the Feliciana Parishes (the "happy land" of the painter John James Audubon) east of the capital city Baton Rouge, itself a town of great charm.

The heart of Southeast Louisiana is, of course, New Orleans. The Crescent City, founded on a "beautiful crescent" of the river by French Canadians in 1718, remains a great and unique destination for tourists.

MISSISSIPPI
LOUISIANA

THE FELICIANAS

Jackson

Bogalusa

FRENCH
CREOLE
COUNTRY

New Roads

TURF AND SWAMP

"RED STICK"

Hammond

Baton Rouge

Lake
Maurepas

Lake
Pontchartrain

Slidell

CRESCENT CITY
REALM

PLANTATION
COUNTRY

New Orleans

BAYS AND
BAYOUS

Thibodaux

Houma

Port Sulphur

SWAMPLAND

Venice

Gulf of Mexico

N

0   40 mi
0   40 km

The area below New Orleans is marked by waterways, fishing and shrimping industries, and the oil business—and small communities known for fun-filled festivals and good times.

Swampland

Entering Terrebonne (*TER-a-bone*) Parish from the west, take State Route 182 to reach Houma (*HOME-uh*). Between Morgan City and Houma, this road follows Bayou Black. Driving along, you'll notice portions of the dark water covered by a bright green film. This substance, known as duckweed, may look like slime to you, but to ducks, it's dinner. A close examination of the plant reveals a mass of tiny four-petaled flowers. One of the world's smallest flowering plants, duckweed makes a tasty salad for ducks and geese. As part of America's WETLAND Birding Trail, Terrebonne Parish boasts five birding sites, including the Mandalay Wildlife Refuge and the Pointe-Aux-Chien Wildlife Management Area.

Because of its many waterways, **Houma** is sometimes called the Venice of America. Its navigable bayous and canals serve as streets for shrimp boats and various vessels that glide by the town's backyards. The parish was established in 1834 on the banks of Bayou Terrebonne (which means "good earth"), and more than half of it is water. Houma is named for a Native American tribe that settled here during the early eighteenth century. Later Cajun settlers arrived and were joined by English, German, and Irish families.

Houma rebounded rapidly from the heavy-duty flooding, wind damage, and power outages resulting from hurricanes Katrina and Rita. In fact, positioned as the town was between the areas of the two storms' impact, Houma

AUTHOR'S FAVORITES IN SOUTHEAST LOUISIANA

Cajun Man's Swamp Tours & Adventures, Gibson

Chauvin Sculpture Garden, Chauvin

French Quarter, New Orleans

Garden District, New Orleans

Grand Isle State Park, Grand Isle

Laura, A Creole Plantation, Vacherie

Louisiana State University, Baton Rouge

Ponchatoula Country Market, Ponchatoula

Rural Life Museum and Windrush Gardens, Baton Rouge

Mardi Gras
New Orleans, Jan 6 through Fat Tuesday

The Audubon Pilgrimage
St. Francisville, Mar
(225) 635-6330
westfelicianahistory.org/pilgrimage

Jackson Assembly Antiques and Art Show
Jackson, Mar
(225) 634-7155
Jacksonassemblyantiquesshow.com

Independence Sicilian Heritage Festival
Independence, Mar
(985) 969-5916
Indysicilianfest.com

Amite Oyster Festival
Amite, Mar & Apr
(985) 969-5340
Amiteoysterfestival.com

Tennessee Williams/New Orleans Literary Festival
New Orleans, Mar
(504) 581-1144
tennesseewilliams.net

French Quarter Festival
New Orleans, Apr
(504) 522-5730
fqfi.org

Jazzfest
New Orleans, Apr & May
(504) 410-4100
nojazzfest.com

Ponchatoula Strawberry Festival
Ponchatoula, Apr
(800) 917-7045
Lastrawberryfestival.com

Angola Arts and Crafts Show and Sale
Angola State Penitentiary
Angola, Apr & Oct
(225) 635-6330
Angolarodeo.com

The Great Louisiana Bird Fest
Covington, Apr
(985) 626-1238
Northlakenature.org/birdfest/

Louisiana Iris Rainbow Festival
New Orleans, Apr
(504) 658-4100
Noma.org

Blessing of the Shrimp Fleet
Lafitte, Apr & May
(504) 689-4101
townofjeanlafitte.com

Thibodaux Fireman's Fair
Thibodaux, May
(877) 537-5800

Gonzales Jambalaya Festival
Gonzales, May
(225) 647-2937
or (800) 680-3208
jambalayafestival.net

Bayou Lacombe Pirogue Races
Slidell, June
(800) 634-9443

Cajun Heritage Festival
Raceland, June
(985) 228-0845
cajunheritagefestival.com

Louisiana Catfish Festival
Des Allemands, June
(985) 758-7542
Louisianacatfishfestival.com

July 4th Boat Parade
New Roads, July
(225) 638-5360
newroads.net

International Grand Isle Tarpon Rodeo
Grand Isle, July
tarponrodeo.org

Angola Penitentiary Inmate Rodeo
Angola State Penitentiary
Angola, Oct & Apr
(225) 635-6330
Angolarodeo.com

Greater Baton Rouge State Fair
Baton Rouge, Oct
(225) 755-3247
Gbrsf.com

The Southern Garden Symposium
St. Francisville, Oct
(225) 635-6330
Southerngardensymposium.org

Voice of the Wetlands Festival
Houma, Oct
(985) 798-5665

French Food Festival
307 East Fifth St.
Larose, Oct
(985) 693-7355
lacajunbayou.com

The Myrtles Plantation Halloween Extravaganza
St. Francisville, Oct
(225) 635-6330
or (800) 809-0565
Myrtlesplantation.com

Wooden Boat Festival
Madisonville, Oct
(985) 845-9200
Woodenboatfest.org

Tangipahoa Parish Fair
Amite, Oct
(800) 542-7520
or (985) 748-8632

Washington Parish Free Fair
Franklinton, Oct
(985) 839-5228
Freefair.com

Fanfare Southeastern Louisiana University
Hammond, Oct
(985) 543-4366
Southeastern.edu

New Orleans Film Festival
New Orleans, Oct
(504) 309-6633
neworleansfilmsociety.org

Three Rivers Art Festival
Covington, Nov
(985) 327-9797
Threeriversartfestival.com

Destrehan Plantation Fall Festival
Destrehan, Nov
(985) 764-9315
Destrehanplantation.org

Festival of the Bonfires
Lutcher Recreational Park
Lutcher, Dec
(800) 367-7852
festivalofthebonfires.org

Christmas in the Country
St. Francisville, Dec
(225) 635-6330
stfrancisvillefestivals.com

Christmas in New Orleans
New Orleans, Dec

served as a base for helicopter pilots all over the state as they carried on rescue missions in the desperate post-hurricane days.

A delightful way to acquaint yourself with the local flora and fauna is to take a swamp cruise, and the region offers several choices. For a swamp tour with a unique slant, try **Cajun Man's Swamp Tours and Adventures** (985-868-4625; cajunmanadventures.com), headquartered on State Route 182, about 15 miles west of Houma and 20 miles east of Morgan City at **Bob's Bayou Black Marina**.

Black Guidry, a French-speaking Cajun singer who dishes up music with his commentary and tour, serves as captain for my trek into a beguiling wilderness. "Folks, if you want to know something, ask me," he says. "If I don't know the answer, I'll tell you a lie, and you won't know the difference." It's obvious that he knows this lush area well, and he often checks his crab traps along the way.

Black will take you through a surrealistic world of cypress trees with swaying Spanish moss. You'll see elephant ears, palmettos, muscadine (wild grape) vines, and pretty purple water hyacinths (which rob the water of oxygen and are extremely difficult to control). Black will point out bulrush, which provides nesting areas for snowy egrets, black-crowned night herons, and other birds. You'll probably see cormorants, ibis, blue herons, ducks, cranes, red-tailed hawks, and perhaps bald eagles and pelicans. You may also spot nutrias (fur-bearing members of the rodent family), otters, turtles, snakes, alligators, and other creatures that populate this eerie realm.

Black's "pet" alligators recognize the sound of his boat and come when he calls (unless they're hibernating). Papa Gator, who is 14 feet long, and other members of his family may put in an appearance.

After the boat tour Black will play his guitar and sing for you. A gifted musician, he composes songs and appears on national television. Maybe he'll sing "Crawfish, Crawdads, Mudbugs, and Other Things" (from one of his albums) or a Hank Williams favorite like "Jambalaya," whose famous line "Son of a gun, we're gonna have big fun on the Bayou!" takes on added relevance in this setting.

During the musical session Black will show you his Cajun accordion made from part of a wooden chest, diaper pins, and other materials of opportunity. Cajuns are noted for their resourcefulness; they are also known for their friendliness, zest for life, strong family ties, and cooking skills.

The swamp cruise, narrated in either French or English, takes about two hours and costs $25 per adult and $15 per child ages twelve and younger. Children under age 2 cruise free. Call ahead because tour times vary, and reservations are required.

Voice of the Wetlands

Lending his talent and energy to bring awareness to Louisiana's coastal and cultural erosion, two-time Grammy nominated musician *Tab Benoit* from Houma formed Voice of the Wetlands in 2003. An annual VOW festival, the only event in Louisiana to address the loss of the state's coast and culture, takes place in Houma during mid-Oct. Look for Tab's musical releases including Voice of the Wetlands with Dr. John, Tab Benoit, Cyril Neville, George Porter Jr., Anders Osborne, Big Chief Monk Boudreaux, Houma native Waylon Thibodaux, and other artists.

If you're game for another tour, visit *Wildlife Gardens* (5306 North Bayou Black Dr.; 985-575-3676; wildlifegardens.com) in *Gibson*. North Bayou Black Drive runs parallel to State Route 182. Owned by Betty Provost, the preserve is populated with numerous animals from South Louisiana. The family pets range from nutrias, bobcats, raccoons, and deer to ducks and black swans. The natural swamp setting in Gibson is also home to great horned owls, pheasants, exotic chickens, alligators, and alligator loggerhead turtles.

Here, depending on the season, you can give bread to the white-tailed deer, perhaps scratch their velveteen horns, and watch their fawns being bottle-fed. Watch out for Clarence, a 90-pound alligator loggerhead turtle. The family also operates an alligator farm, and visitors can touch the babies and observe the different stages of alligator growth.

On a self-guided tour, you'll see an authentic trapper's cabin with furnishings. Guided tours are available for groups. Admission is charged.

Betty also offers bed-and-breakfast. "Guests can stay in one of our four little rustic cabins nestled in the swamp," she says. "Our cabins now have screened porches which are a good place to sit and relax." Moderate rates.

After your encounter with the local wildlife, continue on State Route 182 east to *Houma*. While there, take time to drive along Route 311 on the city's western outskirts to see several lovely plantation homes situated along Little Bayou Black.

Stop by *Southdown Plantation House* (1208 Museum Dr.; 985-851-0154; southdownmuseum.org), located about 3 miles southwest of town on the corner of Route 311 and St. Charles Street. This grandiose pink Victorian mansion, trimmed in green, also serves as the Terrebonne Museum. Inside the twelve-room structure, you'll see a colorful Mardi Gras exhibit. Be sure to notice the hall doorways with inserts of stained glass in a sugarcane motif. There is also an exhibit on the Houmas Indians, with handicrafts and photographs.

Getting Grounded

In Southeast Louisiana there are rich powdered loess soil and some remaining mixed hardwood bottomland forest in the area just east of Baton Rouge in the Feliciana Parishes.

Just north, or east of the Mississippi River, the shallow and brackish Lake Pontchartrain is the largest of a chain of lakes leading into the Gulf of Mexico. North of Lake Pontchartrain the land rises to the sandy soil region of the piney woods.

The land along the Mississippi on the West Bank and nearing the Gulf of Mexico on the East Bank is cut by slow-flowing bayous winding through swamps and marshes. Highland occurs on natural levees along watercourses and on old shoreline ridges called cheniers for the oak trees (des chenes) growing there.

Other interesting exhibits focus on local history and the state's native peoples. You'll also see a re-creation of the Washington, D.C., office of the late Allen J. Ellender from Houma, who served almost thirty-six years in the U.S. Senate. Autographed pictures of familiar political personalities line the wall. Senator Ellender's colleagues acknowledged him as the Senate's master chef, and his original gumbo recipe is still prepared in the U.S. Senate dining room. You can pick up a brochure featuring some of Senator Ellender's Creole recipes such as gumbo, shrimp Creole, jambalaya, oyster stew, and pralines.

Guided tours take about an hour. Except for holidays, Southdown is open Tues through Sat 10 a.m. to 3 p.m. Admission.

While in Houma, consider headquartering at ***Grand Bayou Noir*** (1143 Bayou Black Dr.; 985-804-0303; grandbayounoir.com), the home of Judge Timothy Ellender and his wife, Debra. In a setting of stately oak trees, the handsome white Georgian-style home dates to 1936 and fronts Big Bayou Black. The lush grounds feature four acres of cultivated plants including fifteen citrus varieties and twenty-eight species of banana trees along with a vegetable and herb garden. Guests are invited to enjoy the hot tub on the outdoor patio.

In addition to guest rooms in the main house, accommodations include a suite in the adjacent guest wing with a private balcony and entrance. Like the late U.S. Senator Ellender (his uncle), the judge knows his way around the kitchen, and so does his son. Guests can anticipate a gourmet breakfast, served in the main dining room. Starting with a fruit medley, the meal might feature bananas Foster pancakes with smoked bacon plus an egg dish laced with crawfish and garnished with a sky vine blossom and sprig of dill from the property. Actually, most breakfasts here utilize ingredients gathered fresh from the backyard. Moderate.

While in Houma, don't miss *Bayou Terrebonne Waterlife Museum* (7910 West Park Ave.; 985-580-7200; tpcg.org). Start your visit by watching the eight-minute video presentation, which provides an orientation to the facility. Interactive exhibits showcase the area's close link with the seafood and water-transportation industries and spotlight the plight of the vanishing wetlands. Hours are Tues through Fri from 10 a.m. to 5 p.m., and Sat from noon to 4 p.m. If you visit on Tues or Thurs from 5:30 to 7 p.m., you'll hear some toe-tapping Cajun music. Modest admission.

Before leaving town, you'll want to take in some Cajun music and dancing. At *The Jolly Inn* (1507 Barrow St.; 985-872-6114) located in a former warehouse, every out-of-towner gets an honorary Cajun certificate entitling him "to all privileges, duties, and honors of those who love the lifestyle of the Acadian people and culture." One requirement is to be able to dance at least one step of the Cajun two-step. If you don't know how, the locals will gladly share their expertise.

When dinnertime rolls around, you can dig into a boiled seafood dinner or platter of steaming crawfish at *1921 Seafood Restaurant* (1522 Barrow St.; 985-868-7098), just across the street from The Jolly Inn. (It may be my imagination, but the crawfish look bigger in Houma than most other places—maybe because they are not farmed here but trawled from the local bayous.) Restaurant hours run 5 to 10 p.m. daily, except Sun when the restaurant is closed.

Heading south on State Route 56 will take you to *Cocodrie*, a popular spot with anglers and only about thirty-five minutes from Houma. On the way, you'll pass through Chauvin, home of an extraordinary sculpture garden. To see this collection of more than one hundred concrete sculptures, which ranks among the world's top three finest examples of folk art, turn left on State Route 58 at

Hot Weather Tip

Keep your bathing suits and a towel in the car to be ready for a quick dip. North of Lake Pontchartrain, ice-water creeks with local swimming holes can be found—ask at a busy filling station, especially if you see inner tubes hanging around.

Pushepatappa Creek, north of Bogalusa near Varnado, and Big Creek, outside Amite off Highway 16, are both local favorites. Or check out a "tubing" company—you rent a tube, float down a river, and the service picks you up. Try near Franklinton on Highway 25 from Folsom.

You might also find swimming opportunities on the beach at Grand Isle or around False River. Only swim where it is allowed—Louisiana has serious water pollution problems, and you don't want to take a risk.

the traffic light intersection onto Sarah Bridge and cross Bayou Petit Caillou. Then take a right at the first street to 5337 Bayouside Drive. You'll see Nicholls State University Art Studio on the left and the Sculpture Garden on your right.

The ***Chauvin Sculpture Garden*** (985-594-2542; Nicholls.edu/folkartcenter/park.htm) spills over with the incredible creations of reclusive artist Kenny Hill. Hardly anything is known about Hill other than he was a bricklayer by trade and spent about a decade filling this small piece of property with his profound and unique body of work.

Angels and other amazing creatures painted in vivid Cajun colors testify to the artist's obvious struggle with good and evil. This implementation of his vision, loaded with Biblical and political allegory, reflects such torment that it can prove painful to see. Most of all, you want to know more about the man who could create all this, then disappear. Hill reportedly declared his work a story of salvation, saying, "It's about living and life and everything I've learned." The Sculpture Garden is open from 8 a.m. to 5 p.m. Admission is free, but donations are accepted and used to maintain this remarkable collection.

Across the road, you can visit the ***Nicholls Art Studio*** (958-594-2546; Nicholls.edu/folkartcenter) and view its permanent collection by local artists. Hours are 11 a.m. to 4 p.m. Sat and Sun, or by appointment. For more information, call the NSU Division of Art at (985) 448-4597. Nicholls State University is located in nearby Thibodaux.

Afterward, follow State Route 56 to ***Cocodrie***. At ***Coco Marina*** (985-594-6626 or 800-648-2626; cocomarina.com), local charter fishing captains promise good fishing at this facility on the Gulf of Mexico's fruitful fringes. Here you can charter a boat (the marina currently operates ten boats, ranging from 25- to 38-feet in size) for fishing expeditions. A day's catch might include black drum, redfish, speckled trout, sheepshead, cobia, red snapper, flounder, and mackerel. The marina has recorded daily catches of more than twenty-six different species, and a typical weekend haul might bring in a sampling of ten to fifteen species.

Celebrate your catch at the ***Island Oasis Bar*** while enjoying a wetlands sunset. Afterward, you can dine at the ***Lighthouse Restaurant***, which offers seafood specialties. Or you can feast on your own catch in the privacy of your condo. The complex offers accommodations from motel units to studio apartments, and all buildings stand on 12- to 14-foot pilings. The marina is open daily, except for the months of Nov through Mar and major holidays. Rates are standard to moderate.

While in Cocodrie visit the ***Louisiana University Marine Consortium*** (985-851-2800; lumcon.edu). This working research facility also welcomes tourists for free. You will find exhibits on the environment and some aquarium

For the Birds

Grand Isle is for the birds—at least just before and after their great migration over the Gulf of Mexico. In early spring, just after a cold snap, the trees of the island are filled with warblers and songbirds taking their ease after their long trek.

Grand Isle is also a site for the **Audubon Society Christmas Bird Count**, the annual census of birds that takes place all over the United States. The Grand Isle count is always high.

You can see interesting species at any time. Check out the gulls and terns for some western strays. Keep an eye out for scissor-tailed flycatchers (that tail is remarkably long: you can't miss them). You probably won't see an albatross, but one dedicated birder did add one to his life list here.

You can download a map for birding on Grand Isle at Audubon.org, showing which of the small residential streets might lead you to a good venue.

displays and, best of all, a viewing tower that lets you have a gull's-eye view of the surrounding saltwater marshes. Stroll the boardwalks and see the local birds. Hours are 8 a.m. to 4 p.m. daily.

Afterward, return to Houma and follow Route 24 east until you reach Route 1 in Lafourche Parish. Then head south on Route 1, which runs parallel with Bayou Lafourche, known locally as the "longest street in the world." This waterway, busy with the traffic of barges, shrimp boats, and a variety of other vessels, extends to the Gulf of Mexico. A number of Cajun fishing communities line the shore.

Slow down when you reach the little town of **Golden Meadow** (actually you should slow down before you get here because the speed limit means what it says). Watch for a small shrimp boat, the *Petit Caporal*, moored beside Route 1. Named for Napoleon Bonaparte, the century-old boat serves as a monument to the area's shrimping industry. Driving through the area south of Golden Meadow and all the way down to the coast, you'll see a variety of birds—gulls, terns, shorebirds, and such.

Located on the Gulf of Mexico at the end of Route 1, you'll discover **Grand Isle**. A bridge links the narrow 8-mile barrier island to the mainland. You'll drive past fishing camps, homes built on tall pilings, and other beach proper-ties. Grand Isle is noted for its excellent birding, especially during spring and fall when migrating flocks follow the flyway (the migratory interstate for birds from Canada to Mexico), which crosses the island.

Grand Isle State Park (108 Admiral Craik Dr.; 985-787-2559 or 888-787-2559; crt.state.la.us/Louisiana-state-parks/parks/grand-isle-state-park), at the

OTHER ATTRACTIONS WORTH SEEING IN SOUTHEAST LOUISIANA

Afton Villa Gardens
St. Francisville
(225) 635-6773 or (504) 861-7365
Aftonvilla.com
Around the ruins of what had been the
Afton Villa Plantation is now a beautiful
garden to delight the senses. Open Mar
through June, and Oct through Nov.
Admission.

Annie Miller's Son's Swamp Tours
Houma
(985) 868-4758 or (800) 341-5441
annie-miller.com
Locally, this swamp tour has the usual
pleasant patter, as well as comfortable
seats and alligators who appear on
cue. Kids will enjoy this. Reservations
suggested.

Casa de Sue Winery & Vineyards
Clinton
(225) 683-1010
Casadesuewine.com
Tours available (call first) of Louisiana's
first licensed winery; open daily except
Sun.

Destrehan Plantation
Destrehan
(985) 764-9315
Destrehanplantation.org
Built in 1787, this is a fine example
of the Louisiana French colonial-style
plantation house. Careful restoration is
ongoing, supported by a fall festival and
other events. Besides a resident ghost,
you will also find a nice museum shop
for souvenirs.

Edward Douglass White Historic Site
Thibodaux
(985) 447-0915
louisianastatemuseum.org/museum/
ed-white-historic-site
Edward Douglass White, U.S. Supreme
Court chief justice from 1910 to 1921,
was born in this raised cottage, now
maintained as a historic site by the state
of Louisiana.

Global Wildlife Center
Folsom
(985) 796-3585
Globalwildlife.com
Guided covered-wagon tours over 900
acres and a variety of species to see.
Kids will enjoy the visit.

island's eastern tip, offers many seashore recreation opportunities such as fishing, surfing, crabbing, picnicking, and camping. The park is open for overnight RV camping.

You'll have to return north after you've finished fishing and sunning because Grand Isle is the end of the line.

Greater Baton Rouge Zoo
Baton Rouge
(225) 775-3877
Brzoo.org
Spend a pleasant afternoon on the zoo's walkways, then treat yourself to a miniature train ride.

Louisiana Naval War Memorial
Baton Rouge
(225) 342-1942
Usskidd.com
In addition to the USS *Kidd*, the memorial on the riverfront holds the largest collection of ship models in the South. There is a replica of the gun deck of Old Ironsides (the USS *Constitution*) and the pilothouse of an 1880s steamboat, as well as a restored jet.

Louisiana State Capitol Grounds
Near the capitol is a sunken rose garden. The Pentagon Barracks, dating from 1819, once served as dormitories for LSU students back when the school was all-male and had a somewhat military regimentation. By 1906 the Pentagon housed female students and today it holds apartments for legislators.

Sunshine Bridge
Donaldsonville
The Sunshine Bridge over the Mississippi River commemorates the song written by Louisiana governor Jimmie Davis, "You are My Sunshine."

View of Grande Terre Island
From the easternmost tip of Grand Isle you can see across to the onetime location of U.S. Army Fort Livingston. After Jean Lafitte vacated his pirate lair here in 1814, the military fortified his old camp.

West Baton Rouge Museum
Port Allen
(225) 336-2422
Westbatonrougemuseum.org
A plantation cabin, an 1830 French Creole cottage, and a 1904 sugar mill can all be seen and enjoyed here.

Wetlands Acadian Cultural Center
Jean Lafitte National Historical Park and Preserve
Thibodaux
(985) 448-1375
nps.gov/jela/wetlands-acadian-cultural-center.htm
The center, which often features local craftspeople and experts, houses a theater for video presentations as well as detailed displays and artifacts about the Acadians (Louisiana immigrants from French Canada, evicted by the conquering English in the late 1700s).

At Golden Meadow once more, you can vary your route by switching from Route 1 to Route 308 (which also runs parallel to the waterway) on the eastern bank of Bayou Lafourche. Continue driving north toward Thibodaux (*TIB-a-doe*). Two miles before reaching Thibodaux, just off Route 308 on Route 33, you'll find **Laurel Valley Plantation** (985-446-7456). Dating from the 1840s, this complex is America's largest surviving sugar plantation. Head first for the General Store and Museum where you'll see a couple of locomotives, old machinery, and a pen filled with chickens, ducks, sheep, and goats. The store carries prints depicting Laurel Valley Plantation as it looked during the nineteenth century, as well as local arts and crafts. You'll also see vintage items: iron pots, churns, crocks, smoothing irons, farm implements, and pirogues. Laurel Valley Village consists of some sixty weathered structures, including a manor house, school, blacksmith shop, and barns. A cane-lined drive takes you past rows of workers' cabins. Pick up a leaflet at the museum and go exploring on your own. Weather permitting, hours run from 10 a.m. to 3 p.m. Mon through Fri, and noon to 3 p.m. on Sat and Sun.

After leaving Laurel Valley, drive on into ***Thibodaux*** (about five minutes away) to see the town's fine group of Victorian homes and other interesting buildings such as the courthouse, St. Joseph's Catholic Church, and St. John's Episcopal Church. Dating from 1844, St. John's is the oldest Episcopal church west of the Mississippi River. Nearby ***Nicholls State University*** also features an interesting boat-building facility. After touring Thibodaux take Route 308 north toward Napoleonville.

Plantation Country

About 2 miles south of Napoleonville, a town founded by a former soldier of the Little Corporal, you'll find ***Madewood*** (4250 Hwy. 308; 985-369-7151 or 800-375-7151; madewood.com). Dating from the 1840s, this magnificent white-columned Greek Revival mansion features a huge ballroom, handsome walnut staircase, and ornate plasterwork. The home is furnished with period antiques, fine paintings, Oriental rugs, and crystal chandeliers.

"We're the least commercial of the area plantations," says Keith Marshall, "and some of our guests have returned four and five times." He and his wife, Millie, make their lovely plantation home on Bayou Lafourche available for both day tours and overnight lodging. On the grounds you'll see an interesting old cemetery, several plantation outbuildings, and lovely landscaping complete with live oak trees and swaying Spanish moss.

Overnight guests are greeted with wine and cheese. A house tour, an elegant dinner (with candlelight and wine) followed by after-dinner coffee and brandy in the parlor, and a full plantation breakfast are included in the price of a mansion room or the nearby raised bay cottages. Rates are deluxe. With the exceptions of Thanksgiving, Christmas Day, and New Year's Day, Madewood is open daily from 10 a.m. to 4 p.m. Admission is charged.

Depending on your time frame and interests, you can travel farther east to do some plantation hopping along the **Great River Road** (actually composed of several state highways), which parallels both sides of the Mississippi River between New Orleans and Baton Rouge. Along the way you'll see lovely scenery—magnolia, oak, pecan, and willow trees and many of the South's most beautiful plantation homes, like **San Francisco**, with its elaborate Steamboat Gothic design, and the impressive Greek Revival–style **Oak Alley**, with its grand canopy of live oaks. Several of the plantation homes are patterned after Greek temples and feature long oak-lined approaches. Many of these magnificent old mansions offer both tours for daytime visitors and bed-and-breakfast accommodations for overnight guests.

Ride up the River Road to view **Bocage Plantation** (in 2 miles), **Hermitage Plantation** (3 miles), and **Belle Helene** or **Ashland Plantation** (7.5 miles). On your way to Baton Rouge (37 more miles), you will also pass through the community of Carville, which at one time housed the American treatment center for Hansen's disease (leprosy). Carville is named for the family of James Carville, outspoken political operative.

For a rare glimpse into the past, stop by **Laura, A Creole Plantation** (2247 Hwy. 18; 225-265-7690; lauraplantation.com) near Vacherie. Located on the west side of the Mississippi River, this multicolored manor house built in 1805 was named for Laura Lacoul, whose memoirs provide firsthand accounts of a thriving, hard-driving sugar and wine importation business managed for eighty-four years by women—no languorous hours spent sipping mint juleps on Laura's verandas.

To make Laura's colorful, sometimes cruel history come alive for visitors, owner Norman Marmillion and staff tracked down and studied some 5,000 pages of documentation from several states and as far afield as the National Archives in Paris. People find Laura captivating "not because of our ancient moss-draped oaks or a few pieces of furniture," Marmillion notes, "but because our stories transport visitors into the fascinating world of Creole Louisiana." Throughout the house and wine cellar, mannequins depict Laura, various family members, and servants. From baby teeth to voodoo charms, Laura's family artifacts, clothing, photo albums, business ledgers, and slave records reinforce accounts of "the good, the bad, and the ugly" shared by staff members.

Historians regard Laura as the American home of the Br'er Rabbit stories. "Here in our remaining slave quarters, the centuries-old tales of the West African folk hero [Compair Lapin] were first written down in North America, later to be translated, adapted, and become widely known as the American legend,

Br'er Rabbit," Marmillion says. Slaves from Senegal brought the stories to Louisiana during the early 1700s.

Except for major holidays, Laura is open daily from 9 a.m. to 5 p.m. The day's first tour starts at 9:30 a.m. and the last one at 4 p.m. Admission is charged.

From Laura, follow the River Road (Highway 18) west to **Donaldsonville**. First settled in 1750, this little city was a thriving port in the nineteenth century and served as the Louisiana state capital in the 1830s.

In Donaldsonville check out **Framer Dave's Frameshop** (512 Mississippi St.; 225-473-8536; alvinbatiste.com) in the heart of the historic district. The shop is also the gallery of primitive painter Alvin Batiste. Hours are 10 a.m. to 5 p.m. Tues through Fri, and by appointment on Sat.

For a fun Cajun meal, visit **Grapevine Café** (211 Railroad Ave.; 225-473-8463; grapevinecafeandgallery.com). Housed in a restored 1920s building, Grapevine Café also has a rotating gallery of works from local artists as well as the soulful sounds of local musicians. The bountiful menu offers choices like fried green tomatoes topped with crabmeat and remoulade sauce, turtle soup, peppercorn encrusted filet mignon, spinach and andouille stuffed chicken breast, crabmeat stuffed redfish, and white chocolate bread pudding topped with white chocolate sauce. The café also serves beer, wine, and cocktails.

plantationsin themovies

Louisiana appears on the silver screen with great regularity. Fans of Anne Rice might recognize Destrehan Plantation as the scene for parts of the film *Interview with a Vampire*. The Bette Davis–Olivia deHavilland vehicle *Hush, Hush, Sweet Charlotte* took place at Houmas House. Nearby Ashland (also called Belle Helene) was the setting for *The Beguiled* with Clint Eastwood. Oak Alley appears in *Primary Colors*.

Check out Donaldsonville's museum, the old B. Lemann department store building, and the Fort Butler historic site—a Union Army fortification where African-American soldiers served in the Civil War. You can continue following the Mississippi west toward White Castle to visit Nottaway Plantation.

Nottoway (30970 River Rd.; 225-545-2730; nottoway.com) is the biggest plantation house of all.

Nottoway, sometimes called the White Castle, is a splendid interpretation of the Italianate style. The three-story mansion with sixty-four rooms, once the centerpiece of a 7,000-acre plantation, was designed by acclaimed architect Henry Howard. Sugar baron John Hampden Randolph commissioned the

Sugar Palace Pleasures

Photo opportunities abound at **Houmas House Plantation and Gardens** (40136 Hwy. 942; 225-473-9380; houmashouse.com) in Darrow, once known as the "Sugar Palace" because of its extensive sugarcane holdings. This grand plantation home takes its name from the Houmas tribe who occupied a village here when French explorer LaSalle arrived in 1682. The home boasts fourteen Doric columns and a magnificent three-story spiral staircase. With its spacious rooms and comfortable antiques, this is the plantation most appealing to contemporary tastes in interior design.

Start your visit in the gift shop by viewing a presentation on the property's history. Then meander about the extensive grounds, maintained by ten full-time gardeners. Owner Kevin Kelly has added gorgeous gardens, along with exotic plants, statuary, reflecting ponds, and fountains. The site is open daily from 9 a.m. to 7 p.m.

While touring Houmas House, you'll want to savor a meal at **Latil's Landing Restaurant** on the premises. Executive chef Jeremy Langois, who enjoys creating traditional Louisiana dishes with unique touches, collects culinary accolades, too. Langois puts a southern spin on crème brûlée. Here's the recipe for his version of this classic dessert:

Mint Julep Custard Brûlée

2 cups heavy whipping cream
¼ cup bourbon
½ cup blanched fresh mint leaves
2 egg yolks
3 whole eggs
1 cup sugar
Pinch of cinnamon
Pinch of nutmeg
1 cup sugar for brûlée

Scald heavy whipping cream and bourbon. Blanch mint leaves in boiling water for 10 seconds, remove mint leaves and plunge in ice water. Strain and puree leaves with 1 cup of the cream and bourbon mixture. Combine eggs, sugar, cinnamon, and nutmeg in a mixing bowl and add mint puree. Slowly pour the cream and bourbon mixture into the egg mixture, while whisking constantly. Run the mixture through a strainer. Pour into six 6-ounce soufflé cups. Place the soufflé cups in a water bath, and cover with aluminum foil.

Bake at 350 degrees for 30 minutes. Remove from oven, place soufflé bowls on flat pans and immediately refrigerate for 2 hours. Once the custard has cooled, dust the top of each with sugar. Using a blowtorch, carefully caramelize the sugar on top of each of the custards until golden brown. Be careful not to blacken the sugar as it will have a bitter taste. Serve with a dollop of slightly sweetened whipped cream. Yields 6 servings.

house, which was completed in 1859. The 53,000-square-foot home provided plenty of space for the Randolphs' eleven children, staff, and visitors. Cornelia, one of the Randolph daughters, wrote a book about life at Nottoway titled *The White Castle of Louisiana*. You can buy a copy at the gift shop.

Perhaps the home's ornate interior, the setting for exquisite antiques and art, is best exemplified by the grand White Ballroom. This immense room, with its white marble fireplace and Corinthian columns, is a vision in varying shades of white. With its gleaming floor (covered by three layers of white enamel), vanilla-colored walls, and lofty ceiling, this room made an elegant backdrop for both balls and weddings. Six of the Randolph daughters were married in the White Ballroom, and during the past decade some 500 weddings have also been performed here.

At Nottoway, unlike some mansions, visitors are told they may explore after the tour and go through any door that's not closed. Overnight guests are free to stroll through the mansion after hours between 5 and 10 p.m.

Dinner is served in **The Mansion Restaurant**, open to overnight guests, as well as other visitors. For a casual lunch, visit **Le Café**, where the varied menu offers a large buffet as well as a la carte choices of traditional Louisiana cuisine.

germancoast

When Louisiana was a young French colony, it was difficult to attract settlers. Finally some German farmers were enticed and given land along the Mississippi River in the 1760s. This area became known as the German Coast. Soon the Germans intermarried with the French-Acadian exiles who arrived a bit later. That is the reason that Schexnayder is a typical "French" Louisiana name. The name Hymel (pronounced *HEE-mel*, or *EE-mel*) probably began as "Himmel." The little community of Des Allemands (usually pronounced *des-AL-muns*) is just inland on the West Bank of the German Coast—the name des Allemands is French for "Germans."

Overnight guests are served a welcome beverage on arrival and can enjoy a full plantation breakfast the following morning.

Nottoway is open daily for breakfast from 7 a.m. to 10 a.m., lunch from 11 a.m. to 2 p.m., and dinner from 5 p.m. to 9 p.m. Sunday brunch is served from 11 a.m. to 2 p.m. The plantation is closed on Christmas Day. Otherwise, the mansion can be visited daily from 9 a.m. to 4 p.m. Admission is charged. Rates are moderate to deluxe.

When you leave Nottoway, you will exit near the gift shop. To see the world's smallest church (quite a contrast to the South's largest mansion), turn left when you drive out of Nottoway's parking lot. This puts you on Route 405, also called River Road, which runs in front of the mansion and beside the levee.

Proceed toward Bayou Goula and watch for the ***Chapel of the Madonna*** on the left. (My car clocked the distance at 4.3 miles.) A green sign on the road's right side announces: smallest church in the world/madonna chapel. Unfortunately there's no place to park except on the roadside in front of the church, but at the time of my visit some members of a utility crew at work nearby assured me that this was quite all right.

You may feel a bit like Gulliver approaching a Lilliputian chapel as you open the gate of the fence surrounding this miniature church, which is about the size of a large closet. Mounted on the wall to the right of the door, you'll see a wooden box, which should contain a key to unlock the front door. If the key is not there, check the top of the door frame or ask at the house next door.

When I visited, several candles were burning, and three straight wooden chairs flanked each side of the altar. I was told that the church was built in 1890 by a devout woman to fulfill a vow she had made during her daughter's critical illness. An annual Mass is held here on August 15. You can sign a register and make a donation if you wish.

After this brief detour return to Route 1 (there's a cut-through near Bayou Goula) and head north toward Baton Rouge. A few miles north you may want to stop in downtown Plaquemine to see the locks, built in 1900, which once provided the only access to waterways west of the Mississippi. ***Plaquemine Locks*** (no longer in use) linked the navigable Bayou Plaquemine with the Mississippi River. Here you'll see the original lockhouse with exhibits on the river's traffic and history. The facility also features picnic grounds and an observation tower that affords a sweeping view of the Mississippi River. After visiting Plaquemine continue to Baton Rouge, about 15 miles north.

Political Louisiana

The marble halls of the Louisiana State Capitol (the tallest in the country) have heard their share of political gossip. Political aficionados can watch the legislature in action from the galleries and, in the area near the elevators toward the rear of the main floor, speculate on whether the holes in the marble really date from the assassination of Huey Long. Long's statue stands atop his grave, just in front of the capitol. His son, former U.S. Senator Russell Long, posed for the statue.

Also on the capitol grounds is a plaque commemorating Louisianan Zachary Taylor, who was commandant of the U.S. Army barracks here when he was named president in 1848. Supposedly, the letter telling him of his election sat at the post office for several days before Taylor paid the postage due.

"Red Stick"

According to legend, Baton Rouge's name came from a notation on a map used by French explorer Pierre le Moyne, sieur d'Iberville, and his brother, Jean Baptiste le Moyne, sieur de Bienville, who led an expedition up the Mississippi River in 1699. Iberville spotted a tall cypress pole smeared with animals' blood, which apparently marked the dividing line between the hunting grounds of the Bayou Goula and Houmas Native American tribes who shared this area. When Iberville jotted "le bâton rouge" (French for "red stick") on his map, little did he know that he had named what would become Louisiana's capital city.

Baton Rouge offers many attractions, but most of them hardly qualify as off the beaten path, particularly the *State Capitol* or a major college campus like Louisiana State University. You'll miss some unique places, however, if you bypass them. Many of the city's historic sites are clustered close to the State Capitol, which stands on the north side of the downtown area. You can't miss it—it is thirty-four stories high, the tallest state capitol in the United States. The observation tower on the twenty-seventh floor affords a panoramic view of the city. A special project of Governor Huey P. Long, the Capitol was completed in 1932. (Ironically, Long was later shot on the first floor of this building.)

Don't miss the *Old State Capitol* (100 N. Blvd.; 225-342-0500; louisiana oldstatecapitol.org), which Mark Twain called "an atrocity on the Mississippi." This Gothic Revival castle houses Louisiana's Center for Political and Governmental History. Hours are 10 a.m. to 4 p.m. Tues through Fri, and 9 a.m. to 3 p.m. on Sat. Tours take one hour; modest admission.

You may also want to visit the *USS Kidd* (305 South River Rd.; 225-342-1942; usskidd.com), a World War II destroyer, located downtown on the riverfront at the foot of Government Street. Except for major holidays, hours are 9:30 a.m. to 3:30 p.m. on weekdays, 10 a.m. to 4 p.m. on weekends. Overnight camping is available by reservation. Admission is charged.

batonrouge stars

Joanne Woodward and critic Rex Reed both attended LSU. Filmmaker Steven Soderburgh, whose *Sex, Lies and Videotape* won a Palm award at the Cannes Film Festival, was also a Baton Rougean.

The *Louisiana State University Museum of Art* (225-389-7200; lsumoa .org), which features a collection of more than 3,500 works of fine and decorative arts, is housed in the *Shaw Center for the Arts*. The museum occupies the fifth floor of the Shaw Center, which covers a full city block bordered by North Boulevard, Convention, Third, and Lafayette streets in the heart of downtown Baton Rouge.

Louis Armstrong: From Street Waif to Music Legend

On New Year's Eve in 1912, a young New Orleans boy fired a gun into the air. That was a big mistake—or maybe it was a huge break for the child and for the world of music.

Arrested for disturbing the peace, **Louis Armstrong** was sent to the Colored Waif's Home in New Orleans. While there, he met band manager Peter Davis and received his first formal music training. Released from the home in June 1914, Armstrong went on to become one of the legends in jazz. He died in 1971.

"If he hadn't gone to the home, who knows what might have become of him," our tour guide said. "It might have saved his life."

A cornet and bugle that Armstrong played at the Colored Waif's Home are now on display at the **Louisiana State Museum** in Baton Rouge, along with other Armstrong memorabilia. Born on August 4, 1901, in the rough Storyville District of New Orleans, Armstrong grew up on the streets. His father left the family soon after Armstrong was born. His mother was a domestic servant and part-time prostitute.

As a child, Armstrong dressed in rags and usually shopped in garbage cans. Even then, music was his salvation. He sang with other boys on the streets for tips and flourished in the music program at the Waif's Home.

Look closely at the cornet. It has notches in the non-detachable mouthpiece cut by the young Armstrong to aid his embouchure. Armstrong later described the notchings in an interview before the cornet was relocated.

Several hundred photographs trace Armstrong's career. The collection has quite a few photos of Armstrong as King Zulu at Mardi Gras in 1949, including some recently discovered snapshots that were previously unknown. One touching original photo shows Armstrong returning in triumph to the Waif's Home in the early 1930s. Posing with his teacher Peter Davis, Armstrong is holding the cornet now on display at the museum and grinning in happiness.

Opened February 1, 2006, the Louisiana State Museum is filled with history and interesting artifacts concerning Louisiana. Allow plenty of time for a visit because many visitors are surprised at the exhibits and wide range of topics—from the Louisiana Purchase to Sportsmen's Paradise to Mardi Gras traditions throughout the state and local lore.

Artifacts include a 48-foot wooden shrimp trawler, a Civil War submarine, a record-breaking marlin, a krewe of lawnmowers, a New Orleans Lucky Dog cart, and a huge 30-foot suspended sculpture titled "River of Memory" in the three-story atrium lobby. Louisiana's love for hot sauce is spotlighted in a big cabinet filled with various bottles of the popular food ingredient.

Casinos

Since Louisiana legalized gambling, there have been numerous gambling boats docked throughout the state. As is usual in Louisiana, the introduction of legal gambling was all very exciting, very political, and very controversial. If you like the constant electronic clamor of slot machines and you relish sitting in a room without clocks or windows, you're going to enjoy Louisiana casinos. The ones in Baton Rouge are on the Mississippi River (they are boats, but they seldom cruise) in the Catfish Town vicinity of restored, old-wharf-area buildings.

Located at 100 Lafayette Street across from the Old State Capitol, the handsome Shaw Center serves as a venue for LSU's Laboratory for Creative Arts and Technology, the Manship Theatre, and local Arts Council. Also housed here,

A Dessert for All Seasons

Straight to you from the pastry chef at The Club at LSU Union Square comes this luscious dessert recipe. If you subscribe to the theory of eating dessert first because of life's uncertainty then you'll savor the following all-season treat, Panna Cotta with Strawberry–Vin Santo Sauce, and maybe forget all about lunch.

Italian for "cooked cream," panna cotta is a light, silky egg custard, sometimes flavored with caramel. It's served cold and is especially good in summer with fresh berries on top or drizzled with chocolate sauce. If perchance there's any custard left over, it's also great for breakfast. The chef compares it to crème brûlée without the caramelized top and suggests starting it one day ahead.

Panna Cotta with Strawberry–Vin Santo Sauce

Strawberry–Vin Santo Sauce:

1 pound fresh strawberries, hulled and quartered (about 4 cups)
½ cup sugar
2 tablespoons Vin Santo*
¼ teaspoon vanilla extract
¼ teaspoon (packed) grated lemon peel

Panna Cotta:

¼ cup cold water
4 teaspoons unflavored gelatin
4 cups whipping cream
1 cup sugar
1 tablespoon orange blossom honey

the LSU School of Art Gallery features exhibits by LSU faculty members and students.

Before or after your gallery excursion, you can stop by the LSU Museum Store and/or enjoy a snack or meal at PJ's Coffee House and Wine Bar, Capital City Grill, or rooftop Japanese restaurant Tsunami, which affords a sweeping river view.

Check out an overview of the permanent collection, latest offerings, and upcoming exhibits at the museum's website. LSU Museum of Art hours run Tues through Sat from 10 a.m. to 5 p.m. (hours extended to 8 p.m. on Thurs and Fri), and Sun from 1 to 5 p.m. The museum closes on Mon and major holidays. Admission. The first Sunday of every month is free admission.

After your downtown sight-seeing tour, head toward the city's southwestern corner for a visit to **Louisiana State University**. LSU offers interesting attractions ranging from museums and a live Bengal tiger to Indian mounds

¼ teaspoon vanilla extract
1 tablespoon Vin Santo,* Muscat wine, or cream sherry
2 cups pine nuts (9 ounces), plus more for serving

For the Strawberry–Vin Santo Sauce:

Puree strawberries in food processor. Transfer puree to heavy large saucepan. Mix in sugar, Vin Santo, vanilla extract, and grated lemon peel. Simmer over medium-low heat, stirring often, until sauce is reduced to 2 cups, about 15 minutes. Cool. (Sauce can be prepared two days ahead. Cover and refrigerate.)

For the Panna Cotta:

Pour water into metal bowl; sprinkle gelatin over it. Let stand until gelatin softens, about 10 minutes. Set bowl in saucepan of simmering water. Stir just until gelatin dissolves, about 1 minute.

Combine cream, sugar, honey, and vanilla in heavy, large saucepan. Bring to a boil, stirring until sugar dissolves. Remove from heat. Add gelatin mixture and Vin Santo; whisk until well blended.

Divide 2 cups pine nuts among ten ¾-cup custard cups. Divide cream mixture among cups. Chill overnight.

Set cups in small bowl of warm water to loosen panna cotta, about 20 seconds each. Run small knife between panna cotta and custard cups. Invert panna cotta onto plates. Spoon Strawberry–Vin Santo Sauce over. Sprinkle with additional pine nuts; serve.

Makes 10 servings.

*An Italian dessert wine available at some liquor stores and specialty foods stores.

and a Greek amphitheater. You'll find the campus 1.5 miles south of downtown Baton Rouge, between Highland Road and Nicholson Drive.

Stop first at the visitor information center, located on the corner of Dalrymple Drive and Highland Road, where you can pick up a parking permit (required Mon through Fri) and a campus map.

While on campus, stop by **The Club at LSU Union Square** (225-578-2356) for lunch. Located on Highland Road across from the Parade Ground at 2 Raphael Semmes Road, the eatery is housed in a handsome Italianate-style structure that dates to 1939. The Club offers soups, salads, and sandwiches along with seafood, chicken, beef, and pasta entrees and desserts in an attractive setting, enhanced by easy listening music. Popular choices include the shrimp salad, gourmet burger, or glazed crabmeat sandwich on an English muffin with cheese and fruit. Whatever the talented pastry chef prepares will make a fitting finale for your meal. Maybe panna cotta will be featured when you visit. (See sidebar recipe.) Serving hours are Mon through Fri from 11 a.m. to 2 p.m. Prices are economical to moderate.

Afterward you can visit **Memorial Tower** (225-578-1854; visitbatonrouge .com), built in 1923 as a monument to Louisianans who died in World War I. The 175-foot structure at 131 Johnson Hall also houses permanent collections of the LSU Museum of Art. Chimes ring every quarter hour. Also known as the Campanile.

LSUsports

When the legislature is not in session, the best games in Baton Rouge are usually on the Louisiana State University campus. The Tigers field teams in every possible sport, and they do very well in most. Tiger Stadium earns its nickname "Death Valley" for the steep sides and the roaring hometown crowds. The baseball and basketball teams have gained national honors.

The Tiger Marching Band puts on spectacular halftime shows. It is said that the late governor Huey Long, who was a big LSU booster, wanted LSU to have a band big enough to spell out the full name of opponent Virginia Polytechnic Institute on the field.

He got it.

Take time to stroll to nearby Foster Hall, home of the **Museum of Natural Science** (119 Dalryrmple Dr.; 225-578-2855; museum.lsu.edu), to see dioramas depicting Louisiana's wildlife. On display are mounted specimens of birds, reptiles, and animals, including LSU's original Bengal tiger mascot. (You also can visit the current mascot, Mike VII, who resides in an environmentally controlled home outside Tiger Stadium—a nearby sign reads GEAUX TIGERS!) The museum is open weekdays 8 a.m. to 4 p.m., closed at 2 p.m. on Fri during the school year for research seminars.

Colonial Africans

Recent historical research has revealed that Louisiana has a rich African-connected past. Historian Gwendolyn Midlo Hall's book, *Africans in Colonial Louisiana*, shows that, in the early years of French domination, Africans retained tribal ties, names, and language to a greater extent than realized, especially in this area. The Pointe Coupee district was headquarters for an unsuccessful revolt in 1795—organized not just by African slaves, but also by their white allies, Europeans holding the beliefs of French revolutionaries.

Before leaving campus make a point of seeing the 3,500-seat Greek amphitheater; the avenue of stately oak trees, planted as memorials for LSU alumni killed in World War II; and two intriguing Indian mounds believed to date from 3300 to 3800 B.C.

A short distance northwest of the campus, you'll find **BREC's Magnolia Mound Plantation** (2161 Nicholson Dr.; 225-343-4955; brec.org/index.cfm/park/MagnoliaMoundPlantation), one of the state's oldest plantations. Once a 900-acre plantation extending from Tiger Stadium to the Mississippi River Bridge and back to Highland Road, it now occupies 16 acres. Even though this historic site (owned by the Recreation and Park Commission of East Baton Rouge Parish) is sandwiched between bustling downtown Baton Rouge and LSU, it is more than two centuries removed. In the museum store, a diorama shows the locations of early outbuildings and also the plantation's original boundaries. The 1791 home serves as a lovely example of French Creole architecture. Surrounded by a grove of live oak and magnolia trees, the house stands on a ridge facing the Mississippi levee.

Magnolia Mound, authentically restored, is made of large cypress timbers joined by wooden pegs and packed with *bousillage*. Be sure to notice the quaint iron latches and the carved woodwork. In the dining room you'll see an unusual buffet with locked wine compartments and a Napoleon mirror over the mantel. Other interesting furnishings include an overseer's desk in the plantation office, a pianoforte in the parlor, and an old rope bed. According to the museum's guide, the familiar expression "Good night; sleep tight" originated because some old-fashioned beds used rope-supported mattresses that had to be pulled taut periodically. Mattresses made with Spanish moss were used on plantation beds during summer months and were replaced by feather mattresses for winter.

On the grounds you'll see both a kitchen garden and a crop garden and several outbuildings typical of early plantation life—a detached kitchen, a *pigeonnier,* and an overseer's house.

If you visit on Tuesday or Thursday from October through May, you may see bread or biscuits being made and smell chicken roasting. To illustrate the lifestyle of colonial Louisiana, the staff schedules ongoing activities like quilting and open-hearth cooking demonstrations plus three major events each year. Turning the calendar to December, typical holiday activities at Magnolia Mound include candlelight tours with costumed guides, simple period decorations, and a bonfire on the grounds to guide *le pere Noel*. Except for major holidays, hours run from 10 a.m. to 4 p.m. Mon through Sat, and from 1 to 4 p.m. Sun. Tours start hourly with the day's last tour at 3 p.m. Admission.

If you want to step back into the nineteenth century, drive to the junction of I-10 and Essen Lane, where you'll find the entrance to an outdoor complex called ***Rural Life Museum and Windrush Gardens*** (225-765-2437; lsu.edu/rurallife).

The museum's grounds occupy part of a family plantation that Steele Burden and his sister Ione Burden donated to Louisiana State University. The 450-acre tract serves as a setting for the museum as well as an agricultural research station.

The folk museum consists of more than twenty-five old buildings collected from farms and plantations throughout the state. Instead of a "big house" (most farm families could not afford extravagant residences), you'll see a brick-front overseer's cottage with a parlor, dining room, and two bedrooms. The rooms are furnished with authentic utilitarian pieces. Nearby stands a kitchen, detached from the main house because of the danger of fire.

A row of slave cabins and other rustic buildings paint a picture of austerity. In the sick house, the plantation's infirmary, you'll see rope beds, a tooth

The Wandering River

The reason there is a Pointe Coupee (or "cut point") is that the Mississippi River, in its ceaseless fight to make a beeline to the Gulf, lopped off a turn and created a lake here. Think of the river as a garden hose whipping around on the grass. The force of water is seldom a steady pulse. Also consider the varying composition of the river's bed and its banks—some areas more firm than others, with soil constantly washing away. You can then begin to understand the quandary of the U.S. Army Corps of Engineers as it tries to tame this monster.

The most important building near here is the Old River Control Structure, which keeps the Mississippi from moving into the bed of the Atchafalaya and going south to Morgan City instead of proceeding eastward toward New Orleans. In the great flood of 1927, the Atchafalaya River basin was subject to dreadful flooding from the Mississippi.

Into the Hills

The soil in this region is loess—a rich but powdery mix that tends to form deep gorges. This formed the Tunica Hills region near Angola, where the deep ravines around Little Bayou Sara are the haunt of a large number of bird species, some of the last bottomland hardwood forest, and some buried treasure.

The treasure in question was in the form of grave goods of the Tunica-Biloxi Indian tribe. The Native American group lived in this region in the 1700s and traded extensively with the French. Their graves, with contents of precious objects, contained an assortment of French trade goods, ceramics, beads, and metal, as well as handcrafted items. Ownership of the treasures passed from the person who dug them up to Harvard University and finally to the Tunica-Biloxi tribe, who now house the collection in a museum on tribal land near Marksville.

extractor (ca. 1800), and a shock treatment machine from the 1850s (which generated mild electrical charges for treating arthritis, nervous twitches, and other ailments).

You can also visit a commissary, smokehouse, schoolhouse, blacksmith's shop, gristmill, cane grinder, and sugarhouse. Other structures include a country church, pioneer's cabin, corncrib, potato house, shotgun house, Acadian house, and dogtrot house. The museum's big barn contains hundreds of items, including a voodoo exhibit, a 1905 Edison phonograph, plantation bells, bathtubs, irons, oxcarts, trade beads, an African birthing chair, and pirogues.

Call ahead for a one- to two-hour guided tour for ten or more persons. The museum is open from 8 a.m. to 5 p.m. daily. Admission is charged.

To see an impressive collection of European antiques and architectural elements, head for *Fireside Antiques* (14007 Perkins Rd.; 225-752-9565). Shop hours are Mon through Sat from 10 a.m. to 5 p.m. View the inventory at firesideantiques.com.

Afterward, follow US 190 west to Livonia and into the French Creole country of Pointe Coupee Parish.

French Creole Country

Follow State Route 78 north until it intersects State Route 1. You'll take a left here for *New Roads*, stopping first at nearby *Parlange Plantation* (8211 False River Dr.; 225-638-8410; nps.gov/nr/travel/Louisiana/par.htm) on State Route 1 just north of the State Route 78 intersection. Overlooking False River, a lovely oxbow lake created when the mighty Mississippi River changed its mind, this galleried West Indies–type home built by the Marquis Vincent de Ternant dates from 1750. A National Historic Landmark (a status attained by few structures), Parlange is still a working plantation of 2,000 acres and home to descendants of the original family. On a house tour, you'll see eight generations of Parlange and Brandon family possessions, rare antique furnishings, china, and crystal.

The main salon features unusual corner-hung family portraits. The guide will tell you about Virginie (Mme. Pierre Gautreau), who posed for John Singer Sargent's then-startling *Portrait of Madame X* now housed in New York's Metropolitan Museum of Art. A house tour includes the wine cellar, which contains wooden brick molds used in the home's construction, and *pigeonniers* flanking the entrance. Parlange is open daily by appointment only from 9:30 a.m. to 4:30 p.m. If possible, schedule your visit one week ahead. Admission is charged.

The Felicianas

After crossing the Mississippi River, follow the ferry road (State Route 10, which soon becomes Ferdinand Street) up a hill into **St. Francisville**, a picturesque town in a tranquil setting of live oak, magnolias, and pine trees. A fascinating place to visit, this quaint village in West Feliciana Parish retains its nineteenth-century charm. Many plantation houses, built during the early 1800s, lie tucked away in the surrounding countryside.

About a mile from the ferry, you'll see a sign for **Shadetree Inn** (9704 Royal St.; 225-635-6116; shadetreeinn.com) on your right. Perched on a hill at the corner of Ferdinand and Royal streets, Shadetree offers bed-and-breakfast in three romantic hideaways: The Loft, Sun Porch, and Gardener's Cottage, each with its own ambience, including private parking, private entrance, and private outdoor area. Enticements include a treetop deck along with hammock and swings on the grounds—perfect for sipping coffee, reading, and listening to the birds (whose avian ancestors attracted John James Audubon to this area named Feliciana). You'll enjoy strolling the grounds here and may see squirrels, chipmunks, and deer. A cicada chorus also provides evening music. A continental breakfast of juice, coffee, and pastries with an assortment of jams, jellies, and lemon curd awaits. Moderate to deluxe rates.

Even though you'll want to linger at Shadetree, the village begs to be explored and lends itself beautifully to walking.

Clustered along Ferdinand and Royal Streets, you'll pass lovely houses, antique shops, offices, banks, and churches. The National Historic District contains 146 structures.

You'll see ***Grace Episcopal Church*** (11621 Ferdinand St.; 225-635-4065; gracechurchwfp.org), an English Gothic–style structure surrounded by a canopy of moss-covered oak trees. Fighting came to a halt for the funeral of Union naval officer John E. Hart during the Civil War. Hart had asked for a Masonic burial, and his fellow Confederate Masons honored the deathbed request. A granite slab in the churchyard cemetery tells his story.

Housed in a 1905 bank building, you'll find ***Grandmother's Buttons*** (9814 Royal St.; 225-635-4107; grandmothersbuttons.com), a retail shop with unique bracelets, brooches, earrings, cuff links, and watches. You can browse through the ***Button Museum***, which features multitudes of intricate buttons in pearl, glass, enamel, brass, cut steel, jet lustre glass, celluloid, horn, and pewter—all with pertinent identification.

When owner Susan Davis stepped into her grandmother's sewing room one afternoon more than a decade ago, she had no notion that the buttons she saw there would change both her life and that of her husband, Donny, a former farmer and wildlife biologist. The button jewelry that Susan crafted in an upstairs bedroom blossomed from a budding supplemental income into a booming business for both of them. The couple subsequently hired a designer and production staff and started showing jewelry at major markets across the country. Prominent stores, museum shops, boutiques, and catalogs now carry the Grandmother's Buttons line nationwide.

"Our museum star is the rare George Washington inaugural button," said Susan. "We're also doing more reproductions now, like perfume buttons."

Next, continue to the ***West Feliciana Historical Society Museum*** (11757 Ferdinand St.; 225-635-6330; westfelicianahistory.org), which also houses the town's visitor center, for a map detailing a driving-walking tour of

Battle on the Bluffs

The State Historic Site at Port Hudson in Jackson (236 US 61; 225-654-3775 or 888-677-3400; crt.state.la.us/Louisiana-state-parks/historic-sites/port-hudson -state-historic-site) marks the site of a Civil War battle, one in which African-American troops fighting in the Union Army acquitted themselves well in their first outing. Union troops besieged the Confederate defenders of the high bluffs from May until July 1863, when starvation forced them to surrender.

The site today includes a museum, guided trails, and a picnic area. There are often reenactments with authentically clothed and outfitted soldiers of both sides.

Hours are 9 a.m. to 5 p.m. Wed through Sun except for major holidays. Modest admission.

St. Francisville. While here take time to see the museum's dioramas, displays of vintage clothing, documents, maps, and other interesting exhibits. The museum is open daily from 9 a.m. to 5 p.m. Admission to the museum is free.

Continue to the **Myrtles** (7747 US 61; 225-635-6277; myrtlesplantation.com), an elegant home located 1 mile north of Route 10. The plantation's name comes from the many crepe myrtles on the grounds. The oldest portion of the house was built around 1796 by General David Bradford, leader of the Whiskey Rebellion in Pennsylvania. Later owners enlarged the Myrtles and added wide verandas trimmed in "iron lace," one of the house's trademarks. Inside, you'll see Italian marble mantels, mirrored doorknobs, and Irish and French crystal chandeliers. The house is also noted for its elaborate interior plasterwork—and its resident ghosts.

Overnight accommodations feature beautifully furnished bedrooms and a continental breakfast. Rates are moderate to deluxe. Except for major holidays, the mansion is open for tours from 9 a.m. to 4:30 p.m. daily. Mystery tours are given on Fri and Sat evenings at 6 p.m., 7 p.m., and 8 p.m. Admission is charged.

Opened in 2019, the plantation's **Restaurant 1796** is centered around a 10-foot wood-fired hearth to prepare simple Southern cuisine. The restaurant features farm-to-table dishes with a seasonal menu revolving around locally sourced produce.

Afterward, continue to **Butler Greenwood Plantation Bed and Breakfast** (8345 US 61; 225-635-6312; butlergreenwood.com), a plantation located

The State Pen

Want to see an electric chair? The **Louisiana State Penitentiary Museum** (225-655-2592; angolamuseum.org) has one, and you can see it from 8 a.m. to 4:30 p.m. Mon through Fri. The museum is located at **Angola State Penitentiary**, at the end of Highway 66.

Also on view are exhibits of confiscated prisoner-made weapons, the script of the movie *Dead Man Walking* (the protagonist was an Angola resident), and various guns and paraphernalia, including photos of all those who sparked a firsthand acquaintance with the seat in question. Grim but unique.

The penitentiary hosts an interesting biannual event, the Prison Rodeo, held at the prison each Sun in Oct, plus the third weekend of Apr.

One of the best-known prisoners ever to reside at Angola was Huddie "Leadbelly" Ledbetter, twelve-string guitarist, Louisiana native, and incomparable blues artist. Leadbelly is best known for his composition "Goodnight Irene." His song was good enough to win him a reprieve from Governor O. K. Allen and get him out of Angola.

For additional background, go to angolamuseum.org.

2.2 miles north of town. Watch for a sign on the left marking the tree-canopied drive that leads past a sunken garden and through a parklike setting. Before Hurricane Andrew blew in, says owner Anne Butler, one could not see sky through the arching live oaks—many of which grew from acorns brought from Haiti in 1799 by a planter's family.

A prolific writer whose published works span both fiction and nonfiction, Anne sandwiches in sentences between family responsibilities and guests. Her latest books include *Main Streets of Louisiana*, and *River Road Plantation Country Cookbook*.

On a tour of the English-style house, you'll see a formal Victorian parlor with a twelve-piece matched set of Louis XV rosewood furniture upholstered in its original red velvet. A Brussels carpet, French pier mirrors, and floor-to-ceiling windows topped by gilt cornices echo the room's elegance. Other treasures include a Prudent Mallard bed and dresser, oil portraits, and an extensive collection of vintage clothing. House tours are offered daily from 9 a.m. to 5 p.m. Admission.

Accommodations, which include a continental breakfast, range from the plantation's original detached kitchen of slave-made brick dating from 1796, when Spain ruled the region, and the cook's nineteenth-century cottage to eight cottages set against a lovely backdrop of greenery and a pond where ducks glide and deer come to drink. Rates are moderate to deluxe.

For serious birders, artist-naturalist Murrell Butler offers bird and nature walks. Currently, his local checklist contains 138 species, and 78 of these nest on his property.

After leaving Butler Greenwood, continue north to nearby **Catalpa Plantation** (9508 Old US 61; 225-635-3372). Here, Mary Thompson carries on a tradition of hospitality that goes back six generations. Mary's late mother, Mamie Fort Thompson gave delightful tours of her ancestral home that she described as "lived in, loved, and used."

Just as Miss Mamie shared personal anecdotes while pointing out various pieces and paintings, such as the Thomas Sully portrait of her grandmother Sarah Turnbull from nearby Rosedown Plantation, so does Mary, who offers guests a sherry in honor of her mother.

Much of the home's china, crystal, and other decorative items came from Rosedown. Some beautiful silver pieces only survived the Civil War because "they were wrapped in burlap and buried beneath the pond," Mary explains, showing visitors through her home filled with exceptional antiques such as a rosewood Mallard parlor set, Pleyel piano, Sevres whale-oil lamp, crystal cranberry champagne glasses, antique china, porcelain, and a rare vase from the Vatican.

Mary is delighted to offer tours of her family home by appointment. Admission is charged.

Afterward, you may want to visit the ***Cottage Plantation*** (10528 Cottage Ln.; 225-635-3674; cottageplantation.com). To reach the Cottage continue north on US 61. Watch for a turnoff sign on the right side of the road, and then follow the narrow lane that winds through the woods. You'll cross a small wooden bridge just before you reach the plantation complex.

Definitely off the beaten path, the main house is located in an idyllic setting, thick with trees draped in Spanish moss. If you have trouble locating the Cottage, you might be interested in knowing that Andrew Jackson found it when he and his officers stayed here on their way home after the Battle of New Orleans—without today's road signs.

The 1795 galleried two-story cottage contains most of its original furniture. Outbuildings include the original detached kitchen, one-room school, smokehouse, slave cabins, and other dependencies from bygone days. Guests can stay in six rooms with private bathrooms in the Plantation Main House or choose to stay in Mattie's House, a cottage just a short walk from the Plantation Main House. The plantation has a swimming pool, croquet, and horseshoes for the enjoyment of guests. Each day starts with a full plantation breakfast. Morning coffee is delivered to guest rooms. Except for holidays, tours are offered on Sat and Sun from 10 a.m. to 4 p.m. Rates are moderate.

Consider wandering farther off the beaten path to ***Greenwood Plantation*** (6838 Highland Rd.; 225-655-4475; greenwoodplantation.com) in ***St. Francisville***. Now the home of the Richard Barnes family, this replica of an 1830 Greek

Savvy Eating

North of Lake Pontchartrain the menus reflect Southern specialties. Look for barbecue and fried catfish and ask for sweetened iced tea.

One of the enduring restaurant phenomena in the Florida Parishes is the popularity of the all-you-can-eat catfish place. They dot the highways and all offer the same dining experience: seats at communal tables and endless trips to the buffet for an array of fried seafood, side dishes, and desserts, all served with sweet iced tea or cold drinks (beer is sometimes available). To experience this at its apex, drive up Highway 21 north of Covington to Bush.

The House of Seafood Buffet (81790 Hwy. 21; 985-886-2231) huddles in a blue cement-block building surrounded by a vast parking lot that fills quickly. For about $20 you get catfish plus everything from barbecued ribs to alligator with fried okra and some boudin thrown in. Hours are 4 to 9 p.m. Thurs, 4 to 10 p.m. Fri, and 3 to 10 p.m. Sat.

Revival mansion rose from its 1960 ashes to reclaim the area within its twenty-eight surviving columns. Beautifully restored to original specifications with a copper roof, period furnishings, and silver doorknobs and hinges, Greenwood Plantation served as the setting for six movies, including *North and South*. Visitors can choose from historical, agricultural, or movie tours. Hours run 10 a.m. to 4 p.m. daily. Admission is charged. The plantation also offers bed-and-breakfast accommodations with twelve rooms and a bountiful breakfast to start the day. Moderate rates.

Afterward, return to town and **Rosedown Plantation State Historic Site** (12501 Hwy. 10; 225-635-3332 or 888-376-1867; crt.state.la.us/Louisiana-state-parks/historic-sites/rosedown-plantation-state-historic-site). The property's classic Greek Revival mansion dates to 1835 and was built by Martha and Daniel Turnbull, who patterned the plantation's lovely formal gardens after those they visited on their European honeymoon. They were especially inspired by the gardens at Versailles, and their avenues of shrubs and trees, formal parterres, and classical landscapes reflect a seventeenth-century French influence.

You'll enjoy strolling through these gardens of winding paths with vintage plantings and early varieties of azaleas, camellias, rare trees, and ancient live oaks. Ranked among the nation's most significant historic gardens, Rosedown's gardens are especially delightful in spring.

"Rosedown is one of the most complete antebellum sites in the United States," said a staffer. "We have twenty-eight acres of formal gardens, and the house contains 85 to 90 percent of its original furnishings, which is highly unusual for an antebellum site."

Touring the home, you'll see some lovely period pieces including the music room's original piano and a charming nursery filled with family toys.

The property is open daily from 9 a.m. to 5 p.m., with tours given from 10 a.m. to 4 p.m. Tours take forty-five minutes to an hour and start on the hour. Admission.

To learn about artist John James Audubon, visit **Oakley House** (11788 Louisiana Hwy. 965; 225-635-3739 or 888-677-2838), the focal point of the **Audubon State Historic Site**. West Feliciana's location on the Mississippi Valley flyway lures migrating birds, and Audubon created many of his bird studies while working here as a tutor. Numerous first-edition Audubon prints line the walls at Oakley, restored as a museum with surrounding formal gardens, nature trails, and wildlife sanctuary. Each year during the third weekend in March, St. Francisville hosts an **Audubon Pilgrimage** featuring tours of area plantation homes and gardens. Modest admission. Except for Thanksgiving, Christmas, and New Year's days, hours run from 9 a.m. to 5 p.m. Wed through Sun.

Afterward, follow Route 965 to the **The Bluffs on Thompson Creek** (225-634-6400 or 888-634-3410) with suites within walking distance of golf, tennis, pool, and restaurant. Rates are moderate. Travelers can enjoy steaks, seafood, and more at Palmer's on the Bluff on the premises. For dining and cocktails at the end of a great game, the 19th Hole Bar and Grill offers Palmer's full menu plus a nice assortment of drinks.

Designed by Arnold Palmer, the championship golf course continues to collect accolades. Hundreds of azaleas and native dogwoods supplement the sylvan setting and enhance sweeping swaths of greenery punctuated by high bluffs. Advance tee times are required. Check out thebluffs.com.

From the Bluffs, follow State Route 10 east to Jackson, which offers a host of historical attractions and a winery. In a colonnaded Spanish mission–style structure, travelers can stop by the **Feliciana Cellars Winery** (1848 Charter St.; 225-634-7982) for free tours and tastings. Under the direction of Devin Barringer, the winery currently makes several muscadine vintages plus a sparkling wine and a dry white wine, Blanc du Bois.

Nearby at 1740 Charter Street, the **Old Centenary Inn** (225-634-5050; oldcentenaryinn.com) offers rooms furnished with antiques and equipped with whirlpool baths. Look for the life-size statue of a Scottish Highlander from the British Isles to symbolize the parish's Anglo-Saxon heritage. The handsome

One Big Fair

At the King Cabin a mess of greens is simmering on the back of a woodstove and a pone of corn bread is in the oven. All's fine at **Mile Branch Settlement** and the rambling community of log buildings, assembled from throughout Washington Parish. It is inhabited by folks in nineteenth-century clothes who cook, make soap, grind corn, fuss over chickens, and in general live a pioneer lifestyle for the four days (Wed through Sat) of the **Washington Parish Free Fair** (985-516-7078; thefreefair.com), held the third week in Oct.

The largest free country fair in the nation, this annual event brings to **Franklinton** an enormous number of visitors and depopulates the rest of the parish. There's entertainment on an outdoor stage (amateurs mostly, but with country stars at night) as well as a rodeo, 4-H animals (don't miss the judging of squealing little pigs), and prizes for the best pies, roses, and art. At the Mile Branch Settlement area there is a spelling bee, plus a country store with a big wheel of cheese for slicing, and a log church where you're invited to sing hymns all day. Have a barbecue chicken lunch at the Bowling Green School booth.

Take Highway 25 north from Covington to Franklinton and step back in time. It's probably the best (and one of the few) alcohol-free festivals in the state.

A "Berry" Good Louisiana Breakfast

While in Jackson, don't miss the **Milbank Historic House** (3045 Bank St.; 225-634-5901; milbankbandb.com), a ca. 1836 classic Greek Revival town home that housed the town's first bank. The home, which is open for historic tours, boasts museum-quality antiques. Milbank offers bed-and-breakfast accommodations, and rates are moderate. Guests sleep in Mallard beds and sit down to a full breakfast at a table graced with a candelabra commissioned by Napoleon III.

Overnight guests can enjoy delicious homemade breakfast bread, featuring local seasonal blueberries, strawberries, or ripened persimmons. But, in case you can't wait, here's the recipe:

Strawberry Bread

3 cups all-purpose flour
1½ teaspoons baking soda
1 pinch salt
1 tablespoon cinnamon
1½ cups sugar
3 eggs
1¼ cups vegetable oil
3 cups fresh Louisiana strawberries, sliced
1 cup Louisiana pecans, chopped
1 teaspoon vanilla

In a mixing bowl, combine dry ingredients. Add eggs, oil, strawberries, pecans, and vanilla. Stir until all ingredients are moist. Place in well-greased loaf pans and bake at 350 degrees for 1 hour or until done. Check with toothpick. Enjoy!

mahogany bar embellished with stained glass and brass once served an English pub, and the grilled lift that takes you to the upstairs guest rooms also came from England. The inn offers eight lovely antique-filled rooms and an inviting courtyard plus a full Southern breakfast. Rates are moderate.

Continue to **Centenary State Historic Site** (3522 College St.; 225-634-7925 or 888-677-2364; crt.state.la.us/Louisiana-state-parks/historic-sites/centenary-state-historic-site) for a tour of the restored 1800s home of a former professor with exhibits on pre–Civil War education in Louisiana. Guides interpret early college life and conduct walks across campus. On the way to West Wing Dormitory (complete with historical graffiti), you'll see the remains of the East Wing. Except for major holidays, the site is open Thurs through Sat from 9 a.m. to 5 p.m., and admission is modest.

In **Clinton**, which became the parish seat in 1824, you'll see the **East Feliciana Parish Courthouse**. This stately Greek Revival structure, with twenty-eight columns and a domed, octagonal cupola atop a hipped roof, serves as the town's centerpiece. Be sure to walk around to the back of the courthouse, where you'll see a row of Greek Revival buildings that date from 1840 to 1860. These cottages, collectively known as Lawyers' Row, have also been designated a National Historic Landmark. Nearby, you can take in the Community Street Market held year-round on the first Sat of each month from 8 a.m. to 1 p.m.

From Clinton take Route 10 east until you intersect I-55. Travel south toward Hammond and then take the Springfield exit.

naturewalk

St. Tammany Parish has the Northlake Nature Center, with a pleasant marked nature trail through varying terrain, on Highway 190 near the entrance to Fontainebleau State Park.

Turf and Swamp

Near Hammond you can visit **Kliebert & Sons Alligator Tours** (40511 W I-55 SR; 985-345-3617 or 800-854-9164), an interesting stop (unless you're traveling during winter when alligators hibernate). This unique facility is the world's largest working alligator farm. Harvey Kliebert started the business. After his death on May 15, 2018, his son Mike Kliebert and other family members continued to operate the reptile farm.

The family has been raising alligators for a long time. You'll probably see Crush at almost 15 feet and 1,200 pounds, who was hatched in 1957. The farm's alligators surpass wild alligators in size because they're well fed. Feeding more than 5,000 alligators, a number of which measure from 9 to 17 feet long, requires plenty of food. The alligators eat chicken, nutria, fish, and everything the Klieberts, who trap in winter, bring home.

During June and July, if you're lucky, you may observe a procedure called "taking the eggs," whereby two staff members, using long sticks, retrieve the alligators' eggs. Because these reptiles do not relish relinquishing their eggs, the collection process can prove quite challenging. The eggs are then placed in incubators and hatched to restock the farm.

In addition to alligators, you'll see thousands of turtles as well as a snake pit and a bird rookery. During spring, flocks of egrets and herons nest at the farm. In the gift shop, you can buy alligator meat, sausage, and reptile novelties.

A guided walking tour of the farm takes about forty-five minutes. Weekday tours are done by reservation. Walk-in tours are offered on Sat and Sun.

After visiting the alligators head southeast to nearby **Ponchatoula**—population 7,265. Already recognized as "Strawberry Capital of the World," the town flaunts a new title, "America's Antique City" (americasantiquecity.com). Located at the junction of US 51 and Route 22, Ponchatoula takes its name from Choctaw Indian words for "hanging hair" (a reference to the ubiquitous Spanish moss dangling from area trees).

Ponchatoula's rebirth as an antiques mecca happened in less than three years. Well over 200 dealers offer their wares for shoppers who love poking among yesterday's treasures, antiques, crafts, bric-a-brac, and collectibles. Strolling along the sidewalk, you see changing still-life compositions—a barber pole balanced against an antique pie safe, a rocking chair draped with a crazy quilt, or a hobbyhorse, doll, and vintage buggy.

Stop by the ***Ponchatoula Country Market*** (10 East Pine St.; 985-386-9580; ponchatoulacountrymarket.org) in the heart of town. Housed in an 1854 historic depot, this bazaar offers booths of handcrafted items, antiques, collectibles, homemade jellies, and pastries. Hours are 10 a.m. to 5 p.m. Mon through Sat, and noon to 5 p.m. Sun. Beside the railroad station, you can visit the ***Mail Car Art Gallery***, a restored baggage-mail car featuring the work of local artists. You may want to say hello to the town's mascot, "Old Hardhide." Not your average alligator, this one boasts his own bank account and local newspaper column (in which he espouses opinions that others dare not). He lives in a large wire cage in front of the railroad station.

Across the street, you'll find the ***Collinswood School Museum*** (100 East Pine St.; 985-386-2221; Ponchatoula .com/museum.html). This old-fashioned schoolhouse, which dates from around 1876, contains artifacts and memorabilia pertaining to the area's history. Browse through ***Ponchatoula Feed and Seed*** (180 East Pine St.; 985-386-3506), an old-fashioned store that carries pet, farm, and garden supplies, baby chicks, hardware, wind chimes, gifts, and bedding plants. Store hours are 7:30 a.m. to 5:30 p.m. Mon through Fri, 7:30 a.m. to 5 p.m. Sun.

mardigras, countrystyle

Mardi Gras, the Tuesday before Ash Wednesday, six weeks before Easter, is celebrated in Covington, Slidell, Mandeville, and Bogalusa. Even Bush has a truck parade the prior Saturday. Parade schedules will be in the *Times-Picayune* and in local papers. Bogalusa's parade is the Saturday before Mardi Gras and draws a huge crowd. If you have kids and want to catch lots of throws, consider going to Bogalusa.

From Ponchatoula, take Route 22 east to St. Tammany Parish and the New Orleans Northshore. Here, you'll find charming towns, recreation options galore, enchanting bed-and-breakfasts, dining gems, and more. Stop first in Madisonville,

Weird Roadside Attraction Draws Visitors

Tiny jazz musicians sway to music. A miniature model airplane circles the ceiling of a small toy shop. A motel room lights up to show a youngster jumping on a motel bed.

These teeny wonders are part of the animated dioramas created by the Willy Wonka–mind of Louisiana inventor and artist John Preble at his *Abita Mystery House* (22275 Hwy. 36; 985-892-2624 or 888-211-5731; abitamysteryhouse.com). A natural-born collector and artist, Preble spent a lifetime gathering a huge assortment of odds and ends. He decided to share his wacky wealth with the world in the attraction also known as the UCM (*You-See-Em*) Museum in *Abita Springs*.

"The museum is sort of a hobby that got out of hand," Preble says, standing in the museum's gift shop. Over his head, the ceiling is covered with old circuit and transistor boards with strange mechanical mobiles hanging from them.

"It's just a bunch of stuff geared toward an eight-year-old as far as height and humor," he says. "Kids love it. They understand it …They know I'm nuts."

Preble is far too modest. The talented man has taken what others might consider junk and organized it into a roadside attraction that never fails to amuse—and make visitors stop and think.

Housed in an old gas station and some small cottages connected with covered walkways and paths, the Abita Mystery House is a joyful place that can take hours to tour. "The comment I hear most when people open the door is 'Oh, my God!'" Preble says.

No wonder.

The museum is decorated with tens of thousands of bottles, bottle caps, license plates, springs, motors, old radios, antique postcards, vintage bikes, Southern memorabilia, folk art, pocket combs, barbed wire, garden hoses, ancient arcade machines, and the world's largest collection of paint-by-number paintings. There's also a shrine to Elvis, outdated typewriters, a swan chandelier and all sorts of signs—"Be Strange Not a Stranger," as painted by Preble.

Next to an "abandoned gold mine" sits an old Airstream trailer with a "flying saucer" crashed into it. A family of aliens allegedly lives inside. A little stucco house has been

a lovely waterside town on the northern shore of Lake Pontchartrain with several fine restaurants, shops, and an interesting maritime museum with artifacts from the town's boat-building era, all within a stroll of the riverfront.

Enjoy a casual family lunch or dinner at *Morton's Seafood Restaurant* (702 Water St.; 985-845-4970; mortonsseafood.com). A red-and-white sign alerts diners to hot boiled seafood when arrow is flashing.

Save time for touring *Lake Pontchartrain Basin Maritime Museum* (133 Mabel Dr.; 985-845-9200; lpbmm.org), which also serves as a research covered with glass pieces for the sparkling House of Shards. A colorful Hot Sauce House contains tons of tiny bottles of the Louisiana food favorite.

A 50-foot "bassigator" named Buford—a fiberglass fish with a massive alligator head—rests inside a huge display building. Once a Mardi Gras float, Buford has found a home with Preble. The creature's large shiny eyes (some people think they are bowling balls but the eyes are actually big beach balls painted black) keep watch over the grounds.

As if that's not enough, Preble has fascinating dioramas where visitors push a button and surprising things happen. The main attraction is a 30-foot-long animated diorama called River Road with scenes from along a typical old Southern state highway.

"It's like a humorous 3-D cartoon with a lot of push-button switches," Preble said.

A miniature Mardi Gras parade with teeny folks tossing beads includes Martians in the crowd. An outhouse "library" opens to reveal a surprised man taking care of business. An auto repair shop has a Jeep moving up and down on a lift, as a mechanic waits underneath. A New Orleans jazz funeral has a long black hearse, a group of musicians, tattooed angels overhead, and several skeletons popping out of crypts.

Other miniature moving dioramas include a general store where folks can "Eat Here, Get Gas," a Cajun barbecue shack, mini golf, red neck trailer court, snake farm, and a Southern plantation next to an oil refinery.

Where does Preble come up with such outlandish ideas? "I just think them up and then make them happen," he shrugs.

As for his favorite museum item, Preble doesn't hesitate in answering. A goofy contraption he made of Popsicle sticks sits inside an old movie theater's neon lit ticket booth. Push a button and watch a ball roll down the incredible stick maze.

"Sometimes at night, when no one else is here, I'll be in there pushing that button and watching that ball roll down," Preble says. "I never get tired of watching it."

Except for major holidays, the museum opens daily from 10 a.m. to 5 p.m. Modest admission "if you are over three years old."

center. The facility takes you back to days when the town served as a center for shipbuilding and riverboat traffic between New Orleans and the Northshore. You'll see a full-sized replica of the first Civil War submarine, the Pioneer, predecessor of the famed CSS *Hunley*. The restoration enthusiast will enjoy the collection of vintage and fully operational 1940s-era outboard motors—Johnson Sea Horses, Evinrudes, and Mercurys.

Hours are Tues through Sat from 10 a.m. to 4 p.m., and on Sun from noon to 4 p.m. Modest admission.

Two miles east of Madisonville on Route 22 at 119 Fairview Drive, you'll find ***Fairview-Riverside State Park*** (985-845-3318 or 888-677-3247; crt.state .la.us/Louisiana-state-parks/parks/Fairview-riverside-state-park), which offers great fishing, camping, and picnicking, as well as an old summer home available for touring. Continue on to Mandeville, almost within shouting range.

A short distance southeast of Mandeville, you'll discover ***Fontainebleau State Park*** (62883 Hwy. 1089; 985-624-4443 or 888-677-3668; crt.state.la.us/ Louisiana-state-parks/parks/fontainebleau-state-park), which covers 2,700 acres on the shores of Lake Pontchartrain. The park features the brick ruins of an old sugar mill, and the ***Tammany Trace*** runs through this property. Hours are 6 a.m. to 9 p.m. year-round. To better accommodate campers, closing time is 10 p.m. on Fri and Sat and days preceding holidays.

The park features a white sand beach on Lake Pontchartrain and a 300-foot fishing pier.

You'll want to explore the Tammany Trace, the state's first rails-to-trails project, which stretches almost 31 miles and connects Covington, Abita Springs, Mandeville (crossing through Fontainebleau State Park), Lacombe, and Slidell. A good place to start is the ***Mandeville Trailhead*** (675 Lafitte St.; 985-624-3147) with parking, restroom facilities, and information. By the way, if you visit this site on Sat morning between 9 a.m. and 1 p.m., you'll find a community market with home-baked goods and fresh produce from local vendors.

While here, pop into ***Abita Brew Pub*** (72011 Holly St.; 985-892-5837; abitabrewpub.com) for a burger and Turbodog (a national magazine ranked it America's #1 beer) or a more serious lunch or dinner. Notice the large colorful mural, which depicts real people doing real things here—like biking the Trace. Hours run 11 a.m. to 9 p.m. on Tues, Wed, Thurs, and Sun; 11 a.m. to 10 p.m. on Fri and Sat. The brew pub closes on Mon.

Abita Brewing Company (21084 Hwy. 36; 800-737-2311 or 985-893-3143; abita.com) started on the pub's premises, but outgrew the building and relocated farther up the road. Half-hour brewery tours are offered Wed and Thurs from 2 to 3 p.m., Fri from 1 to 3 p.m., Sat from 10:30 a.m. to 3 p.m., and Sun from 1 to 3 p.m. Self-guided tours are also available from 10 a.m. to 4 p.m. on Mon and Tues, from 10 a.m. to 1 p.m. on Wed and Thurs, from 10 a.m. to noon on Fri, and from 10 a.m. to 1 p.m. on Sun.

While tooling around the Northshore, save plenty of time for ***Covington***, a town that oozes with artsy charm and lures travelers with its great restaurants and shops, inviting bed-and-breakfasts, and a unique microbrewery.

In the town's historic district, you may want to stop by some of the ***Lee Lane Shops***. These Creole cottages, dating from the nineteenth century, have been converted to specialty shops that carry antiques, art, gifts, clothing, and other items.

Don't miss *H. J. Smith's Son General Store* (308 North Columbia St.; 985-892-0460) in downtown Covington. This old-time country store, which also features a museum, sells everything from ox yokes and cast-iron stoves to plantation bells. On the front porch you'll see a buckboard and an inviting swing. Other merchandise consists of cypress swings, oak rockers, wood-burning stoves, and various hardware and farm supplies. Inside the store a corncrib more than 150 years old serves as a display area for kerosene lamps, crockery, and cast-iron cookware.

"There are not a lot of stores like ours left," says Jack Smith, who remembers the "old guys sitting in rocking chairs on the front porch and spinning yarns." Jack and his brothers carry on a family business that started in 1876. The museum contains hundreds of items from yesteryear, such as an old metal icebox, a century-old cypress dugout boat, and a cast-iron casket. A hand-operated wooden washing machine, old cotton scales, and various vintage tools are also on display.

Alligators—Up Close and Personal

Picture yourself holding an alligator, or feeding one, or even watching one hatch from an egg. These adventures and more await at *Insta-Gator Ranch & Hatchery* (74645 Allen Rd., Covington; 985-892-3669; insta-gatorranch.com), where "you can get up close and personal with alligators," promises owner John Price. The facility features some 2,000 alligators swimming in crystal-clear water.

Both entertaining and educational, the tour starts with an interesting overview of the life of the alligator—all the way back to dinosaur days. Afterward, when the tour guide hops into the pen and brings out an alligator (and yes, he tapes the mouth shut), you can get your picture taken holding it.

John and his staff work closely with Louisiana Wildlife and Fisheries in this program, developed to conserve the American Alligator species and save the state's wetlands. Louisiana leads the world in alligator production—and preservation. "It's a win-win situation," says John, describing an alligator ranching program that results in a population twice as large as would otherwise occur. Visitors get a first-person report of the alligator industry and see action film footage made in the wild, which shows the egg harvesting. In only one year, hatchlings grow from less than 1 foot to alligators more than 4 feet long. John harvested his first stock of alligator eggs in 1989—and still has all ten fingers.

Reservations are recommended. Call ahead for tour times. Admission.

Nearby, **Covington Brewhouse** (226 Lockwood St.; 985-893-2884; covington brewhouse.com), a walk-in brewery and museum in a century-old building, makes an interesting stop. The building was once the old Alexius Bros. Hardware building, also a gymnasium, and a cotton processing warehouse. In case you're wondering what happens to the grains used in the brewing, they go to a lot of happy cows. The brewing grains are donated to local farms for use as fresh food for the livestock. Free brewing tours are offered every Sat at 11:30 a.m. and 12:30 p.m. After touring, visit the Tasting Room to sample some fresh brews.

Drive along Rutland Street in the downtown historic district, and you'll see some of Covington's charming homes like **Camellia House Bed & Breakfast** (426 East Rutland St.; 985-264-4973; camelliahouse.info). Innkeepers Linda and Don Chambless welcome guests to their raised Louisiana-style cottage, a great place to swing on the porch or float in the pool.

Nearby, you'll find **Blue Willow Bed & Breakfast** (505 East Rutland St.; 985-892-0011; bluewillowbandb.com), fronted by a white picket fence and an inviting front porch. Hosts Maureen and Tom Chambless invite you to slow down the pace here, sip coffee in a private plant-filled courtyard, and enjoy a Continental-plus breakfast at your leisure. (Maybe they'll give you a ginger plant to take home for your garden.)

Before leaving Covington, enjoy some fine dining and French cuisine at **Annadele's Plantation Restaurant** (71495 Chestnut St.; 985-809-7669; ann adeles.com). Beef lovers will want to order the special-cut filet that arrives on a sizzling platter. Try the blue-cheese mashed potatoes, a popular side item here. Moderate to expensive. This former plantation home on the Bogue Falaya River also offers bed-and-breakfast accommodations with four spacious suites upstairs. Deluxe rates.

St. Tammany Parish boasts a wonderfully remote and mysterious spot for getting off the beaten path—**Honey Island Swamp** on the eastern edge of the parish between Louisiana and Mississippi.

To reach Honey Island Swamp, head toward Slidell in the state's southeastern corner. A good way to explore this pristine wilderness is to take one of **Dr. Wagner's Honey Island Swamp Tours** (41490 Crawford Landing Rd.; 985-641-1769 or 504-242-5877). Tours depart from Crawford Landing, about 5 miles east of Slidell on the West Pearl River. Dr. Paul Wagner is a wetlands ecologist who started the business, retired, and entrusted the tour company to longtime staff members who will introduce you to this wild 250-square-mile region.

Because it attracted large swarms of honeybees, early settlers called the place Honey Island. One of America's least explored swamps, this area is home to a large variety of plants and wildlife—and maybe even the mysterious swamp monster, Wookie. Some hunters and anglers swear that they've seen the creature, which they consistently describe as about 7 feet tall and covered with short hair, longer at the scalp. Wookie supposedly walks upright and leaves four-toed tracks. So far nobody on the tours has spotted said creature, but if it exists, then this wild and dense area seems an appropriate environment.

Although you may miss Wookie, you'll see some of the swamp's resident and migratory birds: herons, ibis, egrets, bald eagles, owls, and wild turkeys. Crawfish, turtles, alligators, wild boar, deer, and otter also live here.

Biologists and a staff of naturalist native guides serve as stewards of the Louisiana Nature Conservancy's White Kitchen Preserve, and the tour includes a visit to this beautiful area, teeming with wildlife. This area contains a rookery, a wood-duck roost, and an active bald eagle nest where generations of eagles have come for some fifty years.

A number of visitors return to see the swamp's seasonal changes. In spring and summer, the place becomes lush like a rain forest, but cool-weather months offer improved visibility. Regular tours are offered morning and afternoon, by reservation. Additional tours, also requiring reservations, are available. A typical tour takes about two hours. The staff offers a hotel pickup service from New Orleans—complete with narration to and from the swamp. Call for tour rates and reservations.

Just five minutes from Honey Island, travelers will find sanctuary and a warm welcome at **Woodridge Bed & Breakfast** (40149 Crowe's Landing; 985-863-9981 or 877-643-7109; woodridgebb.com). Set against a backdrop of century-old live oak trees, this former academy in **Pearl River** offers five spacious suites. Debbi and Tim Fotsch rescued the private school, which closed in the early 1990s, and transformed it into an inviting bed-and-breakfast.

Be sure to notice the intricate Mardi Gras gowns and trains (one with a Greek theme) hand-stitched by Debbi, a doll collection, and other interesting exhibits. A balcony, where early birds can enjoy coffee and pastries, affords access to the suites, each with a motif of its own. Later, a gourmet breakfast is served family style. Moderate rates.

Continue to nearby **Slidell**. In Slidell's **Olde Town**, look for the **Passionate Platter Cooking School** (2104 First St.; 985-781-4372). Located in an eggplant-colored house, the facility offers hands-on cooking classes for kids and adults, lunch and garden tours, private gourmet meals, aromatherapy, garden and planting supplies, and more. Owner and chef Linda Franzo, who provides recipes with all classes, offers a schedule of activities as well. Class prices vary depending on the size.

Leaving Slidell puts you on the doorstep of New Orleans, a city anticipating your visit more than ever. So take nearby I-10 and cross the twin-span bridge over the end of Lake Pontchartrain into America's Paris.

Crescent City Realm

New Orleans, famous for its food, music, festivals, architecture, and history, is a city like no other. New Orleans has been described as magical, rambunctious, debonair, flamboyant, seductive, and, yes, decadent—but most of all, it's fascinating.

Spring is an ideal time to visit New Orleans—it's no secret that summer days can fall in the sweaty and sweltering category.

Before beginning your exploration of the Crescent City, throw away your compass. New Orleans's confusing geography takes a while to master. Natives refer to upriver as uptown and downriver as downtown; the two other major directions are lakeside (toward Lake Pontchartrain) and riverside. You can get a good view of the crescent from **Moonwalk**, a promenade that fronts the French Quarter and overlooks the Mississippi River.

A word of caution: As you explore New Orleans, it's best to stick to the beaten path, avoiding any questionable areas. New Orleans can appear deceptively safe, so don't forget to exercise the same caution that you would in any major city.

If New Orleans is your exclusive destination, consider coming by plane or train. An Amtrak excursion with sleeping car, which includes meals and other

Actor's Pyramid Grave Waiting in Oldest Cemetery

The pyramid-looking grave is huge and seems quite out of place in this historic cemetery. I was told that locals don't much care for it, thinking it too grand and ostentatious.

The man who paid for it is not dead yet. He just wanted it to be ready for when he departs this world. Actor **Nicolas Cage** had this 9-foot pyramid built for his final resting place near voodoo queen Marie Laveau in New Orleans' oldest cemetery, **St. Louis Cemetery No. 1**. The Latin inscription means "Everything From One."

You'll have to pay a tour guide to take you through the late 1700s Cemetery No. 1 near the French Quarter. Vandalism in the famous burial ground was such a problem that licensed tour guides now must accompany visitors and keep a close watch for any mischief, such as that seen in the movie *Easy Rider*, which was partially filmed in the cemetery.

America's Most Haunted City

New Orleans offers many ghostly sites, tours of its historic cemeteries called "cities of the dead," and a variety of Halloween activities. On your next trip to "America's Most Haunted City," check into *Hotel Monteleone* (214 Rue Royale; 504-523-3341 or 800-535-9595; hotelmonteleone.com), a legendary French Quarter hotel. Long known as a literary landmark, the hotel staff has welcomed such guests as William Faulkner, Tennessee Williams, Truman Capote, and Ernest Hemingway.

amenities, will allow you to arrive rested and ready to tackle the Big Easy. For reservations and information call (800) 872-7245 or visit amtrak.com. In this city of precious parking (not to mention the French Quarter's narrow streets), a car has definite drawbacks. United Cabs offer reliable and courteous service; call (504) 522-9771 or visit unitedcabs.com. Also, the St. Charles Streetcar, listed on the National Register of Historic Places, affords an entertaining and inexpensive way to get about. You may want to purchase a pass for a day of unlimited rides.

For comfort and convenience with some marbled opulence thrown in for good measure, plan to stay at *Le Pavillon Hotel* (833 Poydras St.; 800-535-9095 or 504-581-3111; lepavillon.com). Fronted by large columns and ornamented with sculptures and cast terra-cotta garlands, Le Pavillon stands on the corner intersecting Baronne. A member of Historic Hotels of America, this 1907 architectural classic offers spacious rooms and suites along with friendly service. The lobby's crystal chandeliers came from Czechoslovakia and its marble railings from the Grand Hotel in Paris. Each of the hotel's seven deluxe suites features a different decor. From antique to Art Deco, all furnishings, paintings, and accents carry out the room's theme.

Guests can take a dip in the rooftop pool and relax on the patio with its sweeping view of the Mississippi River. You can compensate for the fat grams from delicious New Orleans cuisine in the free fitness center. Rates are moderate to deluxe.

After settling in, start your sight-seeing session in the nearby French Quarter with beignets and cafe au lait at *Cafe du Monde* (800 Decatur St.; 504-587-4544; cafedumonde.com). Located in the French Market, the eatery is open twenty-four hours daily (except Christmas Day). Afterward, stroll through the Vieux Carré (*view-ka-ray*), as the old French Quarter also is known. Save some time to watch the street performers in Jackson Square with its famous artists' fence. Clopping through the quarter, straw-hatted mules pull surreys and carriages—a relaxing way to see the stately tri-towered *St. Louis Cathedral*, outdoor cafes, and "frozen lace" galleries.

New Orleans Museum Honors World War II Heroes

When Navy corpsman Leo H. Sheer's landing craft was sunk on its way to Omaha Beach on D-Day, the young sailor was forced to swim ashore amid heavy gunfire.

Arriving safely on the beach, Sheer began collecting first-aid pouches from the bodies of dead soldiers to help save the wounded. He hung six of the dead men's pouches on his equipment belt.

Today, Sheer's blood-stained web belt is displayed at the **National World War II Museum** in New Orleans. And it is artifacts such as this that help put a human face on the terrible time in our history.

Since its opening, the museum has quickly grown into one of New Orleans' main attractions. Why New Orleans? Because New Orleans was where more than 20,000 of the famed Higgins boats were made.

The shoebox-shaped landing craft carried American troops ashore in the major amphibious assaults of World War II. Supreme Allied Commander Dwight D. Eisenhower once credited Higgins as "the man who won the war for us" because his shallow boat could land on almost any beach.

Noted World War II historian Stephen E. Ambrose, who founded the museum, also wanted the tribute located in New Orleans. Before his death in 2002 from lung cancer, Ambrose had lived about an hour from New Orleans. Ambrose spent decades researching and writing about World War II, Eisenhower, and D-Day, authoring books such as *Citizen Soldiers* and *Band of Brothers*.

As he collected more than 2,000 oral histories from D-Day veterans, Ambrose realized that the United States had no museum to honor these men and women and the people on the home front. The museum he founded presents the war from the viewpoint of regular soldiers, nurses, factory workers, and folks at home.

Formerly known as the D-Day Museum, the museum officially opened on June 6, 2000. Some 65 million people died in World War II, known as "the war that changed the world."

D-Day on June 6, 1944, marked the invasion of Normandy, France, and the beginning of the end of the war in Europe. D-Day began shortly after midnight with the landing of 24,000 Allied airborne troops.

While in the French Quarter with its many enticements, consider touring the **Beauregard-Keyes House** (1113 Chartres St.; 504-523-7257; bkhouse.org) just across from the Old Ursuline Convent. Frances Parkinson Keyes, author of fifty-one books, lived here while writing *Dinner at Antoine's, Blue Camellia,* and other novels. Docents give guided tours Mon through Sat, from 10 a.m. to

Amphibious landings began around 6:30 a.m. as about 156,000 servicemen from the United States, United Kingdom, Canada, and other Allied countries disembarked from more than 5,000 ships and Higgins boats. They landed into a wall of gunfire from German defenders.

The operation cost US forces 2,499 dead that day alone, with total Allied deaths reaching 4,414. By June 11, with beachheads firmly secured, more than 326,000 troops had crossed with more than 100,000 tons of military equipment. Paris was liberated on Aug. 25, 1944. Germany surrendered on May 8, 1945.

The museum's two primary permanent exhibits focus on amphibious landings on Normandy and in the Pacific. Both feature photographs and newspaper articles, along with cases of weapons, helmets, uniforms, and other historic objects, as well as hundreds of individual stories. Touch screens along the walls offer two-minute video oral histories and cases contain letters, diaries, and objects that belonged to individual soldiers.

A simple metal "cricket" on display was carried by 22-year-old Private Ford McKenzie of the 101st Airborne on D-Day. Worn around his neck on a string, the cricket would make a clicking sound like the insect. "One click of the cricket was supposed to be answered with two clicks," McKenzie explained in the display. "If you didn't click back, it was assumed you were the soon-to-be-dead enemy."

The museum's 250-seat Solomon Victory theater presents a moving spectacle billed as a 4-D experience that is far more than a film.

Narrated by actor Tom Hanks, "Beyond All Boundaries" is a multisensory presentation with smoke, simulated snow, shaking seats, and other special effects. The high-tech flourishes are blended with graphic war footage and photographs to trace the war's cause, its execution, and its tragic toll.

A 1940s-era radio sits alone on the stage and begins at the real beginning—December 7, 1941, "a day which will live in infamy."

Voicing the words of American warriors and war correspondents are some of Hollywood's most recognizable actors—Kevin Bacon, Patricia Clarkson, Viola Davis, Gary Sinise, Neil Patrick Harris, Tobey Maguire, Brad Pitt, John Goodman, Blythe Danner, Jennifer Garner, Justin Long, Elijah Wood, and Wendell Pierce.

"People are visiting us because they want to understand what their mothers and fathers, grandfathers and grandmothers went through," said Stephen Watson, chief operating officer for the museum. "It's a way of honoring the generation that paid the price for our precious freedom."

3 p.m. on the hour. Tours last about 45 minutes. The gift shop offers a wide selection of the author's books. Admission is modest.

Afterward, take a break at nearby ***Napoleon House*** (500 Chartres St.; 504-524-9752; napoleonhouse.com). This interesting old building houses a bar and cafe. You can study the menu, printed on fans with faces of Napoleon and

Josephine, while listening to classical music in the background. Try the house specialty, an Italian muffuletta—a great sandwich with meats, cheeses, and olive salad. Call ahead for hours.

For a great way to get acquainted with this fascinating section, sign up for a walking tour by a ranger from the *French Quarter Visitor Center–Jean Lafitte National Historical Park and Preserve* (419 Decatur St.; 504-589-3882 ext. 221; nps.gov/jela/French-quarter-site.htm). Tours last about sixty minutes, so wear your walking shoes. Except for Christmas Day and Mardi Gras, the tours take place daily at 9:30 a.m. and are free. "It's first come, first served" for the first twenty-five persons to show up. A ranger talk is offered at 9:30 a.m. Tues through Sat in the visitor center courtyard. This is a great way to learn more about New Orleans' history and culture. The center is open Tues through Sat 9 a.m. to 4:30 p.m. Closed on federal holidays and Mardi Gras.

fishing

Everyone who fishes in Louisiana and is between the ages of sixteen and sixty is required to have a fishing license. You can purchase one at most sporting goods stores and bait shops; a one-day license is available for about $5 (add $17.50 for saltwater) for out-of-state visitors.

Bienville House Hotel (320 Decatur St.; 504-529-2345 or 800-535-9603; bienvillehouse.com) makes a convenient and cozy base for exploring the French Quarter. You'll find it only a short stroll or cab ride away from antiques shops, jazz showcases, blues clubs, and great restaurants. For hotel dining, try *Beach-bum Berry's Latitude 29* (504-609-3811; latitude29nola.com), a full-service upscale Tiki bar and restaurant. The menu offers modern Polynesian cuisine and creative cocktails.

Created from two eighteenth-century warehouses, this 80-room hotel exudes an old-world ambience, and features a heated saltwater pool. Moderate to deluxe.

After browsing through the French Quarter's antiques shops, art galleries, and boutiques, consider taking a stroll along Riverwalk and visiting *Audubon Aquarium of the Americas* (1 Canal St.; 504-565-3033; audubonnatureinsti tute.org/aquarium), where you can get nose to nose with a shark, see white alligators, and hold a parrot in the Amazon rain forest. Hours are 10 a.m. to 5 p.m. Tues through Sun. Admission.

Afterward, walk down Canal St. This wide avenue divides the French Quarter from "American territory" in uptown New Orleans. On Canal, hopefully you can catch the St. Charles Streetcar for a ride through the *Garden District*. Bumping along you'll see handsome nineteenth-century villas, Greek Revival mansions, and raised cottages surrounded by magnolias and ancient

Tujague's Tantalizing Tastes

Something about New Orleans spells food. While you're exploring the French Quarter, stop by the city's second oldest restaurant, **Tujague's** (823 Decatur St.; 504-525-8676, tujaguesrestaurant.com). The restaurant opened its doors in 1856 and soon became a favorite spot for workers from the nearby French Market. Be sure to step into the antique bar to see the massive ornate mirror, shipped from Paris in 1856.

Presidents Roosevelt, Truman, and Eisenhower, and French president de Gaulle have enjoyed Tujague's, and so can you. From appetizer through dessert, today's owners carry on the Tujague family's tradition of serving fine fare in the Creole manner. The restaurant's seven-course meals evolve from such staples as shrimp remoulade and a superb brisket of beef presented with a red horseradish sauce.

Straight from this classic New Orleans neighborhood restaurant to you, here's the recipe for Tujague's signature dish.

Tujague's Boiled Brisket of Beef

6–7 pounds choice brisket of beef
2 onions, quartered
1½ ribs celery, quartered
1 head garlic, peeled
1 bay leaf
1 tablespoon salt
15 black peppercorns
2 green onions, quartered
1 carrot, quartered
1 bell pepper, quartered

Sauce ingredients:

1 cup ketchup
½ cup prepared horseradish
¼ cup Creole mustard

Note: Here are the two most important steps to produce a tender, juicy, tasty brisket: (1) Buy a quality, well-trimmed brisket, never frozen. (2) Simmer the meat (not a hard boil).

Place the brisket in a large soup pot, cover with cold water, add the remaining ingredients, and simmer for 3–4 hours until beef is tender. Remove beef and slice. Serve with a sauce made by combining the ketchup, prepared horseradish, and Creole mustard.

For vegetable soup, skim and strain the beef stock. Add 3 tablespoons tomato paste, 2 sliced tomatoes, and your favorite vegetables. Cook until vegetables are tender, and serve. We have found a little okra adds a distinctive taste to the soup. Cut and cook okra first in the oven or a saucepan to remove slime.

Any stock left after soup is made can be frozen and stored for future soups and sauces. Makes approximately 1 gallon soup.

live oaks. This lovely area, with its lush landscaping and extravagant gardens dotted with statuary and fountains, makes a fine place to stroll. By walking you can better admire the ornamental iron fences with their geometric and plant motifs.

Or, you can take a short stroll to **Commander's Palace** (1403 Washington Ave.; 504-899-8221; commanderspalace.com), one of the city's renowned restaurants. Housed in a Victorian mansion, the famous eatery has been offering refined Creole fare and an elegant jazz brunch in a chandelier-hung space since 1880.

Making Groceries

New Orleans is a city that, like Napoleon's army, moves on its stomach. To get in the spirit of things, learn to "make groceries"—a local expression that's a rough translation of the French *faire le Mare*.

There is a farmers' market every Sat from 8 a.m. to noon on the corner of Girod and Magazine Streets featuring fresh produce, a local chef using market goods to prepare dishes for tasting, lots of baked goods, jellies, and more. There's also coffee so you can make this a breakfast. There is an uptown farmers' market Tues from 10 a.m. to 1 p.m. at Broadway and Leake Avenue and a mid-city version on Thurs evening from 4 to 6 p.m. at Orleans Avenue by Bayou St. John.

Langenstein's (1330 Arabella St.; 504-899-9283; langensteins.com), uptown off St. Charles Ave., is the uptown grocery of choice. It has good meats, seafood, and produce and a deli department that prepares lots of local specialties: boiled seafood, gumbo, red beans and rice, oyster dressing for your turkey, and pies. They will ship for you.

Most eccentric supermarket? *Dorignac's* (710 Veterans Blvd.; 504-834-8216; dorignacs.com) in Metairie. Although the late "Mr. Joe" Dorignac no longer sits in the coffee shop consulting the Racing Form (at one point he owned a good string of runners), his all-inclusive inventory still holds. The aisles are jam-packed, and you can find one of every local product here first. There's an incredible array of vegetables, including things like those hard-to-find artichoke stalks that make a special dish around St. Joseph's Day. Good butchers, too.

For health food try the **Arabella Station Whole Foods Market** (5600 Magazine St.; 504-899-9119; wholefoodsmarket.com). It is a full-size grocery with organic vegetables and meat and a deli with fresh-made New Orleans specialties, albeit in healthful form.

For wines consult **Martin Wine Cellar** (504-899-7411; martinwinecellar.com) for a huge selection and a regular schedule of tastings each Saturday. Four locations: 3500 Magazine St.; 714 Elmeer at Veteran's Blvd. in Metairie; 2895 Hwy. 190 in Mandeville; and 7248 Perkins Rd. in Baton Rouge.

On St. Charles Avenue you may want to visit **Audubon Park** in a pretty setting with ancient live oaks, flower-filled gardens, and wandering lagoons. The 400-acre urban park also offers a golf course, tennis courts, and picnic facilities as well as walking and jogging paths. At Cascade Stables in the park, you can rent a horse and go galloping off along a tree-shaded trail that offers glimpses of St. Charles Avenue.

Don't miss nearby **Audubon Zoo** (6500 Magazine St.; 504-581-4629 or 800-774-7394; audubonnatureinstitute.org/zoo). Noted for its simulated barrier-free natural habitats, the zoo also makes a delightful outing, complete with peanuts, popcorn, and more than 1,800 animals. Zoo hours are 10 a.m. to 4 p.m. Tues through Fri, and 10 a.m. to 5 p.m. on Sat and Sun.

Magazine Street, which runs parallel to the Mississippi River, offers some of the country's most unique shopping opportunities. You can stroll along 6 miles of intriguing antiques shops, art galleries, boutiques, clothing stores, home decor shops, and more. Fortunately, Magazine Street survived Katrina without flooding.

As You Like It Silver Shop (3033 Magazine St.; 504-897-6915; asyoulikeit silvershop.com) offers strictly estate silver and specializes in matching flatware patterns for both discontinued and active patterns. You'll also find sterling silver tea services, tureens, goblets, bowls, and other hollowware items. Hours are 11 a.m. to 5 p.m. Mon through Fri, 10:30 a.m. to 5 p.m. Sat. Farther down the street you can browse through antiques at **British Antiques** (5415 Magazine St.; 504-895-3716). Hours are 10 a.m. to 5 p.m. Mon, 11:30 a.m. to 4:30 p.m. on Thurs, and 10 a.m. to 5 p.m. on Fri and Sat.

You'll come across some excellent buys in English and French antiques, furniture, paintings, china, crystal, silver, collectibles, and souvenirs. You'll also pass brass dealers, bookstores, restaurants, and specialty shops. Even though most of the stores don't have fancy facades (some even resemble junk shops), you can find some quality merchandise at bargain prices.

The **New Orleans Museum of Art** in City Park (1 Collins C. Diboll Cir.; 504-658-4100; noma.org) has interesting holdings, especially in decorative arts, with a good selection of European as well as South American and African work to complement its American collections. While you're there, be sure to check out NOMA's handsome **Sydney and Walda Bestoff Sculpture Garden**, which is free to the public and open daily from 10 a.m. to 6 p.m. for summer hours (Apr 1 to Sept 30), and 10 a.m. to 5 p.m. for winter hours (Oct 1 to Mar 31). The seven-acre setting showcases a world-class collection of modern and contemporary sculpture set among City Park's moss-festooned oaks.

Museum hours are Tues through Fri 10 a.m. to 6 p.m., Sat 10 a.m. to 5 p.m., and Sun 11 a.m. to 5 p.m.

New Orleans Hurricane Exhibit Packs Powerful Punch

Scrawled on well-worn blue jeans are a man's name, social security number, blood type, wife's name, hotel where she was evacuated for safety, and the hotel phone number.

Claudio Hemb wanted to ensure that his body would be identified and his family notified if he perished in Hurricane Katrina's floodwaters.

The exhibit, "Living with Hurricanes: Katrina and Beyond" at the **Louisiana State Museum** in New Orleans' French Quarter, brings home the devastating power of hurricanes. In 2005, Hurricane Katrina and the aftermath flooded 80 percent of New Orleans and took an estimated 1,500 lives.

"We knew right after the storm that we had to collect artifacts because we were going to do this exhibit," says Karen Leathem, museum historian. "It was such a significant event, not only for us but for the entire state and for the nation as well."

Although the catastrophe was precipitated by a natural event, "it was really a human-made disaster," Leathem says. "We wanted to explain why it happened and what we need to do to make sure it never happens again."

Opened in October 2010, the permanent exhibit greets visitors with a powerful emotional punch beginning with the lobby of the circa 1791 Presbytère building. Originally the residence of Capuchin monks, the Presbytère became part of the Louisiana State Museum in 1911.

Positioned exactly as it was when floodwaters destroyed his home, a ruined Steinway baby grand piano that belonged to legendary New Orleans musician Fats Domino is a lobby centerpiece. For days after Katrina hit, people feared the rock-and-roll pioneer had died when his Lower Ninth Ward home was flooded to the roof.

A well-known homebody, Fats Domino and his wife Rosemary didn't evacuate before the hurricane but were later rescued by boat and taken to a shelter in Baton Rouge. Almost everything the couple owned was lost. Fats Domino died on October 24, 2017, at age 89.

Colored stripes on the museum lobby walls depict water levels reached by the rising waters. Standing beneath the lines is a stark reminder of how people became trapped and drowned.

The ceiling is hung with hundreds of glass bottles filled with notes in homage to those who perished. Blue glass hands interspersed among the bottles honor volunteers who came to the city to help in the rescue and rebuilding.

Four galleries inside the museum contain artifacts, dramatic footage, and interviews with survivors. In the first gallery, visitors learn the geographical facts about living in a city that is below sea level and surrounded by water.

Visitors move through an Evacuation Corridor overhearing residents' voices weighing options as Katrina approaches. A state-of-the-art Storm Theater shows Katrina's full fury with dramatic footage of the hurricane onslaught.

Gallery Two takes visitors past a leaking floodwall and into an attic and onto the roof of a house surrounded by rising floodwaters. When his family evacuated to Houston as Katrina bore down on New Orleans, Claudio Hemb stayed behind to secure his French Quarter business.

The day after Katrina devastated the city, Claudio set out on bicycle to reach his Lakeshore home about seven miles away, inking vital info on his pants in case he didn't make it. Fortunately, he did.

Framed in a glass shadow box is a hatchet that a mother and daughter bought two days before Katrina. Trapped in the small attic of their St. Bernard Parish home, the two used that hatchet to chop through the roof to be seen and rescued by boat.

On the "Mabry Wall," housing complex resident Tommie Elton Mabry wrote on his apartment walls with a black felt tip marker to record his ordeal starting with the day before Katrina hit and continuing for weeks afterward. Museum staff preserved his journal before the building was demolished.

A mud-encrusted teddy bear illustrates the personal possessions that were lost and the hope that former owners of those beloved items survived the catastrophe. A garage door shows the markings of rescuers who note that two cats and one dog were found dead inside.

"Do not remove. Owner will bury," says a red painted message.

Seats from the heavily damaged Louisiana Superdome are a reminder of where an estimated 35,000 people sought refuge and rescue.

"The number of people combined with the stifling heat and the breakdown of plumbing systems created notoriously miserable conditions as the sports stadium came to symbolize failed emergency response systems," a placard notes.

Gallery Three explains the forensics of Katrina and shows through digital animation how the levees failed. "The levees failed because of poor design and poor construction," Leathem says. An estimated 70 percent of New Orleans occupied housing was damaged by Katrina.

Gallery Four deals with recovery and promotes preparedness. "Seeing what happened here brought up discussions on how disasters are handled," Leathem says.

"Disasters happen around us all the time," she concludes. "We need to know how to manage disasters and also what we should be looking for from our local government."

For more information, contact the Louisiana State Museum at (800) 568-6968; louisiana statemuseum.org.

Return of an Icon

A Bus Named Desire? Nope. Doesn't resonate. You've got to admit that streetcars, with a mystique all their own, help define New Orleans. These city icons, especially those on the historic St. Charles line, represent much more than a way to reach a destination.

"I'll tell you what the St. Charles streetcar means to this city. It's a symbol—and a spirit," said resident writer Marda Burton. "Those old green cars have been trundling along the Avenue for so long, making noise and holding up traffic, that when they were gone it just didn't seem like New Orleans anymore."

After Katrina wreaked her havoc, service on the city's three streetcar lines came to a screeching halt, as did everything else. The Riverfront Line bounced back less than two months later, and then came a portion of the Canal Line with the entire route in place by the following spring. But the return of the St. Charles Line, which required replacing the overhead electrical system, took more than two years.

During that grim period, the New Orleans Regional Transit Authority (RTA) provided bus service for the identical route used by the St. Charles streetcars. Still, buses run on ordinary streets—not the neutral ground (median). And folks missed their favorite fleet.

"Everybody rode those streetcars: visitors, sightseers, locals going to and from work, late-night revelers, even Mardi Gras krewes. The Riverfront streetcars and the new Canal Street to City Park streetcars went back on line fast, but they simply weren't the same," Burton explained. "We still expected to see those old 1923 Perley Thomas greens rounding the corner of Canal Street and St. Charles Avenue. Now that they're back, we can really feel like New Orleans is back, too."

You'll find **Contemporary Arts Center** (900 Camp St.; 504-528-3805; cacno.org) in what is fast becoming New Orleans's art district, just a few blocks above the French Quarter. The C.A.C. hosts theater as well as art exhibits. Be sure to stroll the galleries of Julia Street—New Orleans has a vibrant and active art community.

Art lovers can explore a neighborhood of museums, galleries, and more in the **Warehouse Arts District**, sometimes called "the Soho of the South." Prominent in the area's arts explosion is the **Ogden Museum of Southern Art** (925 Camp St.; 504-539-9650; ogdenmuseum.org) featuring five floors of the world's most comprehensive collection of Southern art. (Tip: Start on the top floor and work your way down.)

Consider headquartering at the **Renaissance Arts Hotel** (700 Tchoupitoulas St.; 504-613-2330). A virtual art gallery in itself, the hotel features rotating exhibits and original art in each room. Three Dale Chihuly chandeliers hang in its handsome lobby, and the Arthur Roger Gallery is located on the first floor.

So it was with great glee that locals and visitors celebrated on November 10, 2007, when the legendary St. Charles Line reopened all the way to Napoleon Avenue in Uptown. Full service started the next day at dawn's early light. Soon after the first car stopped at St. Charles and Common at 5:27 a.m., a group of Loyola sorority sisters jumped aboard and memorialized the happy moment with photos, delighted they could once again roll along St. Charles Avenue.

The entire 13-mile length of St. Charles Avenue opened again on June 22, 2008, when streetcar service resumed along the traditional route through the neighborhoods of South Carrollton to Claiborne Avenue.

The St. Charles route makes it easy to reach some great galleries, museums and restaurants. But when it comes down to this celebrated icon, why bother with a destination? It's all about the easygoing ride, the history, the charm. As for these vintage vehicles, who cares about hard wooden seats when you're bumping along St. Charles, mesmerized by the Garden District's magnificent mansions and glorious landscapes?

The streetcars always have the right of way, so RTA officials urge everyone to watch out for them. Look both ways before turning left at any corner on St. Charles Avenue. Streetcar service runs between Canal Street and Carrollton and Claiborne Avenues seven days a week.

During daytime hours, cars run every 7 to 15 minutes, daily. Visit norta.com for hours and information on streetcar fares, routes and schedules. Unless you have an RTA Pass or Jazzy Pass, you'll need exact change. The passes allow you to board RTA streetcars and buses as often as you want with no need to worry about exact fare.

Call New Orleans RTA RideLine at (504) 248-3900 or visit norta.com for the nearest distributor.

Visit the ***Chalmette Battlefield*** (504-281-0510; nps.gov/jela/Chalmette-battlefield.htm) to learn more about the ***Battle of New Orleans***. Chalmette is now part of the many-sited ***Jean Lafitte National Park***. Military history buffs will enjoy this one: Here's where the Duke of Wellington's brother-in-law, General Pakenham, came to his end during the British defeat. This is what started Andrew Jackson on the road to the White House.

From the French Quarter go east on Rampart Street, then on St. Claude Avenue, which actually becomes St. Bernard Highway and leads you right to the park at 8606 West St. Bernard Highway. A few miles farther is the ***Isleños Center***, also in Jean Lafitte National Park. Here you can learn the history of the Canary Islanders who settled the area. Sometimes the local docent demonstrates how to skin a nutria or coypu, a local wild rodent. Warning: It's not for the squeamish.

New Orleans has such a rich stock of nineteenth-century housing, it can offer the very best in accurately furnished period homes. Try ***Gallier House***

(1132 Royal St.; 504-274-0746; hgghh.org), home of architect James Gallier, or the **Hermann-Grima House** (820 St. Louis St.; 504-274-0746; hgghh.org). There is also one in-town plantation, the **Pitot House on Bayou St. John** (1440 Moss St.; 504-482-0312; louisianalandmarks.org).

Traditional jazz can be heard nightly at **Preservation Hall** (726 St. Peter St.; 504-522-2841; preservationhall.com) where fans sit on benches and pay a modest fee for pure music. If you decide to hit the clubs, expect to be out late—New Orleans music hits its stride after midnight. There is sometimes a van service that operates between clubs; ask at a club to see if it is still rolling.

At some point during your visit, schedule a boat ride to experience the mighty Mississippi's romance and majesty. Describing the Mississippi, Mark Twain called it "not a commonplace river, but in all ways remarkable." For a taste of Mr. Twain's river, you can choose a short ferry trip or a longer excursion on the *Creole Queen*, the *Natchez*, or another of the local riverboats. Some cruises combine sightseeing with jazz, dinner, or Sunday brunch.

Bays and Bayous

Cross over the river to **Gretna**, once a small community of railroad workers and German immigrants. Near the river is the **City of Gretna Visitor Center** in the old depot area (337 Huey P. Long Ave.; 504-363-1580 or 888-447-3862; gretnala.com). There is a railroad exhibit there and nearby is the **Gretna Historical Society Museum** (209 Lafayette St.; 504-362-3854; gretnala.com), which encompasses three nineteenth-century cottages, properly furnished, and the David Crockett Fire House, built in 1859. The pumper wagon still shines, and even if the Dalmatian on board is ceramic, the costumed volunteer firemen are real—most are current or former volunteer firemen. Nearby, you'll find a blacksmith shop and the **German American Cultural Center** (519 Huey P. Long Ave.; 504-363-4202; gacc-nola.org). **The Gretna Heritage Festival** (504-361-7748; gretnafest.com) takes place here the first full weekend in Oct.

Look for the life-size bronze statue of New York Giants star Mel Ott in front of the visitor center. The **Gretna Farmers' Market** (300 Huey P. Long Ave.; gretnafarmersmarket.com) takes place every Sat from 8:30 a.m. to 12:30 p.m. with a monthly Art Walk scheduled the second Sat of each month from Sept through May.

When it's time for a break from boisterous New Orleans, head for the banks of **Bayou Barataria**, about 30 miles south. The little fishing village of **Jean Lafitte** "where there be dragons" (just like the kind bordering the unknown on ancient maps), makes an excellent escape. The local dragons must be the gentle sort, because people in Lafitte don't feel the need to lock doors and often leave keys in their cars. The year's big crime might involve a shady aluminum-siding deal.

Both Gulf and inland fishing charters are available locally, and the inn's staff can help with sea-plane and fishing packages. Just ten minutes away you'll find the **Jean Lafitte National Park Barataria Unit** (6588 Barataria Blvd.; 504-689-3690; nps.gov/jela/barataria-preserve.htm) in Marrero. You'll see an interpretive center with a good video on early area inhabitants and extensive displays on the local environment and the cypress timber industry (which decimated the indigenous trees in the area). Other enticements include several hiking trails, all of them enjoyable. There is also a canoe trail, and close by are canoes for rent. Rangers guide regular free tours.

The most popular trail is the Bayou Coquille–Marsh Overlook, especially spectacular when ringed with iris in spring (unless saltwater intrusion prevents it, as proves to be the case following active hurricane seasons). It ends on high ground with an aerial view of the marsh and the skyscrapers of New Orleans in the background—and perhaps an alligator nearby. Those little black "pickles" you see are nutria droppings. Watch for the rooting armadillos with their little piggy ears. If you have one afternoon to go to the country, go here.

Hungry? On the West Bank of the Mississippi and downriver from New Orleans, look for boiled seafood such as shrimp, crabs, and crawfish. You may have to be shown how to pick a boiled crab, but it's worth it. Add some crackers and cold beer and you have an instant picnic.

Stop at small bakeries for fresh French bread. Look for homemade hogs-head cheese (Creole Country is a good New Orleans brand). Be on the lookout for roadside stands that sell "Creole" (home-grown) tomatoes or strawberries in season.

Rare Treasures on Royal Street

In the French Quarter, you'll find six blocks of the country's finest antiques shops, unparalleled art galleries, and superb restaurants. Royal Street Guild merchants offer a unique experience when it comes to antiquing.

Serious collectors should not miss **M. S. Rau Antiques** (630 Royal St.; 504-523-5660 or 888-557-2406; rauantiques.com). With an inventory that equals or surpasses many museums, M. S. Rau ranks as one of the world's premier dealers in antiques. The huge showrooms carry everything from silver pieces by Tiffany & Co., original Renoir and Monet paintings, and exquisite estate jewelry to mirrors, Venetian glass chandeliers, and stunning historic pieces like the rare Henry Clay Rosedown Plantation armoire, originally created for the White House. Visit the website to browse through recent acquisitions.

A po'boy sandwich on French bread can be ordered dressed (with lettuce and tomato) and with gravy (for roast beef). Po'boy Nirvana? Softshell crab.

For help in planning your visit, click on neworleansonline.com, the city's official tourism website. Here, you can book a room in your preferred location and price range, get restaurant information, and order a free New Orleans Official Visitor's Guide.

Places to Stay in Southeast Louisiana

BATON ROUGE

Baton Rouge Marriott
5500 Hilton Ave.
(225) 924-5000
or (800) 842-2961

Cajun B&B
1253 N. Cicero Ave.
(225) 413-3777
cajunbb.business.site

The Cook Hotel & Conference Center
LSU Campus
3848 West Lakeshore Dr.
(225) 383-2665
or (866) 610-2665
thecookhotel.com

Hampton Inn
4646 Constitution Ave.
(225) 926-9990

Hilton Baton Rouge Capitol Center
201 Lafayette St.
(225) 344-5866

Hotel Indigo
200 Convention St.
(225) 341-1515
ihg.com

The Stockade Bed & Breakfast
8860 Highland Rd.
(225) 769-7358
or (888) 900-5430
thestockade.com

Watermark Baton Rouge
150 Third St.
(225) 408-3200
marriott.com

COCODRIE

Coco Marina
106 Pier 56 Ct.
(985) 594-6626
or (800) 648-2626
cocomarina.com

COVINGTON

Annadele's Plantation Bed & Breakfast
71495 Chestnut St.
(985) 809-7669
annadeles.com

Best Western Northpark Inn
625 N Hwy. 190
(985) 892-2681
or (877) 766-6700

Blue Willow Bed & Breakfast
505 E. Rutland St.
(985) 892-0011
bluewillowbandb.com

Camellia House Bed & Breakfast
426 E. Rutland St.
(985) 893-2442
camelliahouse.net

Land-O-Pines Family Campground
17145 Million Dollar Rd.
(800) 443-3697
camplop.com

DARROW

Inn at Houmas House
40136 Hwy. 942
(225)-473-9380
houmashouse.com

DONALDSONVILLE

Raylin House of Donaldsonville
129 Lessard St.
(225) 939-4740

Victorian on the Avenue Bed and Breakfast
117 Railroad Ave.
(225) 473-1876
the-victorian-on-the-avenue
.com

ETHEL

St. Gemme de Beauvais
4302 Quiet Ln.
(225) 634-3245
or (225) 721-1514
stgemmedebeauvais.com

FOLSOM

Maison Reve Farm
76251 Hwy. 1077
(985) 769-8103

HARVEY

Best Western Westbank
1700 Lapalco Blvd.
(504) 366-5369
or (800) 528-1234

Travelodge by Wyndham
2200 Westbank Expy.
(504) 521-7602

HOUMA

Crochet House
301 Midland Dr.
(985) 879-3033
crochethouse.com

Fairfield Inn by Marriott
1530 Martin Luther King
Blvd.
(985) 580-1050

Grand Bayou Noir
1143 Bayou Black Dr.
(985) 873-5849
grandbayounoir.com

Hampton Inn
1728 Martin Luther King
Blvd.
(985) 873-3140

JACKSON

Milbank Historic House
3045 Bank St.
(225) 634-5901
milbankbandb.com

Old Centenary Inn
1740 Charter St.
(225) 634-5050
oldcentenaryinn.com

LAPLACE

Holiday Inn LaPlace
4284 Hwy. 51
(985) 618-1600

NAPOLEONVILLE

Madewood
4250 Hwy. 308
(985) 369-7151
or (800) 375-7151
madewood.com

NEW ORLEANS

Bienville House Hotel
320 Decatur St.
(504) 529-2345
or (800) 535-9603
bienvillehouse.com

Grand Victorian
2727 St. Charles Ave.
(504) 895-1104
or (800) 977-0008
gvbb.com

Hampton Inn
3626 St. Charles Ave.
(504) 899-9908

Hotel Monteleone
214 Royal St.
(504) 523-3341
or (866) 338-4684
hotelmonteleone.com

InterContinental New Orleans
444 St. Charles Ave.
(504) 525-5566
ihg.com

Le Pavillon Hotel
833 Poydras St.
(504) 581-3111
or (800) 535-9095
lepavillon.com

Macarty House
3820 Burgundy St.
(504) 267-1564
macartyhouse.com

Maison Perrier Bed & Breakfast
4117 Perrier St.
(504) 897-1807
maisonperrier.com

Prytania Park Hotel
1525 Prytania St.
(504) 524-0427
prytaniaparkhotel.com

Queen Anne Hotel
1625 Prytania St.
(504) 524-0427
thequeenanne.com

R&B Bed & Breakfast
726 Frenchmen St.
(504) 943-9500
rbbedandbreakfast.com

Renaissance Arts Hotel
700 Tchoupitoulas St.
(504) 613-2330

Rose Manor Inn
7214 Pontchartrain Blvd.
(504) 282-8200
rosemanor.com

St. Charles Guest House
1748 Prytania St.
(504) 523-6556
stcharlesguesthouse.com

Sully Mansion
2631 Prytania St.
(504) 891-0457
or (800) 364-2414
sullymansion.com

PORT ALLEN

Quality Inn
131 Lobdell Hwy. I-10 and
Hwy. 415
(225) 343-4821

SLIDELL

La Quinta Inn
794 E I-10 SR
(985) 643-9770
laquintaneworleansslidell
.com

Woodridge Bed &
Breakfast
40149 Crowe's Landing
(985) 863-9981
or (877) 643-7109
woodridgebb.com

FOR MORE INFORMATION

Ascension Parish Tourism
Commission
6967 Hwy. 22, Sorrento 70778
(225) 675-6550 or (888) 775-7990
tourascension.com

Bayou Lafourche Area Convention
and Visitors Bureau
4484 LA 1, Raceland 70394
(985) 537-5800 or (877) 537-5800
lacajunbayou.com

Bogalusa Chamber of Commerce
608 Willis Ave., Bogalusa 70427
(985) 735-5731
bogalusa.org

East Feliciana Parish Chamber of
Commerce
P.O. Box 573, Clinton 70722
(225) 634-7155
eastfelicianatourism.org

Gonzales Welcome Center
1006 W. Hwy. 30, Gonzales 70737
(225) 647-9566

Grand Isle Tourism Department
2757 Hwy. 1, Grand Isle 70358
(985) 787-2997
townofgrandisle.com

Houma Area Convention and Visitors
Bureau
114 Tourist Dr., Gray 70359
(800) 688-2732
houmatravel.com

Jean Lafitte National Park Barataria
Unit
6588 Barataria Blvd., Marrero 70072
(504) 689-3690
nps.gov/jela/barataria-preserve.htm

Jefferson Convention and Visitors
Bureau
1221 Elmwood Park Blvd., Ste. 411,
New Orleans 70123
(504) 731-7089 or (877) 572-7474
experiencejefferson.com

New Orleans Convention and Visitors
Bureau
2020 St. Charles Ave.,
New Orleans 70130
(504) 566-5011 or (800) 672-6124

New Orleans Tourism Marketing
Corporation
(504) 524-4784
neworleans.com

Pointe Coupee Office of Tourism
727 Hospital Rd., New Roads 70760
(225) 638-3998 or (800) 259-2468
pctourism.org

St. Charles Parish Economic
Development and Tourism
Department
15012 River Rd., Hahnville 70057
(985) 783-5140
stcharlesparish-la.gov

ST. FRANCISVILLE

Butler Greenwood
8345 Hwy. 61
(225) 635-6312
butlergreenwood.com

Cottage Plantation
10528 Cottage Ln.
(225) 635-3674
cottageplantation.com

Greenwood Plantation
6838 Highland Rd.
(225) 655-4475
greenwoodplantation.com

Hotel Francis
1 Lakeside Dr.
(225) 635-3821

Myrtles
7747 Highway 61
(225) 635-6277
myrtlesplantation.com

St. James Tourist Center
1094 US 61, Gramercy 70052
(225) 562-2525 or (800) 367-7852
stjamesla.com

St. John Parish Administration Office
1801 West Airline Hwy., LaPlace 70068
(985) 652-9569
sjbparish.com

St. Tammany Tourist & Convention Commission
68099 Hwy. 59, Mandeville 70471
(800) 634-9443
louisiananorthshore.com

Tangipahoa Parish Tourist Convention and Visitors Bureau
13143 Wardline Rd., Hammond 70401
(985) 542-7520 or (800) 542-7520
tangi-cvb.org

Visit Baton Rouge
359 Third St., Baton Rouge 70801
(800) 527-6843
visitbatonrouge.com

West Baton Rouge Convention and Visitors Bureau
2750 North Westport Dr., Port Allen 70767
(225) 344-2920 or (800) 654-9701
westbatonrouge.net

West Feliciana Parish Tourist Commission
11757 Ferdinand St., St. Francisville 70775
(225) 635-4224
stfrancisville.us

Local newspapers: *Amite Tangi–Digest*; The *Baton Rouge Advocate* (check the Friday "Fun" section for events, restaurant reviews, and so on); *Bogalusa Daily News*; *Covington News–Banner*; LSU student paper, the *Daily Reveille*; *Franklinton Era Leader*; The *Gambit Weekly* has another event calendar; *Hammond Daily Star*; *Houma Today*; *Kentwood News–Ledger*; The *OffBeat Magazine* has music listings; The *Pointe Coupee Banner* of New Roads; the *Ponchatoula Times*; *St. Francisville Democrat*; *St. Helena Echo* in Greensburg; *St. Tammany Farmer*; *Thibodaux Daily Comet*; *Times–Picayune* has a daily calendar of events; the *Watchman* in Clinton; the *West Side Journal* of Port Allen; and the *Zachary Plainsman-News*.

WWOZ community radio (FM 90.7) sponsors a phone line for recorded information on performances: (504) 840-4040.

Shadetree Inn
9704 Royal St.
(225) 635-6116
shadetreeinn.com

THIBODAUX

Dansereau House
506 St. Phillip St.
(985) 227-9937
dansereauhouse.com

WHITE CASTLE

Nottoway
30970 Hwy. 405
(225) 545-2730
nottoway.com

Places to Eat in Southeast Louisiana

ABITA SPRINGS

Abita Brew Pub
72011 Holly St.
(985) 892-5837
abitabrewpub.com

Abita Springs Café
22132 Level St.
(985) 400-5025
abitaspringscafe.com

AKERS

Middendorf's
30160 Hwy. 51
(985) 386-6666
middendorfsrestaurant.com

BATON ROUGE

Capital City Grill
The Shaw Center
100 Lafayette St.
(225) 381-8140
capitalcitygrill.net

Chimes
3357 Highland Rd.
(225) 383-1754
thechimes.com

Drusilla Seafood Restaurant
3482 Drusilla Ln.
(225) 923-0896
or (800) 364-8844
drusillaplace.com

Juban's
3739 Perkins Rd.
(225) 346-8422
jubans.com

Louisiana Lagniappe
9990 Perkins Rd.
(225) 767-9991
louisianalagniappe
restaurant.com

The Club at LSU Union Square
2 Raphael Semmes Rd.
(225) 578-2356
dineoncampus.com

Mike Anderson's Seafood
1031 West Lee Dr.
(225) 766-7823
mikeandersons.com

Parrains Seafood
3225 Perkins Rd.
(225) 381-9922
parrains.com

Sammy's Grill
8635 Highland Rd.
(225) 766-9600
sammysgrill.com

Tsunami
The Shaw Center
100 Lafayette St., 6th Fl.
(225) 346-5100
servingsushi.com

BUSH

The House of Seafood Buffet
81790 Hwy. 21
(985) 886-2231

CHAUVIN

Coco Marina
106 Pier 56
(985) 594-6626
or (800) 648-2626
cocomarina.com

COVINGTON

Acme Oyster House
1202 N. Hwy. 190
(985) 246-6155
acmeoyster.com

Annadele's Plantation Restaurant
71495 Chestnut St.
(985) 809-7669
annadeles.com

Coffee Rani
234-A Lee Ln.
(985) 893-6158
coffeerani.com

Dakota Restaurant
629 Hwy. 190
(985) 892-3712
thedakotarestaurant.com

Gallagher's Grill
905 S. Tyler St.
(985) 892-9992
gallaghersgrill.com

Mattina Bella
421 E. Gibson St.
(985) 892-0708
mattinabella.com

Ristorante Del Porto
205 N. New Hampshire St.
(985) 875-1006
delportoristorante.com

Toad Hollow Café
207 N. New Hampshire St.
(985) 893-8711
toadhollowcafe.com

CROWN POINT

Restaurant des Familles
7163 Barataria Blvd.
(504) 689-7834
desfamilles.com

DARROW

Latil's Landing Restaurant
at Houmas House
Plantation
40136 Hwy. 942
(225) 473-7841
houmashouse.com

Le Café
40136 Hwy. 942
(225) 473-9380
houmashouse.com

DONALDSONVILLE

Café Lafourche
817 Veterans Blvd.
(225) 473-7451
cafelafourche.com

Grapevine Café
211 Railroad Ave.
(225) 473-8463
grapevine.cafe

HARVEY

Cleopatra Mediterranean Cuisine
2701 Manhattan Blvd.
(504) 361-1113
cleocuisine.com

Copeland's of New Orleans
2333 Manhattan Blvd.
(504) 364-1575
copelandsofneworleans
.com

HOUMA

531 Liberty
531 Liberty St.
(985) 223-2233
531liberty.com

1921 Seafood Restaurant
1522 Barrow St.
(985) 868-7098

Bayou Delight
4038 Bayou Black Dr.
(985) 876-4879

Big Al's Seafood
1377 W. Tunnel Blvd.
(985) 876-4030
bigalsseafood.com

Boudreau & Thibodeau's Cajun Cookin'
5602 W. Main St.
(985) 872-4711
bntcajuncookin.com

Christiano Ristorante
724 High St.
(985) 223-1130
or (985) 223-1103
christianoristorante.com

The Jolly Inn
1507 Barrow St.
(985) 872-6114
jollyinn.com

MANDEVILLE

Benedict's Plantation
1144 N. Causeway Blvd.
(985) 626-4557
benedictsplantation.net

MARRERO

Chateau Orleans Po Boys
2324 Barataria Blvd.
(504) 347-1177
chateauorleanspoboys.com

NAPOLEONVILLE

Madewood
4250 Hwy. 308
(985) 369-7151
or (800) 375-7151
madewood.com

NEW ORLEANS

Arnaud's
813 Bienville St.
(504) 523-5433
arnaudsrestaurant.com

Brennan's
417 Royal St.
(504) 525-9711
brennansneworleans.com

Cafe du Monde
800 Decatur St.
(504) 587-0840
cafedumonde.com

Commander's Palace
1403 Washington Ave.
(504) 899-8221
commanderspalace.com

Doris Metropolitan
620 Chartres St.
(504) 267-3500
dorismetropolitan.com

Emeril's Restaurant
800 Tchoupitoulas St.
(504) 528-9393
emerilsrestaurants.com

Galatoire's
209 Bourbon St.
(504) 525-2021
galatoires.com

GW Fins
808 Bienville St.
(504) 581-3467
gwfins.com

K-Paul's Louisiana Kitchen
416 Chartres St.
(504) 596-2530
kpauls.com

Mother's
401 Poydras St.
(504) 523-9656
mothersrestaurant.net

Muriel's Jackson Square
801 Chartres St.
(504) 568-1885
muriels.com

Napoleon House
500 Chartres St.
(504) 522-4152
napoleonhouse.com

Rebirth Restaurant
857 Fulton St.
(504) 522-6863
restaurantrebirth.com

Rum House Caribbean Taqueria
3128 Magazine St.
(504) 941-7560
therumhouse.com

The Steakhouse at Harrah's
8 Canal St.
(504) 533-6111
caesars.com

Tujague's
823 Decatur St.
(504) 525-8676
tujaguesrestaurant.com

Upperline Restaurant
1413 Upperline St.
(504) 891-9822
upperline.com

NEW ROADS

Hot Tails
1113 Hospital Rd.
(225) 638-4676
hottailsrestaurant.com

Ma Mama's Kitchen
124 West Main St.
(225) 618-2424

Morel's
210 Morrison Pkwy.
(225) 638-4057
morelsrestaurant.com

Southern Chicks Café & Daiquiris
1630 Hospital Rd.
(225) 618-5683
southernchickscafe.com

ST. FRANCISVILLE

The Bluffs on Thompson Creek
14233 Sunrise Way
(225) 634-6419
thebluffs.com

Magnolia Cafe
5687 Commerce St.
(225) 635-6528
themagnoliacafe.net

Restaurant 1796
at the Myrtles Plantation
7747 US 61 N.
(225) 635-6278
myrtlesplantation.com

St. Francisville Inn
5720 North Commerce St.
(225) 635-6502
stfrancisvilleinn.com

SUNSHINE

Roberto's River Road Restaurant
1985 Hwy. 75
(225) 642-5999
robertosrestaurant.net

THIBODAUX

Fremin's
402 W. Third St.
(985) 449-0333
fremins.net

Politz's Restaurant
535 St. Mary St.
(985) 448-0944

Spahr's Seafood
601 W. Fourth St.
(985) 448-0487
spahrsseafood.com

VACHERIE

Oak Alley Plantation Restaurant and Inn
3645 Hwy. 18
(225) 265-2151
or (800) 44-ALLEY
oakalleyplantation.com

WHITE CASTLE

Nottoway
30970 Hwy. 405
(225) 545-2730
nottoway.com

Ourso's Seafood House
32010 Hwy. 1
(225) 716-4455

Index